ON FANTASY ISLAND

CONOR GEARTY

ON FANTASY ISLAND

Britain, Europe, and Human Rights

OXFORD
UNIVERSITY PRESS

OXFORD
UNIVERSITY PRESS

Great Clarendon Street, Oxford, OX2 6DP,
United Kingdom

Oxford University Press is a department of the University of Oxford.
It furthers the University's objective of excellence in research, scholarship,
and education by publishing worldwide. Oxford is a registered trade mark of
Oxford University Press in the UK and in certain other countries

Published in the United States of America by Oxford University Press
198 Madison Avenue, New York, NY 10016, United States of America

British Library Cataloguing in Publication Data
Data available

Library of Congress Control Number: 2016939532

ISBN 978-0-19-878763-1

Printed and bound by
CPI Group (UK) Ltd, Croydon, CR0 4YY

To Éile Úna

ACKNOWLEDGEMENTS

The idea for this book first came to me when I was invited by the Wyndham Trust to give its Corbishley Lecture for 2014. I delivered the lecture on 6 November 2014 at LSE, under the title 'On Fantasy Island'. I am very grateful to the Trust for the invitation to give the talk, and to LSE for hosting it. The book that has grown out of that one-off event is a culmination of conversations I have had over many years with colleagues and friends, about the Human Rights Act and its true meaning in UK domestic law. Prominent among these have been Jonathan Cooper, David Davis, Francesca Klug, John Phillips, and so many colleagues at the law department at LSE that it would be invidious to single out even a cluster of them for special mention. As ever my human rights graduate students have been a stimulus to deep thought in ways that have really helped even without their fully knowing this to be the case. Professor Aoife Nolan has read the book in draft from start to finish and I owe her special thanks for the extensive, helpful improvements that she suggested. On the web front, Caroline Mockett has been an imaginative and valued colleague in creating and then supporting the www.onfantasyisland.co.uk which we launched before the book was published and where parts of it have been regularly posted. I am grateful to her, and to Asmaa Akhtar and Zoe Paxman at LSE's Institute of Public Affairs for helping me to exploit the web's potential so as to spread the ideas that are to be found more fully developed here. Lastly I'd like very much to thank Oxford University Press, in particular my editor Alex Flach, for supporting the book from the start and for being so open to fresh ways of disseminating its content via the web before official publication.

TABLE OF CONTENTS

PREFACE

On 23 June 2016 the UK voted in a referendum to leave the European Union. Turnout was high, 72.2%, and the result close but decisive: 51.9% for Leave as against 48.1% for Remain. The Prime Minister immediately announced his resignation, to take effect just as soon as his successor could be chosen. The Labour opposition was thrown into disarray, members of the parliamentary party seeking to remove their own leader Jeremy Corbyn but finding themselves at the time of writing unable to do so. Scotland—which had voted to remain—began immediate planning to distance itself from the rest of the UK. On the Saturday immediately following the result, foreign ministers of the founding member countries of the European Union came together to consider what actions to take, and in the days that followed a series of debates, discussions, and emergency sessions were held in Brussels, Luxembourg, and across the capitals of Europe. As Europe debated, markets wiped millions off the value of shares, and the pound sterling fell to lows not seen for a generation. On the Monday after the Thursday result, an anxious House of Commons reflected on the implications of what the people had decided.

The architects of the Out, or Brexit, vote, meanwhile, were nowhere to be seen. After a short vague statement, Conservatives Boris Johnson and Michael Gove disappeared almost entirely from public view, giving no interviews, issuing no plan—or even suggestion of a plan—of how to proceed, and not even engaging in the parliamentary discussion on what was to happen next. Within days it became disconcertingly clear that neither these mainstream campaigners for Brexit nor their allies had the slightest idea of what to do next. Nor did the government. The result being wholly unexpected, no plan B had been put in place. After a few days of policy-immobility, a sort of provisional answer appeared in the form of the Conservative politician Oliver Letwin, whose enormous responsibility it suddenly became to execute the people's wishes to depart from the market on which so much of British trade depended.

This book is about a fantasy island which thinks it can go it alone so far as human rights are concerned, and which has fooled itself into believing that while with the poet John Donne no man is an island, a country as great as the UK can indeed be exactly that in a metaphorical as well as a geographic sense: a place of safety and separateness, one that is immune to the pressures of the outside world, and onto whose shores the waves of globalization never break. The same instinct to celebrate the lonely courage of an ancient island people is behind the Brexit vote. Time and again during the referendum campaign, rational arguments about risk were met with a grand contempt for the very idea that expertise could matter in a struggle as great as this for the restoration of ancient British freedom. Migration would finally be brought irrefutably under control and (it was implied) sharply reduced. The beloved National Health Service would receive an infusion of cash —previously bound for the hated Brussels bureaucrats—that would take it out of intensive care and restore it to rude good health. Trade deals with the world would roll in as nation states reacted to the opportunities afforded by a free Britain for a renewal of old commercial ties and the development of new ones. The European Union itself would quickly come round, acknowledging that the specialness of the UK warranted access to its single market without the disciplines required of every one of its other members. All those who said otherwise—world leaders like the US President Barack Obama; governors of banks around the world; the leaders of global financial institutions—were simply being made to parrot the views of the British political establishment so as to help this 'elite' win a referendum that would, if they had their way, merely confirm the country's ongoing subjugation to 'abroad'. The vote was not about dreary economic facts: it was about 'taking back control', about 'democracy' and 'freedom'.

As I write, the consequences of this collision between fact and fantasy are being played out not only in the shocks being delivered to trade, the currency, and the stock market but also on the streets where a rise in racially motivated hate crime has been reported. The next target being sized up for destruction is also coming into view, the Human Rights Act and (quite possibly in the new climate) the European Convention on Human Rights on which that measure is based. Here the topic of this book connects directly with the events I have just been describing. For years human rights law has been the object of scorn among a wide range of Right-leaning politicians, and their supporters in the traditional print media. The arguments against the law have been broadly the same as those that have ended up driving the UK decision to leave the European Union; this book analyses these in no little detail in the pages that follow. Now that the larger European entanglement has been successfully seen off, the time has come for finishing the unfinished business of human rights destruction. The driver is UK domestic politics, in particular the needs of the pretenders to the prime ministership so abruptly vacated by David Cameron. The electorate here is not now the people, but rather Conservative MPs initially and thereafter the Conservative Party membership generally. Neither community is enthusiastic about human rights in general or the Human Rights Act in particular. Here is another example of foreign intrusion, an alien contamination that needs now to be washed away altogether so that the UK's fresh start can be properly made. Much of this book is taken up with showing how wrong-headed this critique of the Human Rights Act is ('fantasy' is a polite way of putting it) and how impossible it is to step out of the world in this way.

How has the UK reached the point that it has, where invented versions of a golden past are being allowed to drive the country into an (in every sense) impoverished future? The answer is the same so far as both the EU and human rights are concerned. A country's political leadership cannot spend decades attacking an idea and the set of institutions behind that idea and then expect the electorate to follow it when it suddenly changes tack and asks voters to support that which had been previously derided and abused. This is exactly what Mr Cameron and his colleagues asked so far as the European Union was concerned. No political leader in the UK has had an unqualified good word to say about Europe since Edward Heath, and he left office in 1974. Even Tony Blair's enthusiasm was tempered by a perceived need to fall in with rather than work to change the anti-European prejudice that had become normal in the long period of conservative hegemony from 1979 to 1997. This was why the Remain campaign was so negative, so rooted in what became known as Project Fear: a sudden conversion to the values of the European Union would have looked ridiculous to an electorate brought up on a cross-party consensus (ostensibly shared even by closet pro-Europeans) about how awful Europe really was.

It is the same with human rights. As Chapter 1 of this book shows, the Human Rights Act has been friendless from the moment of its enactment, unsupported by the government that created it, attacked by the Conservative opposition, savaged by the newspapers, and eventually now facing the possibility of repeal—victim of the same forces that have swept the UK out of Europe.

Or have they? In the days after the referendum result, much attention has focused on turning the fantasy of British independence into reality. When they are victorious, even fantasists cannot avoid facts forever. However hard they try to hide, Messrs Johnson and Gove and their gang of Brexiteers will eventually have to explain what they plan to do. It was their desperation to avoid this that led them to be so anxious that the Prime Minister they had destroyed should stay on to do their work for them, so that he could engage in the detailed work of extrication that is so far beneath men so wedded to the abstract big picture as these philosopher–journalists (an invitation Mr Cameron rightly declined). There is now talk of delaying pulling the trigger on the exit discussions. Conservatives so keen on exit last week seem intent on hanging around in the cloakroom for years before finally retrieving their sovereign clothes and marching off into the dark night of freedom.

Things are not as easy as they look when fantasy collides with fact. The Human Rights Act may yet survive. The UK's membership of the European Union might even as well. After the Roman Empire had converted to Christianity one emperor stood out against the change, seeking to turn back the clock to the old pagan ways. Julian lasted just three years, and Christianity came back stronger than ever. Maybe as Prime Minister one or other of the Brexiteers or near Brexiteers is fated to play the role of King Canute, whose wisdom in showing that he could not resist the tides has long been misunderstood as stupidity.

CONOR GEARTY
London
1 July 2016

PART I

INTRODUCTION

1

WHY THE HUMAN RIGHTS ACT MATTERS

This book is concerned with a law that has been under sentence of death since May 2015, a measure as remarkable for the enemies it has attracted as for the successes it has enjoyed.

The Labour government responsible for enactment of the Human Rights Act in 1998 immediately began to row back from its implications, delaying its introduction for nearly two years, and—when it was finally grumpily brought in—treating it as though it were some kind of alien intrusion on British law rather than a flagship New Labour project for which so many of them had worked just a few years before.[1] The Conservatives (or Tories as they are often called) were opposed as they were concerned about the potential effect on parliamentary sovereignty. They were anxious also (though to a lesser degree than is now the case) about the Bill's suspect European pedigree. (The Human Rights Act does, with its talk of rights being rooted in the European Convention on Human Rights.) Even the Liberal Democrats, usually dependably in favour of anything that involves an increase in checks and balances, were critical because it had not gone far enough, a malnourishing half a loaf when the whole (more rights; better enforcement) should have been on offer. The press quickly grew to hate the Act when they discovered to their horror that it was not just about publishing what they liked in an exciting

---

[1] J Gordon and F Klug (eds), 'Special Issue on the Tenth Anniversary of the Human Rights Act' [2010] (6) *European Human Rights Law Review* 568–630 has many useful essays tracking the immediate reception of the Act.

On Fantasy Island: Britain, Europe, and Human Rights. First Edition. Conor Gearty.

American 'Watergate' kind of way, but that it also allowed people to claim a right to privacy to stop the exposure of their celebrity lives for commercial gain.[2] With every movie star, footballer, and famous author that successfully relied on the Act, so the frustration of the papers dependent on such gossip for their survival grew stronger. Expanding their criticisms even further, in the eyes of many in the press human rights became political correctness gone mad, the Act itself a charter for thugs and terrorists.[3] When hatred of things European tottered to the centre stage of British politics from the sceptical fringe, this quasi-European fall-guy already lay prostrate on the floor, an easy target for further, cost-free bashing. And so the promise of repeal in the current government's manifesto for the 2015 election, with its demise a matter of time it might be thought. But this is an Act that should not be given up without a fight.

Any law would have had difficulty thriving in the teeth of such antagonism. The Human Rights Act has managed extraordinarily well in the circumstances. From the start, its modest protection was limited not only in terms of the rights which could be protected but also in the way in which these rights—restricted as they were—could be set aside where this was necessary and even (this is what annoyed the Liberal Democrats) be overridden completely by Parliament where the public good (as understood by MPs and peers) demanded it.[4] On the other hand, and by way of compensation for such potential impotence, state authorities were all required in their interactions with the public to act compatibly with the rights set out in the Act ('the Convention' rights—

---

[2] R Clayton and H Tomlinson, *Privacy and Freedom of Expression* 2nd edn (Oxford: Oxford University Press, 2010) is an extensive survey.

[3] See Ch 8. For a sample of these attitudes see C Meredith, 'Daily Express and Mail celebrate the end of human rights, a horrified Twitter despairs' *Huffington Post* 3 October 2014: <http://www.huffingtonpost.co.uk/2014/10/03/daily-mail-daily-express-human-rights-twitter-reaction_n_5925540.html> [accessed 30 October 2015].

[4] Human Rights Act 1998, ss 4 and 14 and European Convention on Human Rights and Fundamental Freedoms, art 15.

that European angle again),[5] and the government was also obliged to identify the human rights implications (if any) of every law that it introduced to Parliament.[6] These two stipulations did not challenge Parliament's intensely protected sovereignty, it was true. They did however give human rights a valuable route into the day-to-day lives of central government departments and the authorities up and down the land that interact with the public every day. Officials gradually grew used to their new obligations, and became if not fond then at least affectionately tolerant of their new duties: it is not unpleasant to be reminded that it was not only in one's private life that one should strive to act with humanity towards one's fellow human being.[7] This essentially was all that the Act was saying, and where that person was someone different (an immigrant; an asylum seeker; a person with mental disabilities; a Traveller) or presumed to be bad (a suspected 'terrorist'; a criminal defendant) or both then the law offered a disciplined insistence on universalism that ran with the grain of, rather than opposed, Britain's view of itself as a free and tolerant country.

Then there were the courts. Everyone knew right from the off that this was where the main responsibility for making the Act work in a sensible way would fall; examples littered the democratic world of judges out of control, imposing their version of justice via some grand claim to know exactly what rights in this or that 'constitutional' document entailed whatever anyone else said, elected or not. On the other hand there were judges so quiescent that in the words of one of them in the United States, the legendary Oliver Wendell Holmes, 'If my fellow citizens want to go to Hell, I will help them. It's my job.'[8]

---

[5] s 6(1).

[6] s 19.

[7] Ministry of Justice, *Human Rights: Human Lives. A Handbook for Public Authorities* (2006) eventually showed a government seeking to get to grips with this legislation in a fair-minded way.

[8] In a letter to Harold Laski, 4 March 1920: M DeWolfe Howe (ed), *Holmes-Laski Letters: The Correspondence of Mr Justice Holmes and Harold J Laski 1916–1935* (London: Geoffrey Cumberlege with Oxford University Press, 1953), vol 1, p 249.

Seeking to avoid these two extremes, British judges trained themselves up conscientiously for their new role. Seminars were held, academics invited to speak, even continental judges asked to explain what adjudicating on rights really entailed. The two-year period before the law came fully into force but after it had been enacted may have been driven by government hesitation but it proved a valuable delay—one that not having occurred in Scotland had produced a few eccentric pronouncements north of the Border.[9] (Northern Ireland with its Good Friday Agreement of which human rights respect was an integral part was in a different place again: more on this later.[10]) For their part, though, the judges in England and Wales were ready from the off, trained up in what the law was really about. This was not what the tabloids told them, but rather entailed delivery of respect for the dignity of all, albeit (Parliament's instruction again) in a way that was to be subject to the sometimes aggravating constraints that could continue to be imposed by the people through their representatives in the shape of laws before which even human rights were to be required to bend. In other words: dignity for all unless Parliament specifically decided to dispense with it in particular circumstances.[11]

The result has been an unexpected triumph, a masterpiece of judicial self-consciousness, on the whole delivering rights at the right times while bending to the will of Parliament where that will has taken an unequivocal legislative shape. Much of what appears in this book is critical of the British judges in the past—it has to be when one of the revived fantasies of recent years has been how marvellous the judges of the old common law were before this European rights contamination took hold. So it is right and just to pause at the very start of the

---

[9] See Ch 6.

[10] See Ch 11.

[11] My own *Principles of Human Rights Adjudication* (Oxford: Oxford University Press, 2004) deals with the period of transition after enactment and before implementation as well as with the early cases that set the tone for much of what followed. See generally K S Ziegler, E Wicks, and L Hodson (eds), *The UK and European Human Rights: A Strained Relationship?* (Oxford: Hart Publishing, 2015).

story to acknowledge the remarkable achievement of the judges from all UK jurisdictions in bedding down the Act, intervening in difficult circumstances to force the rights of the marginalized, the dispossessed, the hated onto centre stage—but doing so in a way which has not amounted (one or two early mistakes aside) to a judicial rights revolution. The result has been clear guidance for public authorities, a judicial empowerment of their shift to rights-respecting decision-making, and—if we had to quantify such things—a likely consequent decrease in the misery of the lives of those whom democracy can too easily forget, but a decrease that is achieved without any consequent damage to (or even intrusion upon) the prosperous world inhabited by the majority.

The human rights insight is that none of us has a guaranteed space among the fortunate, that the border between affluence and misfortune is more porous than we assume. Human rights are for us all but likely to be called upon only when we need them. And rich and fortunate though we might seem, these are not guaranteed conditions: we will grow old, we may be visited unexpectedly by the police, an onset of mental ill-health may leave us vulnerable; our lives may change suddenly for the worst. When the editor of The Sun—so casual with the lives of so many in search of a headline; leader of the popular charge against human rights law—emerged from the courtroom in which her fall from power at the hands of a police investigation had just been confirmed to complain about the infringement of her human rights, it was difficult not to stifle a smile but important to try to do so: human rights are for us all for sure, but for each of us individually on that rainy day that we hope never comes.[12] Even the greatest cheerleader against

---

[12] M Mansfield, 'Rebekah Brooks needn't worry about her right to a fair trial' Guardian 18 March 2012: <http://www.theguardian.com/commentisfree/2012/mar/18/rebekah-brooks-worry-fair-trial> [accessed 30 October 2015]. And for The Sun's own reliance see News Group Newspapers Ltd and others v Metropolitan Police Commissioner [2015] UKIPTrib 14_176-H: <http://www.bailii.org/uk/cases/UKIPTrib/2015/14_176-H.html> [accessed 31 March 2016]; [2016] UKIPTrib 14_176-H: <http://www.ipt-uk.com/docs/NGN%20v %20MPS%20Approved%20Judgment%20on%20Remedy.pdf> [accessed 31 March 2016].

human rights, *The Daily Mail*, has not been below deploying the law it despises to advantage when it finds itself needing to strike against authority.[13]

The Human Rights Act does more than merely focus the minds of administrators and guide the judges to better, more compassionate decision-making, important though each of these impacts is. It stands for a series of important claims about Britain's true place in the world. Indeed it might well be these assertions that have proved its undoing; as the naturalized British poet and Anglophile T S Eliot put it, 'Humankind cannot bear very much reality.'[14] If we leave aside for now this piece of legislation's politically astute respect for parliamentary sovereignty, it is clear that the Human Rights Act is a document that is profoundly subversive of the partisan national interest. To put it mildly some people—often quite powerful people—do not like this. So how does the Act have this effect?

First there is its determination to obliterate the difference between Brits and the rest. Gone is the imperialist claim of Lord Palmerston at the time of the Don Pacifico affair in the mid-nineteenth century that a British subject 'in whatever land he may be, shall feel confident that the watchful eye and the strong arm of England will protect him, against injustice and wrong'.[15] Human rights replaces 'Gunboat diplomacy' with humanitarian intervention where the targets of the action ostensibly at any rate (more on hypocrisy and double standards later) are precisely not British at all. It is under human rights law that British soldiers are held to account if things go wrong (a bit of unnecessary killing here; an outbreak of torture there) whereas in the past it would have been the 'natives' whatever were the facts on

[13] *Miller v Associated Newspapers Limited* [2016] EWHC 397 (QB): on appeal to the Supreme Court.

[14] *Four Quartets*: <http://www.coldbacon.com/poems/fq.html> [accessed 30 October 2015].

[15] For his full speech to Parliament on affairs in Greece, made on 25 June 1850, in the course of which this famous remark was made see <http://www.historyhome.co.uk/polspeech/foreign.htm> [accessed 30 October 2015].

the ground. This is a huge ask of a state that was still in living memory top dog across the world, that held this position for generations, whose wealth is built upon making the international rules to suit itself, and for whom the weakness of others was for centuries something to be exploited rather than remedied.

Second comes the Human Rights Act's role as passport to the wider world of ordinary European nationhood to which the collapse of Empire has now fated Britain to belong. Again this is tough on a country whose twentieth-century story, the one it so often tells itself, is one of heroic and singular defence of the Continent against evil. In the early days of the European Court of Human Rights a judgment against a repressive common law decision of the House of Lords on contempt of court provoked the wrath of another adopted Brit, F A Mann. He had been forced to flee Nazi Germany and had settled in Britain, becoming a famous and highly influential solicitor: what right had these judges (naming the countries from which the majority votes came) to challenge 'one of the greatest contributions the common law has made to the civilized behaviour of a large part of the world'?[16] Mann may have a point here, but it is not one he would recognize: the case reflects a precipitous fall from grandeur, Lord Grantham slumming it in the kitchen fighting over food with servants of whose existence just a short while before he had been uncertain. Even more than the European Union, the European Convention on Human Rights—with its forty-seven equal members and its court with a single judge drawn from each place no matter how large, powerful, or great its history—is for many evidence of decline before it even opens its judicious mouth. It is much easier to savage the messenger than understand the news it is bringing, both particular (this or that verdict) and general (Britain's modest place in the world as one European state among many, equality having replaced exceptionalism).

---

[16] F A Mann on *Sunday Times v United Kingdom* (1979) 2 EHRR 245 in (1979) *Law Quarterly Review* 348–54, at pp 348–9.

Third there is the internationalism that the Human Rights Act takes as a given. One of the large-scale achievements of the liberal global order has been the amassing of a set of standards about good behaviour which are manifest in legal obligations to behave properly. International law used not to be about this, the obligation on states to respect the rights of those within their power. In its Victorian pomp it busied itself with the regulation of the conduct of nations, its vigilant oversight always stopping at the front door.[17] Relics of this old approach remain, pre-eminently in the United Nations' caveat about the domestic autonomy of its member states, but the veil is often pierced these days by energetic human rights inspectors, popping up as UN monitoring committees, special rapporteurs on some moral aspect of life, or as the Secretary General's representative on a knotty global question, all demanding the subject state change its tack. Infuriating to countries keen to hide authoritarian tendencies or embarrassed by illegal occupation, these rights interventions have often proved unpopular in Britain too, notoriously with regard to Northern Ireland but also whenever they appear to involve the assertion of oversight over what the visitor calls human rights but which the government sees as its policy choices. The Special Rapporteur on Adequate Housing Raquel Rolnik found herself at the centre of much governmental and journalist anger along these lines in 2014, 'the Brazilian nut'[18] who had the temerity to claim that this country's rules on housing benefit might breach the state's obligations to its poorest people. One government Minister even went so far as to describe her report as a 'misleading Marxist diatribe'.[19]

---

[17] See further on the nineteenth-century story M Koskenniemi, *The Gentle Civilizer of Nations: The Rise and Fall of International Law 1870–1960* (Cambridge: Cambridge University Press, 2004).

[18] J Groves, 'The Brazilian nut strikes again: IDS anger as former Marxist Raquel Rolnik attacks his benefit cuts' *Daily Mail* 5 July 2014: <http://www.dailymail.co.uk/news/article-2681313/The-Brazil-Nut-strikes-IDS-anger-former-Marxist-Raquel-Rolnik-attacks-benefit-cuts.html> [accessed 30 October 2015].

[19] This was Kris Hopkins: see <http://www.theguardian.com/society/2014/feb/03/ministers-savage-un-report-abolition-bedroom-tax> [accessed 30 October 2015].

The Human Rights Act does not directly engage with this international world, one where a mere South American woman can seek to hold the UK to account in this substantive way, but it talks the same language, normalizes the binding of a once-great Leviathan with restraints whose tightness is determined by others, one minute a European judge, the next a tenacious UN-appointed academic. Where will it end? And so does one of the great achievements of the liberal international order, the growth of international human rights, become for such critics a thing to be deplored rather than, as surely it should be, celebrated.

So we have these three related dispensations: international human rights law; the European Convention on Human Rights; and the Convention's domestic incarnation in the shape of the Human Rights Act. Each is drawn from the same cloth, dividing opinion in the sharp way they do because all three start a conversation which cannot but lead to discussion of Britain's smallness on the world stage and its relative inability to act in the sovereign manner many continue to claim as its birthright. There is a marked difference here between the New Labour model of Britain that dominated politics from 1997 through to 2010 (the Human Rights Act being one of its first legislative achievements) and the more determined but inward-looking brand of politics that has followed the Blair project's collapse. Tony Blair and Gordon Brown led administrations that embraced internationalism and largely accepted international constraints (and their domestic incarnation in law) as part of what modern Britain had become, punching above its weight perhaps but doing so from within the featherweight division. (Indeed it was probably an over-awareness of this weakness that caused its downfall—joining the world heavyweight champion to win what looked like some easy victories in the Middle East only to end up abject partners in chaos.) David Cameron and his ministerial team have from the start, but especially since shaking free of the Liberal Democrats in 2010, been Little Englanders writ large on a UK stage, forsaking a rational centre-right grouping in Europe for a loose collection of Europhobes much further to the right,[20] treating Scotland as a mere (possibly even a dispensable) tool in a trivial political game against Labour, and largely ignoring Wales and Northern Ireland unless violence in the latter wakes them up. They have ratcheted up their anti-foreigner rhetoric to see off the UKIP threat from the Right (one rooted in attitudes very similar to those of their own continental allies) while preaching to the world about good behaviour without stopping to think seriously about whether, these days, anyone is listening.

Parliament may be sovereign in law but it can as easily legislate for a return of British global power as it can mandate the sun to travel around the earth. Both interventions are constitutionally possible but in different ways (almost equally) laughable. This country is surrounded by large facts that it simply cannot control: the European project across the Channel, the refugee crisis further south, the neoliberal global movement driven by financial institutions and their corporate advocates that appears to have escaped national control everywhere; the human rights movement with its regional manifestation in both the European Convention and (more recently) the EU Charter of Rights that seek in the name of human dignity to counter some of the worst excesses of these large-scale changes.

None of these can really be challenged by even the most confident Little Englander schooled in the triumphs of Agincourt and Churchill (of whom one of their most polemical members has written a biography[21]). It turns out that despite all earlier appearances, antagonists of human rights do not plan, after all, to withdraw from the European Convention on Human Rights. The Raquel Rolniks of this world will keep on coming or trying to come and denying entry will make the country look North Korea silly—an isolated farmer shouting at passers-by to keep out wielding a giant shotgun while his family

---

[20] 'Conservative MEPs form a new group' BBC 22 June 2009: <http://news.bbc.co.uk/1/hi/uk_politics/8112581.stm> [accessed 30 October 2015].
[21] B Johnson, *The Churchill Factor: How One Man Made History* (London: Hodder and Stoughton, 2014).

ekes out a dull and dreary life behind him. Britain can do nothing at all about the facts around it. But guess what: it can bash the little kid in the playground who stands for what these large truths reflect but who is wholly at the mercy of the local bullies. Parliament made the Human Rights Act all by itself. In none of its forms did Europe demand it. Repeal is noisy but safe, even if it means nothing at all, or is disguised by a supposed move towards better rights protection.[22] Only on a fantasy island could such a proposal be treated with a straight face.

In a powerful recent report, the European Union Committee of the House of Lords made a plea to government to 'think again' before persevering with the plan to remove the Act and replace it with a British bill of rights about which its inquiry had 'raise[d] serious questions' as to 'feasibility and value'.[23] This book is about the true place of the Human Rights Acts in Britain, but to get to this we must first confront these fantasies; exposing them tells us more about Britain today than it does about human rights themselves. At the time of writing the execution has been stayed, the plan foiled perhaps by exposure to fact. If so this book may be less an obituary than preparation for a second coming. Let us hope so.

---

[22] Commission on a Bill of Rights: The Choice Before Us (December 2012) gives a sample of the arguments for and against the Human Rights Act but is memorable mainly for a strong defence of the Human Rights Act from two of the Commission's members, Phillipe Sands QC and Baroness Helena Kennedy: <http://webarchive. nationalarchives.gov.uk/20130128112038/http:/www.justice.gov.uk/downloads/about/ cbr/uk-bill-rights-vol-1.pdf> [accessed 31 March 2016]. For a recent argument for change along these lines see J Fisher, The British Bill of Rights: Protecting Freedom Under the Law (London: Politeia, 2015).

[23] European Union Committee, The UK, the EU and a British Bill of Rights (12th Report of 2015–16, HL 139, 9 May 2016) Summary.

PART II

THE FANTASIES

2

THE MYTH OF THE MARVELLOUS PAST

In Gray's Inn Hall on 20 October 2015, the distinguished Oxford professor John Finnis gave a coruscating lecture, on the theme of *Judicial Power, Past, Present and Future*.[1] The paper on which the talk was based is brilliant. It oozes contempt for judges who have been near-deified by others (such as the late Lord Reid, Lord Scarman, and even Lord Bingham of Cornhill, whose book 'applicants to read law in Cambridge and Oxford all read'). Finnis condemns the most renowned Human Rights Act decision of all (on the detention of terrorist suspects: the Belmarsh case[2]) as having missed an absolutely key point about possible deportation, obvious to the professor but no trace of which 'appears in the hundreds of pages of argument and judgment' that the proceedings produced. Above all the talk draws its main strength from homage paid to a common law so ancient that it was already centuries old when the two principal actors in this dramatic professorial intervention Sir Francis Bacon and Sir Edward Coke were at their professional peaks—the late sixteenth and early seventeenth centuries. John Finnis applauds the limited role of the courts, whose judges have as their job only 'to adjudicate between parties who are in

---

[1] See <http://judicialpowerproject.org.uk/john-finnis-judicial-power-past-present-and-future/> where there is a link to the full paper [accessed 9 November 2015]. For an excellent response see M Elliott, 'Judicial Power in Normative, Institutional and Doctrinal Perspective: A Response to Professor Finnis' 5 November 2015: <http://publiclawforeveryone.com/2015/11/05/judicial-power-in-normative-institutional-and-doctrinal-perspective-a-response-to-professor-finnis/> [accessed 18 March 2016].

[2] See Ch 5.

dispute about their legal rights and obligations by applying—to facts agreed between them or found by the court after trial—the law that defined those rights and obligations at that time past when the matter of their dispute (the cause in action) arose'. The courtroom is no place for interventions or public interest argument. An old friend whom the speaker met at Oxford, now on the bench in a Commonwealth jurisdiction, gives judgments that are 'authentic' and 'admirable' while the European Court of Human Rights in Strasbourg is made up of (the professor does not quite say) fools, unaware of the most straightforward of points which are 'well-known to philosophers'. Its record shows that it should have listened more to a now long-gone British colleague, the 'oft-dissenting' Gerald Fitzmaurice.

Apart from Lady Hale (for whom this will be no surprise) and a long-forgotten Lady Hatton ('a wealthy widow who became Coke's second wife'), there are no women at all, not as judges in the cases cited but neither in any of the articles or books referred to in the written record of the lecture. And if the common law is a man's world, it is also a privileged one. Law students go to 'Cambridge or Oxford'. The Strasbourg Court has a misguided view of the Convention on Human Rights as a 'living instrument', an idea the playing out of which has meant that that Court (in a startling turn) must bear 'a substantial responsibility' for the refugee crisis that was taking place in the Mediterranean at the time the professor was delivering his lecture. The economic circumstances of the moment or the turmoil caused by tyranny or imperialist violence can never be part of this version of the common law's role in the world. It sits aloof in the law courts, waiting to try cases, its judges too polite to ask about the coincidence of the affluence of all those who appear before them (other than defendants en route to jail) and too well educated to notice the connection between what they do and the world they read about in their *Times* or *Telegraph*.

John Finnis's view of the law is coming back into fashion. The talk he gave served to launch a judicial power project organized by a right-leaning think tank and with many well-known scholars on its academic advisory council.[3] For those exasperated by the Strasbourg Court and all this endless talk of human rights, that ancient code of laws beckons as an agreeable home for serious discussion, a place of safety for the intelligent sceptic of the limitations—one might almost say the *stupidity*—of modern life. Indeed to take an example from one of the papers just mentioned, the *Telegraph*, Charles Moore was quick to draw on Finnis's remarks as his inspiration for a critique of those of the judges who embrace the activism of rights language before choosing to end his piece with this paean of praise for the old ways:

> Against this, England (Scotland is not the same) has something quite different. It is called the Common Law. Because we developed and spread it, it remains the basis for the law of more than two billion people across the globe today. It is called 'Common' for the same reason that the House of Commons is so named. It is common to us, in virtue of being the English people.[4]

This new mood of common law revivalism has extended into politics and onto the bench itself. As we shall see in Chapter 12 no less august a body than the Supreme Court has been turning to the common law with new-found enthusiasm. During the debate on the Queen's Speech directly after the election of the new Conservative administration in May 2015, the incoming Secretary of State for Justice and Lord Chancellor Michael Gove used irony in order to praise (by seeming to damn) the past in a way that was clearly designed to destabilize the (human rights) present:

> I did think that there was an element of the lurid in the description of what would happen if we were to tamper in any way with the Human Rights Act. To listen to Labour Members at some points one would have thought that prior to 1998 this country was a lawless wasteland in which

[3] See <http://www.policyexchange.org.uk/item/judicial-power-project-academic-advisory-council> [accessed 9 November 2015]. Two of the eleven members of the council are women.

[4] 'Our top judges have become too powerful—we need to rein them in' *Telegraph* 24 October 2015: <http://www.telegraph.co.uk/news/politics/11951936/Our-top-judges-have-become-too-powerful-we-need-to-rein-them-in.html> [accessed 9 November 2015].

the innocent were put to the sword and no one had any recourse to justice, and that after 1998 we entered a land where the rule of law was at last respected, after decades, if not centuries, of arbitrary rule.[5]

The Lord Chancellor was able in his speech to draw on the critique of serving and recently retired judges to buttress his case against the Human Rights Act about which 'distinguished Supreme Court justices [had] expressed concern'.[6] We shall come later to the way some of these judges have extra-judicially let themselves go in a Finnis-type way about the European Court of Human Rights and the negative impact these speeches have had on perceptions of human rights at home. At the root of this type of critique is frequently to be found a hankering after our golden past. To take a prominent example, to the President of the Supreme Court Lord Neuberger 'there is no doubt that the common law was in many ways the origin and promoter of individual rights', with its only problem being (and the reason for the turn to rights) that 'it developed such rights in a somewhat haphazard and leisurely way'.[7] In his recent, beautifully written Hamlyn lectures, the celebrated Court of Appeal judge Lord Justice John Laws sings a Finnis-style hymn of praise to the old common law, arguing both that it is the unifying principle of the constitution with its 'insights' of 'reason, fairness and the presumption of liberty' and that 'its distinctive method has endowed the British State with profoundly beneficial effects'.[8] The recently retired Lord Chief Justice Lord Igor Judge took a not dissimilar line in a lecture at University College London where he defended the courts from executive interference against a background of unquestioned acceptance of the fact of the 'independence of judicial decision making' as 'an integral structure of

[5] HC Debs, 28 May 2015, col 291.

[6] Ibid.

[7] 'The Role of Judges in Human Rights Jurisprudence: A Comparison of the Australian and UK Experience': Supreme Court of Victoria 8 August 2014, para 2: <http://sup remecourt.uk/docs/speech-140808.pdf> [accessed 4 November 2014].

[8] J Laws, *The Common Law Constitution* (The Hamlyn Lectures 2013) (Cambridge: Cambridge University Press, 2014), at p 7 and p 3 respectively.

the constitution'.[9] One of the leaders of the common law resurgence, and a judge specifically mentioned by Michael Gove in his parliamentary remarks, is the former law lord Lord Hoffmann for whom a festschrift has been recently published, celebrating his contribution to the development of English law as both judge and academic; the only chapter specifically about human rights to be found in it is one by a specialist in the field rebutting Lord Hoffmann's critique of human rights law.[10]

This warm retrospective of the common law is underpinned by academic scholarship which often goes so far as to find in it the source of freedom within the British constitution. Important here are the work of scholars like Paul Craig,[11] Jeffrey Jowell,[12] and (of course) John Finnis himself, and also—perhaps even mainly among contemporaries—the very substantial achievements of Trevor Allan at Cambridge, driving through in a lifetime of consistent academic engagement a basic thesis well summed up in the title of his most recent and ambitious opus, *The Sovereignty of Law: Freedom, Constitution*

---

[9] 'Constitutional Change: Unfinished Business' University College London 4 December 2013: <https://www.nottingham.ac.uk/hrlc/documents/specialevents/lordjudgelecture041213.pdf> at para 7 [accessed 10 May 2016].

[10] P S Davies and J Pila (eds), *The Jurisprudence of Lord Hoffmann: A Festschrift in Honour of Lord Leonard Hoffmann* (Oxford: Hart Publishing, 2015). The chapter (at pp 97–114) is by S Fredman, 'Are Human Rights Culturally Determined: A Riposte to Lord Hoffmann'. For a sample of Lord Hoffmann's critical views see 'The Universality of Human Rights' Judicial Studies Board Annual Lecture, 19 March 2009: <https://www.judiciary.gov.uk/announcements/speech-by-lord-hoffmann-the-universality-of-human-rights/> [accessed 25 March 2016].

[11] P Craig, 'The Common Law, Shared Power and Judicial Review' (2004) 24 (2) *Oxford Journal of Legal Studies* 237–57; P Craig, 'Constitutional and Non-Constitutional Review' (2001) 54 *Current Legal Problems* 147–78; Select Committee on the Constitution, *Relations Between the Executive, the Judiciary and Parliament* appendix 5, Paper by Professor Paul Craig on the Rule of Law (Sixth Report; HL 151 of 2006–7): <http://www.publications.parliament.uk/pa/ld200607/ldselect/ldconst/151/15115.htm> [accessed 10 November 2015]. See also for a very well-argued critique from the Conservative perspective J Fisher, *The British Bill of Rights: Protecting Freedom Under the Law* (London: Politeia, 2015).

[12] J Jowell, 'Beyond the Rule of Law: Towards Constitutional Judicial Review' [2000] *Public Law* 671–83; J Jowell, 'The Rule of Law Today' in J Jowell and D Oliver (eds), *The Changing Constitution* 3rd edn (Oxford: Oxford University Press, 1994) ch 3, esp pp 72–3.

and Common Law.[13] The heroes of these common law partisans are the preservers of tradition from days long gone by, not only the Bacons and the Cokes of Finnis's lecture, but also even earlier writers like Bracton and Glanville, with towering presences like those of Blackstone, Dicey, and Maitland stepping in in later times to take us through to the modern era. Dicey in particular—another 'Oxford man' (like so many of these ancient writers) but one who lived on into the near-remembered times of the early 1920s—is hugely influential for the way he sought to work parliamentary sovereignty into a constitution which was to his mind still nevertheless rooted in a common law dedicated to and guarantor of individual freedom. For all these men—contemporary or ancient; Oxford or Cambridge—the common law inevitably and rightly stands centre stage for the sheer vastness of its commitment to freedom, doing human rights better (more nuanced; more sensitive; more respectful of tradition; etc) than human rights has ever managed by itself, especially on the Continent. (With nineteenth-century continental charters in mind, Dicey was particularly critical of 'those declarations or definitions of rights so dear to foreign constitutionalists'.[14])

How true is this version of the common law? It depends on whose freedom we are concerned with, what sort of freedom we have in mind, and which English people it is of whose virtue the common law is the legal embodiment. Certainly this judge-made system has thrived on a premise about respect for property ownership that has long made the political weather, underpinning the intellectual case for the constitutional settlement of the late seventeenth century, and thereafter surviving well into the democratic era as a central assumption of good governance. The common law has also undoubtedly played a central part in facilitating the growth of our market society by

[13] T R S Allan, *The Sovereignty of Law: Freedom, Constitution and Common Law* (Oxford: Oxford University Press, 2013).

[14] A V Dicey, *Introduction to the Study of the Law of the Constitution* 8th edn (London: Macmillan, 1915), at p 116.

showing a strong commitment to freedom of contract, the right of us all to make agreements with whomsoever we wish. (More in Chapter 12 on these ideological dimensions to the common law.) As Finnis says, the nature of its adversarial process is compelling, with its respect for tradition frequently well judged and for that reason effective. As the remarks made a moment ago about the professor's lecture suggest, however, that same common law has not been so good at recognizing any kind of deeper structure to the society out of which arise the disputes that its judges encounter. The sort of deliberate eschewing of the wider context of which Professor Finnis's lecture is such a good example has this large weakness: it is blind to power and privilege and therefore to the commitments to equality and non-discrimination with which those discontented with the status quo seek to achieve change.[15] Historically these ideas have had to fight the common law, not rely on it.

Take as a classic example of this point the Lord Chief Justice for almost the whole of the inter-war period Gordon Hewart, first a baron and eventually a viscount, a liberal politician who had been Solicitor General and Attorney General before being appointed directly to the highest position on the bench in 1922 where he remained until his retirement in 1940. As Lord Chief Justice he wrote a book in 1929 which created an immense stir when it appeared, partly because of the status of the writer but also on account of the power of both its message and the prose used to communicate it. *The New Despotism*[16] is a cry of despair against the 'genuine belief'—one that was in 'certain quarters ascendant'—that 'Parliamentary institutions and the Rule of Law have been tried and found wanting, and that the time has come for the departmental despot, who shall be at once scientific and

---

[15] A point that Allan in his book seeks to address with his idea of the 'rule of law' as 'an ideal of fair and just governance' which imposes 'standards of equality and due process' (p 119). As is often the case in legal analysis, much depends on whether one looks first at the reasoning in cases (which is often fine) and only then (passingly) at the results (which from a claimant's point of view are less so), or the other way round.

[16] Gordon Hewart, *The New Despotism* (London: Ernest Benn, 1929).

benevolent, but above all a law to himself.'[17] Hewart the old school liberal was setting himself against the newly emerging administrative state tasked to push government into the lives of the public further than ever before in a broad public interest of the definition of which these administrators were the initial and often the sole custodians. Crucial to this perspective was Hewart's belief in the long-standing virtue of 'the supremacy of Law'—something 'more than the exclusion of arbitrary power, and something more also than the equality of all citizens before the ordinary law of the land administered by the ordinary Courts'. To Hewart, it also meant that 'in this country, unlike some foreign countries, the principles of the Constitution are, in Dicey's phrase, inductions or generalizations based upon decisions pronounced by the Courts as to the rights of particular individuals'[18]—in other words it reflected the strengths of the common law, with us 'ever since the eleventh century' but now facing the real risk of being 'diminished or destroyed',[19] not at the hands of 'foreign constitutionalists' (some would no doubt say today's problem) but the new despotism of state power.

Powerful language like this must have emboldened litigants before the Lord Chief Justice who sought to call the state to account for the abuse of their rights. But Hewart was a reactionary in every sense: he hated the new administrative state but he despised radical challenges to authority from the Left even more. The police were outside his critical gaze, especially when they were cracking down on public protest. So when attempts to demonstrate outside labour exchanges against mass unemployment in the early 1930s were being constantly thwarted by the police, a full-scale challenge was mounted before Lord Hewart and his colleagues on the High Court, citing back at him his own words and those of Dicey on whom in his book he had strongly relied. This was all to no avail. Interrupting counsel for the police

[17] Ibid at p 14.
[18] Ibid at pp 25–6.
[19] Ibid at p 23.

without even bothering to hear their defence and leading his colleagues on the bench to an immediate ruling (*ex tempore*), Hewart
quickly dismissed the appeal, even going so far as to deny that it raised
any issue of free speech at all: 'This case...does not even touch that
important question.'[20] The 'right of assembly' was 'nothing more than
a view taken by the Court of the individual liberty of the subject', and
here 'the Court' took another view entirely: 'It does not require
authority to emphasise the statement that it is the duty of a police
officer to prevent apprehended breaches of the peace.'[21]

Hewart was unusual in the vehemence with which he spoke against
the modern state in his notorious book but he was absolutely mainstream when it came to the common law's enthusiastic defence
of police denial of rights of free speech and of public protest.
Through the twentieth century the courts were creative, energetic,
and determined—not to protect freedom but in their efforts to support authority against all those who would challenge it from the Left.
In the 1920s, a decade or so before the case just described, the
Communist Party leadership was dispatched to prison on charges of
conspiracy to publish seditious libels so lavishly supported by the trial
judge that the jury took no more than ten minutes to convict.[22] In
later years, the police were retrospectively vindicated in law for incur-
sions into meetings of which they disapproved[23] and for the seizure of
materials from radicals whom they regarded as unacceptably subversive.[24] Looking both further back and forward, to the extent that the
common law embraced within its remit principles of statutory interpretation then these were deployed during both world wars to
empower the executive branch even more than the parliaments of

---

[20] *Duncan v Jones* [1936] 1 KB 218, at p 222.

[21] Ibid at p 223 per Humphreys J.

[22] The story is told in K D Ewing and C A Gearty, *The Struggle for Civil Liberties: Political
Freedom and the Rule of Law in Britain, 1914–1945* (Oxford: Oxford University Press, 2000),
at pp 136–51.

[23] *Thomas v Sawkins* [1935] 2 KB 249.

[24] *Elias v Pasmore* [1934] 2 KB 164.

the day had intended. *Salus populi suprema lex* ('the safety of the state being the highest law') was how one First World War judge put it.[25] During the Second War the phrase 'reasonable cause to believe' (required by the relevant piece of delegated legislation) of a Home Secretary before detaining someone without trial was construed to mean in fact merely thinking he had such a reasonable belief, in the majority decision of a (particularly abject) House of Lords bench.[26] Mr Justice McCowan's puzzlement that he could not instruct a jury to equate the interests of the state with the interests of the government of the day (in a well-known official secrets prosecution in the mid-1980s[27]) was not some maverick intervention by a judge out of kilter with his rights-conscious colleagues but rather a man doing exactly what the common law culture to which he belonged had long demanded: hammer dissidents in court while celebrating the ancient constitution's commitment to rights when at dinner in the Temple or in the Oxbridge common room afterwards. (This is why so few of the protagonists for the common law focus on cases; they are invariably (and given the record necessarily) more comfortable in the realm of theory than of fact.)

What would Dicey have made of these twentieth-century developments? Hero to Lord Hewart and invoked with misty-eyed respect by the contemporary celebrants of the old ways, he was someone for whom the 'rule of law' involved 'the subjection of government to standards of respect for individual freedom and dignity',[28] by which he meant 'the predominance of the legal spirit' as one of his biographers has called it.[29] But of course he was just as bad: freedom was not for the undeserving whatever his theory might seem to demand. One

---

[25] *Michaels v Block* (1918) 34 TLR 438, at p 438. See also *Chester v Bateson* [1920] 1 KB 829.

[26] *Liversidge v Anderson* [1942] AC 206.

[27] *R v Ponting* [1985] *Crim Law Review* 318.

[28] Allan (n 13), at pp 104–5.

[29] R A Cosgrove, *The Rule of Law: Albert Venn Dicey, Victorian Jurist* (London and Basingstoke: The Macmillan Press, 1980), at p 79.

example may make the general point. Dicey's leading work—which went to multiple editions and has helped enormously to shape the twentieth-century perception of the English constitution as a bastion of freedom—made an immense fuss of an obscure (but when the book first came out contemporary) decision from Weston-super-Mare in which the High Court was to be found requiring that the Salvation Army be allowed to march to demand temperance even where their conduct was certain to be opposed by aggressive locals, factions who had been organized into a Skeleton Army so as to make this display of proselytizing teetotal radicalism impossible.[30] Dicey drew from this '[t]he principle, then, that a meeting otherwise in every respect lawful and peaceable is not rendered unlawful merely by the possible or probable misconduct of wrongdoers, who to prevent the meeting are determined to break the peace'.[31] In truth it depended on what kind of 'lawful and peaceable' meeting you were planning. At around the same time as this Salvation Army case, a gathering of Irish Land Leaguers organized by a member of Parliament protesting about injustices in Ireland's land law and calling for reform was banned because a local magistrate took the view that the intended opposition of an Orange mob made it impossible to let it go ahead.[32] Counsel's enthusiastic reliance on the new English case from Weston-super-Mare did him no good in the (Irish) Court of Appeal, and all Dicey could add by way of explanation was a footnoted exception to his 'well estab-lished'[33] principle, namely that this recent Irish case 'carried furthest the right of magistrates to preserve the peace by dispersing a lawful meeting' where it was 'believed that there would be a breach of the peace if the meeting broken up continued assembled, and that there was no other way by which the breach of the peace could be avoided

---

[30] *Beatty v Gillbanks* (1882) 9 QBD 308.

[31] (n 14), at p 174.

[32] *O'Kelly v Harvey* (1883) 15 Cox CC 435.

[33] (n 14), at p 174.

but by stopping and dispersing the meeting'.[34] There you have it, the common law's golden rule: 'no to mob rule, unless it is our mob'.

There are far more examples of the Irish case in the law reports than there are of victory for the Salvationists (whose radicalism went only so far, after all, as to demand that the working class be sober as well as poor). In *Despard v Wilcox*,[35] an assembly from the Women's Freedom League had gathered in Downing Street with the intention of presenting a petition to the Prime Minister and was in due course cleared by the police with a number of arrests made. Subsequent legal proceedings vindicated the police action: in vain did the Suffragette activists rely on *Beatty v Gillbanks* to argue that they were exercising their ancient common law rights. Judges have always been reactionary, hardly surprising when we recall that their job is to uphold the law, a code of control that you do not need to be Michel Foucault to see is by definition made up of the spoils of the victory of an already concluded political battle. The seventeenth century witnessed the courts being largely supportive of the determination of various Stuart kings to identify a legal basis for the extension of their royal power. Sir Edward Coke was notoriously sacked in 1616 for defiance of the King in circumstances well described in Professor Finnis's Gray's Inn lecture and was not a fan of royal power thereafter—but most judges were not like Coke and stayed safely on the bench, upholding this and that exercise of regal power until the fall came, first in the middle of the century and conclusively with the flight of the Stuarts near its end. Residues of the courts' role as a judicial buttress to royal power continued into the eighteenth century, albeit slowly transforming themselves as the decades progressed into unquestioning supporters of that new source of executive power, cabinet (and prime ministerial) government. True, we have a persistently remembered ruling by Lord Mansfield on slavery,[36] and also a renowned decision on state power

---

[34] Ibid at p 175 n 19.

[35] (1910) 26 TLR 226; cf *Pankhurst v Jarvis* (1910) 26 TLR 118.

[36] *The Case of James Sommersett* (1771–2) 20 St Tr 1.

by Lord Camden and his colleagues on the Court of Common Pleas around the middle of the century.[37] But 'one swallow does not a Summer make'—the most dependable guarantors of liberty during the heady days of late eighteenth-century revolt were politicians like John Wilkes and the brave jury members that defied judicial instructions to acquit him and men like him time and time again. The great repression that followed the French Revolution and survived through the long and drearily authoritarian prime ministership of Lord Liverpool was rarely troubled by any kind of libertarian reaction from the courts. Even after male suffrage was achieved, the courts continued in their most reactionary mode through the hundred years that followed, denying women any opportunity to secure participation in the political process[38] and even trying to strangle the Labour Party at birth through denying it the right to have its members of Parliament paid out of union funds.[39] The twentieth century did not come out of nowhere.

A passing reference was made earlier to the moral framework of the common law, the principles that keep it afloat, mentioning two of these—the right to respect for property ownership, and freedom of contract. The point of recalling these again now is to stress that while it may be true that the common law was 'in many respects ethically aimless',[40] in certain important ways it most definitely was not: it is just that progressives (and human rights advocates) do not care very much for the ethic they find so sharply defined and deeply embedded. Anthony Lester himself—the source of the remark just quoted—has done important work with the lawyer Geoffrey Bindman to show

---

[37] *Entick v Carrington* (1765) 19 St Tr 1030.

[38] '[I]t was a principle of the unwritten constitutional law of the country that men only were entitled to take part in the election of representatives to Parliament': *Nairn v The University Court of St Andrews* 1907, 15 SLT 471, at p 473.

[39] *Amalgamated Society of Railway Servants v Osborne* [1910] AC 87.

[40] A Lester, 'The European Court of Human Rights after 50 Years' in J Christoffersen and M R Madsen (eds), *The European Court of Human Rights: Between Law and Politics* (Oxford: Oxford University Press, 2011) 98, at p 100.

quite how much work Parliament had to do to undo a commitment to freedom that allowed employers perfectly lawfully to discriminate against people from different ethnic backgrounds, and permitted dance halls, hotels, and pubs to refuse them entry and lodgings to refuse to take them.[41] In an earlier work, the late Bob Hepple explained why the 'victim of job discrimination who seeks redress in the courts of law is likely to be frustrated. The major reason for this is that the judge-made common law does not recognise racial discrimination as a distinct legal wrong in itself.'[42] This was an area that required statutory intervention, as did that of the freedom to incite racial hatred, cloistered under the common law in the absence of a threat to the peace until 1965. There is an important point that arises out of this last remark. The common law did defend the freedom of some but it was on a perennially partial basis. Thus, as the line of cases already mentioned has already demonstrated, this solicitude for liberty of speech did not mean that radical interventions of an undesirable sort had to be tolerated. As the Home Secretary said in 1924, defending the prosecution of the Communist Party leadership for seditious libel earlier referred to, the convicted men had not been engaged in the 'right type of freedom of speech'.[43] This mysterious notion was the ancient liberty which gave you 'the right to a full propagation of your opinion, provided you do not try to damage the Constitution'.[44] Communists were at one with women, workers, blacks, and Irish, all of them the wrong kind of people to enjoy the 'commonalty' of the common law. Parliament tamed the King. The 'People' eventually tamed Parliament. And then Parliament tamed the common law. And a good thing too.

[41] A Lester and G Bindman, *Race and Law in Britain* (Cambridge, Mass: Harvard University Press, 1972).

[42] B Hepple, *Race, Jobs and the Law in Britain* (London: Allen Lane, 1968), at p 91.

[43] HC Debs, 1 December 1925, col 2093.

[44] Ibid.

Now we must not lull ourselves into any kind of belief that the story told here is ancient history, some kind of shout from an antediluvian past. Professor Finnis's lecture and its popular reception may be thought to show clearly enough that this is not the case. There is a final point to cover, a myth within a myth that needs now to be nailed. The argument runs something like this: it concedes that all that I have said here is true but goes on to claim that the judges have in recent times changed, that the common law had reshaped itself well in advance of the arrival of all this human rights talk, and as a result it can now to be trusted to approach liberty with a new perspective, one rooted in a different set of values than might have governed in the past. We don't need human rights because we have this new vibrant, decent, reformed common law, one that disowns its own murky past while being (in some complicated way) rooted in it. But if this is true today, then it is only *because* of the Human Rights Act, not *despite* it. The last full decade before enactment of the Human Rights Act was the 1980s, a time that was (as many will recall) notorious for the extension of authoritarian state power at the expense of workers, demonstrators, Irish political activists, nuclear disarmament campaigners, and many others besides. The late Margaret Thatcher strode the stage as Prime Minister imposing her will via strong police and secret service interventions which had a series of negative impacts on freedom. Where was the glorious modern reformed common law when all this was happening?

3

THE SEDUCTIVE POWER
OF THE PRESENT

The year 1988 ought to have been one of celebration for the courts, the common law and the British constitution generally. Instead, the 300th anniversary of the original bill of rights that had marked the final victory of Parliament over the King in 1688 was greeted with relative silence from those whom one would have expected to be jubilant, and a cascade of critical commentary from those who were not. Books on the urgent need for reform proliferated, with anxious titles like *Time for a New Constitution*[1] and *The Coercive State.*[2] Pressure groups were formed which, looking deliberately east to the Soviet Union and its satellite states, sought to capture in their very names the depth to which freedom and liberty were believed to have fallen: *Samizdat*[3] and *Charter 88.*[4] *Glasnost in Britain?* was published, an edited collection inspired by the appearance of Russian intellectuals at the

---

[1] R Holme and M Elliott (eds), *Time for a New Constitution 1688–1988* (Basingstoke: The Macmillan Press, 1988).

[2] P Hillyard and J Percy-Smith, *The Coercive State: The Decline of Democracy in Britain* (London: Fontana Press, 1988).

[3] Out of which grew B Pimlott, A Wright, and T Flower (eds), *Politics for a Change* (London: W H Allen, 1990), hoping to create a 'popular front of the mind' as Ross McKibbin noted in his review of the book (1990) 12 (16) *London Review of Books* 7–8, 7: <http://www.lrb.co.uk/v12/n16/ross-mckibbin/what-a-progressive-government-will-have-to-do> [accessed 23 November 2015]. The campaign was one with which the late Ben Pimlott was closely involved: <http://www.theguardian.com/news/2004/apr/12/guardianobituaries.politicsphilosophyandsociety> [accessed 17 November 2015].

[4] See <https://www.opendemocracy.net/ok-tags/charter-88> [accessed 17 November 2015].

On Fantasy Island: Britain, Europe, and Human Rights. First Edition. Conor Gearty.

Edinburgh festival.[5] The magisterial legal philosopher Ronald Dworkin intervened with ideas that were to take shape within a couple of years as *A Bill of Rights for Britain: Why British Liberty Needs Protection*.[6] As Dworkin's title illustrates, all this anxious scrutiny engendered by the memory of 1688 gave the British movement for a new human rights law the powerful kick-start that it needed to get the campaign for innovative rights legislation properly under way. As we shall see later in this chapter, around this time some of the judges were becoming aware that their usual satisfaction about the status quo was no longer convincing, even (increasingly) to themselves. Despair about the past in 1988 can rightly be regarded as one of the parents of the 1998 Human Rights Act.

The contrast with 2015 and the 800th anniversary of Magna Carta has been stark. This occasion has produced an overflow of state-organized joy. A large international conference (the 'Global Law Summit') attracted 2,000 'leaders in law, business, government and academia from around the world' to central London.[7] On the anniversary day itself a pilgrimage to the original site of the signing of the document (Runnymede, in Surrey) was made by an array of dignitaries headed by the Queen, the Duke of Edinburgh, and Prince William, and including the Prime Minister David Cameron who spoke of the principles behind the document shining 'brighter than ever' in today's Britain. There were fly-pasts by British fighter planes old and new, a programme of recitals and music that included excerpts from Gilbert and Sullivan's *Trial by Jury*.[8] At the invitation of a senior judge, the Master of the Rolls Lord Dyson, the Queen unveiled a plaque marking the event. Whereas in 1988 the judiciary had remained lurking in their

---

[5] See N Buchan and T Sumner (eds), *Glasnost in Britain? Against Censorship and in Defence of the Word* (Basingstoke: The Macmillan Press, 1989).

[6] London: Chatto and Windus, 1990.

[7] See <http://magnacarta800th.com/events/the-global-law-summit/> [accessed 23 November 2015].

[8] See <http://www.theguardian.com/uk-news/2015/jun/15/magna-carta-leaders-celebrate-800th-anniversary-runnymede> for a full report [accessed 17 November 2015].

tents devoted in their avoidance of media attention, senior figures from the bench like Lord Dyson were in 2015 to be found at events home and away, celebrating the past like cheerleaders at an American football game. Lord Neuberger—currently President of the Supreme Court—took the chairmanship of the Magna Carta Trust. The jovial face of the former Master of the Rolls Sir Anthony Clarke graced the home page of the Global Law Summit, writing of Magna Carta as that 'enduring symbol of freedom', one that represents 'the fundamental rights that lie at the very heart of our open and democratic societies as they have developed over the long centuries from Runnymede'.[9] Lord Judge, the former Lord Chief Justice, spoke at the Summit ('Magna Carta: Luck or Judgement?') and later lectured at Salisbury Cathedral on 'Magna Carta and the Law'.[10] The current Supreme Court member Lord Sumption preferred the title 'Magna Carta: Then and Now' for his address on the topic to the Friends of the British Library in March 2015.[11] And this is only scratching the surface of judicial speechmaking.[12]

Why the difference? There were Conservative administrations in power on each occasion it is true, but the country could be said to have been in a very different place in 1988, one from which it has now unequivocally emerged. The response to the memory of 1688 had been what the obituarist of one of those most closely involved in the *Samizdat* initiative Ben Pimlott has called 'a sharp cry against the "the bleak age" of Thatcherism'.[13] Attention focused on the political leader who gave

---

[9] <http://magnacarta8ooth.com/articles/the-continuing-importance-of-magna-carta/> [accessed 23 November 2015].

[10] See <http://www.salisburycathedral.org.uk/events/2015-magna-carta-lectures-magna-carta-and-law-lord-judge> [accessed 23 November 2015].

[11] See <https://www.supremecourt.uk/docs/speech-150309.pdf> [accessed 23 November 2015].

[12] Cf an academic treatment that neatly avoids these self-congratulatory traps and so manages to provide a powerful account of human rights which draws on the tradition epitomized by Magna Carta: F M Klug, *A Magna Carta for All Humanity* (London: Routledge, 2014).

[13] Kenneth O Morgan at <http://www.theguardian.com/news/2004/apr/12/guardianobituaries.politicsphilosophyandsociety> [accessed 17 November 2015].

the era its name. *Charter 88* complained of the dominance of the then Prime Minister Margaret Thatcher, and the risk that under her aggressive watch the political system had veered into destructive authoritarianism. It was this concern that accounted for the movement's strength in academic, journalistic, and progressive circles, and even among some Conservatives. The checks that had been put in place by the constitutional settlement of 1688—between parliament and the executive—and which had been copper-fastened so far as the judges were concerned by the later Act of Settlement of 1701 were perceived to have failed, with the result that an eastern European political climate was thought to be beckoning even while that very model of government was fast disappearing in its place of origin. Constitutional concerns remain in 2015 of course but they are of a very different order.

Acting in their traditional real-life manner (as opposed to what the high theory discussed in the last chapter seemed to demand and the speeches celebrating Magna Carta in 2015 casually assumed), the judges that had had so little to say in 1988 had been complicit in the decline of liberty that had come to worry so many at the end of the 1980s, and with a brief reminder of which we ended the last chapter. Mrs Thatcher's drive towards more executive power at the expense of freedom was legitimized by judicial imprimatur at every stage in the process; if liberty was indeed 'ill in Britain' as Ronald Dworkin famously claimed in 1988,[14] then the courts were acting less as a cure than as enthusiastic exacerbator of the malady. The glum litany of failure is a long one, including as it does the following shabby highlights: permitting the banning of nuclear disarmament marches when that movement was at its height (so much for *Beatty v Gillbanks!*);[15] empowering the police to do whatever it took to defeat the industrial action of the coalminers in a bitter dispute in 1983–4

[14] 'Devaluing Liberty' *Index on Censorship Special Issue* 17 (8) (1988), at pp 7–8: <http://www.tandfonline.com/doi/abs/10.1080/03064228808534496?journalCode=rioc20> [accessed 18 November 2015].

[15] *Kent v Metropolitan Police Commissioner* The Times 15 May 1981. For *Beatty v Gillbanks* see Ch 2.

(including expanding the common law to permit picketers to be turned away from still-working collieries at which they proposed to protest);[16] ordering the *Guardian* to reveal its sources for stories about the arrival of American nuclear missiles in Britain, and then overseeing the prosecution (and jailing) of the woman employee found to have been responsible;[17] (as we mentioned in Chapter 2) begging a jury to convict in a secrets case on the basis that the interests of the state could not be separated from those of the government of the day;[18] upholding a ban on trade unions at the government's Communications Headquarters (GCHQ) despite acknowledged procedural flaws on supposed grounds of 'national security' of which the government itself—in the shape of the Minister for the Civil Service (no other than Margaret Thatcher)—was permitted to be the sole judge;[19] sanctioning a series of aggressive police raids on the offices and homes of those responsible for reporting the launch of an expensive spy satellite in defiance of parliamentary rules governing when such matters should be made public;[20] and upholding a media ban on a lawful political party Sinn Féin, censorship which also extended to those whose views coincided with the party's aims.[21]

The cloak of false principle and ancient authority which (as again we saw in Chapter 2) had so long disguised these partisan warriors as being somehow above the fray just about survived these various incidents, albeit it is true at some cumulative cost, a fraying of a different sort. The judges were increasingly being seen not as above but rather as part of the problem and some of the judges were

---

[16] *Moss v McLachlan* [1985] IRLR 76.

[17] *Guardian Newspapers Ltd v Secretary of State for Defence* [1985] AC 339. See K D Ewing and C A Gearty, *Freedom Under Thatcher: Civil Liberties in Modern Britain* (Oxford: Oxford University Press, 1990), at pp 139–43.

[18] *R v Ponting* [1985] *Crim Law Review* 318. The jury refused, famously acquitting the accused.

[19] *Council of Civil Service Unions v Minister for the Civil Service* [1985] AC 374.

[20] Ewing and Gearty (n 17), at pp 147–52.

[21] *R (Brind) v Secretary of State for the Home Department* [1991] 1 AC 696.

beginning themselves to see that the critics might have a point. What had ripped the camouflage away completely by 1988—adding to the indignation of the activists but also on this occasion and most damagingly being understood as self-evidently ridiculous by members of the general public who take no great interest in politics and law—was the *Spycatcher* affair. A former MI5 operative Peter Wright had set about writing a book of this title recounting in some detail (and despite the Official Secrets Act) stories from his time in the service, and making in particular two incendiary claims: that MI5 had, the decade before, conspired to destabilize the Labour administration of Harold Wilson, and (just as shockingly) that its former chief Sir Roger Hollis had been a Soviet double-agent. The government's reaction was to set about preventing the book's publication at all costs, deploying the law of confidence in a global assault on proposed publishing outlets. The Cabinet Secretary Sir Robert Armstrong appeared in the mid-1980s in the guise of a roving litigant as he toured the world seeking injunctions wherever he happened to touch down, on one occasion (in the course of an Australian cross-examination with a young lawyer who was to become Australian Prime Minister, Malcolm Turnbull) giving the world a famous new phrase, conceding he had been 'economical with the truth' about a particular matter rather than (as others, less refined, might have put it) simply lying. With failure after failure mounting abroad (and no effort even being made in the home of free speech, First Amendment America), the courts in Britain found themselves being drawn ever deeper into the quagmire of litigation in which the government was already drowning. Recklessly compliant to the wishes of state power in their usual manner, they joined in the repressive campaign, but to catastrophic effect.

Excerpts of the book were banned from the British newspapers; new contempt laws were devised by the judges to ensure general compliance with orders which had been made only against specific papers; libraries were instructed on what books to hold; interlocutory relief was used as a device to close down debate. Eventually on 30 July 1987 the House of Lords—then the UK's supreme judicial body—

ordered continuing temporary restrictions on the book's reporting, indeed hardened these somewhat, despite a by now widespread awareness (thanks to foreign publication or reportage) of what the book had to say.[22] True, it was a narrow win for the authorities—three votes to two—but the majority's decision not only to make the order but not even to offer reasons until they returned from their holidays not only caused uproar but invited ridicule as well. The courts found themselves roundly condemned and the perception of their performance as poodles of power persisted notwithstanding subsequent grumpy acceptance of the newspapers' actions in later proceedings.[23] Meanwhile it fell to the European Court of Human Rights to restore a degree of balance to the debate, deploying the right to freedom of expression to acknowledge that with publication already having taken place worldwide, this was a publications horse than had long since bolted from the national security stable.[24]

The bridge from the despair of 1988 to the judicial hubris of 2015 began to be erected in the early 1990s when a final hurricane of bad behaviour left the judges ethically homeless: if the *Spycatcher* debacle began the move of the senior judiciary towards an embracing of the human rights idea, the miscarriage of justice cases that emerged soon after made reform impossible to avoid. It is hard now to imagine the dramatic impact of the revelations that came time after time in the early 1990s of Northern Irish convicted 'terrorists' against whom on closer reflection it was apparent that there was either no credible evidence at all or, even if there was, not enough for guilt ever to have been established beyond reasonable doubt.[25] The 'Birmingham

---

[22] *Attorney General v Guardian Newspapers Ltd* [1987] 1 WLR 1248.

[23] *Attorney General v Guardian Newspapers Ltd (No 2)* [1990] 1 AC 109.

[24] *Observer and Guardian v United Kingdom* (1991) 14 EHRR 153; *Sunday Times v United Kingdom (No 2)* (1991) 14 EHRR 229.

[25] For a near contemporary account from a journalist who had been in the front line of reportage of these events see J Rozenberg, *The Search for Justice: An Anatomy of the Law* (London: Hodder and Stoughton, 1994), ch 7 ('When Justice Miscarries'). All the details referred to in this paragraph can easily be followed up there.

Six', 'the Guildford Four', 'the Maguire Seven' were the infamous Irish cases, and these were then followed by a succession of British-based revelations: for a while it looked to concerned members of the general public as though more of the convicted were 'fitted up' or made the victims of fabricated confessions than there were prisoners legitimately in jail. The role of the judges in all this was either as passive legitimizers of state abuse or—more scandalously—as drivers of the wrong convictions in the first place and (when these were secured) as actors determined to save institutional face by keeping them in jail at any cost. Mr Justice Bridge felt able to share with the jury in the Birmingham case his belief (as the trial judge) in the defendants' guilt. Lord Denning MR—possibly the most celebrated judge of his (or any other) day—explained a refusal to allow a civil action by one set of Irish prisoners to proceed because if they were right about what they said 'an appalling vista' would unfold before the judges' and the country's eyes, one which by implication we simply had to refuse to see. The Lord Chief Justice Lord Lane led the Court of Appeal in denying any miscarriage in the Birmingham case despite the evidence adduced in this review of the case pointing firmly in the opposite direction. When the public clamour for justice grew impossible to resist in these arguments, the government itself began to concede the cases rather than risk trying to persuade the judges to recant.

As we have seen and the Magna Carta remembrance events showed, the speeches of today's senior judiciary reflect a renewed confidence, both in the common law and in their own ability to manage it, that is at odds with the taste left in the public mouth by this series of judicial debacles. The current crop of senior judiciary appear honestly to believe that they now put real flesh onto the common law bones of equality and justice, bones onto which, in the bad old days (that are rarely explicitly noted but always in the background), mere partisanship (for class; for gender; for security) used resolutely to cling. These many celebrations of today are understandably (though not excusably) happier speaking of ancient history than of the disturbing, more immediate past of which we have just had a brief glimpse. As we shall see in Chapter 7, far from acknowledging that the Strasbourg Court has helped the common law renew itself from its recent low, some of today's serving and former judges have not been above using their celebration of Magna Carta as a route into some noisy berating of the 'Johnny foreigners' on the Strasbourg Court for their failure to understand the true genius of the English way of doing things.

A point made at the end of Chapter 2 bears repeating. What is rarely acknowledged or appreciated in the midst of all this contemporary and somewhat shrill talk of common law quality and Strasbourg inadequacy is just how much the civil libertarian advances of today's judges (real enough as we shall see so far as the late 1990s and first decade of the 2000s is concerned) are down not to some renaissance of ancient indigenous sensitivity but to the fact of the Human Rights Act itself. It has been the true game-changer, from its conception in the political sphere, its adoption as a sensible proposed reform by the senior judiciary, and (perhaps most of all) its subsequent enactment followed as this was by the long period of training undergone by the whole judiciary before it came into force, on 2 October 2000. Politicians like Michael Gove and academics like John Finnis (both of whom we encountered in Chapter 2) can join today's judges in praise of the common law for its steadfast commitment to principle, its universality, and the depth of its fairness. But—to make the point just made again in a slightly different way—the common law that they and we see today does not stand apart from the Human Rights Act, just as it is not removed from earlier benign legislative interventions to correct its many mistakes (some of which were mentioned in Chapter 2). This ancient English code of 'unwritten' law has in the past fifteen years grown through the Act, drawing from it the inspiration to make its claims for justice truer than they have ever been before. The common law has needed the Human Rights Act more than the human rights movement has ever needed the common law, just as it has needed earlier legislative interventions to modify its intrinsic unfairness.[26]

---

[26] See Ch 2.

One of the more interesting questions about repeal, and one to which we will return in Chapter 12, is how many of these human-rights-based improvements to the common law will survive the measure's likely repeal. That issue is indelibly linked to the wider one of a changing judicial culture, a subject that squarely belongs here, in this chapter on what sort of human-rights-inspired common law we really have today. But before we turn to that, a word or two is required on the great judicial journey to human rights, without the occurrence of which the political destination—legislation on a new human rights law—might never have been reached.

A series of key judicial appointments in the immediate post-*Spycatcher*, post-miscarriages-of-justice era set the tone for the reform agenda that was about to be taken up. Lord Lane finally retired as Chief Justice and in his place came Baron Taylor of Gosforth, Peter Taylor, a barrister from the North-Eastern Circuit, and a man who bore the scars of miscarriages of justice on his back, having been involved as a prosecutor in some of the more notorious of these cases. He brought a fresh atmosphere to the ancient post he held, relaxing an old judicial rule about engaging with the media and proving himself an adept performer on the public stage before his retirement due to ill-health in 1996. (He died the following year.) By the time of his unfortunately premature departure, Taylor had been joined on the bench by figures who were to go on to change the character of the judiciary, men like Tom Bingham (who succeeded the trial judge in the Guildford Four and Maguire Seven cases John Donaldson as Master of the Rolls in 1992 and went on to be Chief Justice), Lord Harry Woolf (Master of the Rolls and then Lord Chief Justice), and Sir Stephen Sedley (High Court and then Court of Appeal). Among them all a single woman managed to squeeze onto the bench, the former academic Brenda Hale who joined the Family Division as a High Court judge in 1994 and who now sits on the Supreme Court as Baroness Hale of Richmond. Now of course it is true that the engagement of these judges (and a few others) in the public sphere—making speeches in favour of change; giving interviews; writing books—was not typical: the vast majority of judges remained what they had always been, quietly successful barristers from privileged backgrounds whose elevation reflected their triumph in a race to the top so rarefied that it was vulgar even to acknowledge it was taking place. But these were the judges among them who occupied the key positions, who made the judicial weather—and their orientation was towards reform.

Under their guidance that weather was turning sharply towards human rights. Lord Taylor had used a very early speech to raise the issue when he was Chief Justice, declaring in his Dimbleby Lecture towards the end of 1992 that 'We should have the courage of our treaty obligations and incorporate the convention.'[27] Lord Bingham as Master of the Rolls gave a talk as part of a debate which was based on an earlier lecture and was afterwards published in the very establishment *Law Quarterly Review*, simply entitled 'The ECHR: Time to Incorporate'.[28] The original discussion may have taken place in a traditional legal environment, but chaired by the then famous TV presenter Sir Robin Day and with cameras trained on his every word, Lord Bingham (as he then wasn't) knew exactly what he was doing. The same was true of Lord Woolf who coupled his work on the simplification of legal processes via the reform of the language of civil procedure with a strong advocacy of incorporation as the right route forward for the country. Certainly it seemed to be that for the judges: nothing marked the break with the past more clearly than this embracing of a new language of universality and human dignity, one that seemed to speak more directly to people than did the old unchallenged but now jaded verities of the past. Their advocacy drew other parts of the profession in: in 1993, the Law Society's Council unanimously came out in favour of incorporation.

It will already be clear from the way these interventions were phrased that the push was for a very specific kind of bill of rights,

[27] See Rozenberg (n 25), at p 213, where a long extract from the speech is given.
[28] (1993) 109 LQR 390.

one which rather than reinventing human rights for the British chose to draw on the already existing European Convention on Human Rights and Fundamental Freedoms, a Council of Europe multilateral treaty agreed in Rome in 1950 and coming into force in 1953, overseen in Strasbourg since the late 1950s by its own regional tribunal, the European Court of Human Rights (with, until the late 1990s, an ancillary European Commission on Human Rights as well). The idea was accordingly more modest than it might have been, a way of rationalizing rather than revolutionizing the law, less radical change than the removal of an anomaly which permitted the Strasbourg Court to hold British policy and law to account against the Convention's rights in a way that British judges were at that time prevented from doing because that same Convention was not explicitly part of domestic law. (Individuals had been able to take the country to this court since 1966.) Delay, expense, and loss of control resulted, negatives that you did not need to be a revolutionary to see needed addressing.

A very neat trick was being pulled off here. Judicial partisanship for what would clearly be a large-scale reform of the law expressed itself with astute modesty when its promoters were laying out the details among their fellow professionals, while all the while the big picture being painted for the public was of a judiciary intent on radical change. Whether by calculated design or by happy accident, it was a brilliantly performed makeover, the leading judicial protagonists for rights being conservative among conservatives, while at the same time looking radical to those who hankered after the radical. As we will see in Chapter 5, the turn to rights by these key judges gave Labour a breathing space in which to develop its own commitment to incorporation, freed by judicial support for the same end from the risk of being dubbed extremist by their political opponents.

There was more going on, though, than merely a human-rights-based transformation of judicial opinion. We turn back now to this wider question of judicial culture, of the sort of body the judiciary has become. The polls did not point to a sustained decline in the respect owed the judiciary as a result of its descent to the low ebb of the late 1980s and early 1990s. It was more a case of an elite community (including in this number the judges themselves) that had lost the belief that was needed for the judges to do their job with the confidence that was required. Even without *Spycatcher* and the miscarriage of justice cases, the change might have come anyway. True the men (and very occasional woman) that populate the senior judiciary today are on the whole drawn from the same class and the same educational backgrounds as their predecessors: the changes have been not in the replacement of these people with something entirely new but in how their equivalents today see the world. The new broom that was whirling through the inner denizens of judicial power in the late 1980s and early 1990s was not just sweeping out specific individuals, it was removing a whole generation—men who had like Lords Lane, Donaldson and Bridge served in the Second World War (Lane had been a decorated pilot; Donaldson a commissioned officer in the Royal Signals; Bridge a captain in the army) or at very least had done compulsory military service. The end of the latter in 1960 meant that lawyers who came of age in that decade were free of that shared male experience which had bonded those who had gone before. They were also, of course, exposed to a changed culture which could not be entirely avoided even by those insulated by privilege in the successive medieval cloisters in which they spent their schooling, their legal studies, and their careers. Early judicial outriders like Lord Scarman (who had argued for a declaration of rights as early as 1975)[29] and Nicolas Browne-Wilkinson (who had fought the consensus in the *Spycatcher* debacle from the lower courts with a degree of courage) became the norm. As already noted, under Lord Woolf's tutelage, the language of court procedures became easier for laypeople to navigate. The top courts became more open and accountable, particularly with the establishment of a new Supreme Court, separate from the House of Lords and consequently aware of its

---

[29] L Scarman, *English Law: The New Dimension* (London: Stevens, 1975).

institutional image in a way that the appellate committee in the upper house had never been.[30] The common law even began to develop its own, indigenous human rights commitment—coincidentally at the same time as enactment of the Human Rights Act but purporting nevertheless to stand apart from it.[31] Simultaneously, principles of access to justice were developed which gave the chance of justice to far wider ranges of people—many of them vulnerable—than might previously have had such opportunities.[32]

In Chapters 9 and 10 we track in detail the way in which the common law and the Human Rights Act have been developed by this new generation of judges. The evidence will be laid out later but it seems reasonably clear that there is a difference between 2015 and 1988: the common law is in a better state now than it has been in the past. This provokes another question, though: if the judges are indeed better equipped to do justice than were their predecessors, not least because of the Human Rights Act itself, will these improvements last? More specifically, if the positive changes in the substance of the common law that we will be discussing owe their origin at least in part to the 1998 Act, can they survive its repeal? Having gone forward will the common law now change gear and move into reverse? We examine the whole question of the sort of effect that removal of the Human Rights Act would have in Chapter 12. Such questions as these are inevitably subsumed in the wider issue of whether the judges would want this to happen. Glorious recalling of the distant past is a bad sign so far as future direction is concerned. We must not take today's judicial perspective on human rights for granted; today is always on its way to becoming tomorrow. By way of conclusion to

[30] See <https://www.supremecourt.uk/> [accessed 27 November 2015].

[31] See eg R (Simms) v Secretary of State for the Home Department [2000] 2 AC 115. See in particular the judgment of Lord Hoffmann on the effect of the Human Rights Act: 'the principles of fundamental human rights which exist at common law will be supplemented by a specific text, namely the European Convention on Human Rights and Fundamental freedoms' (at p 131).

[32] See eg R (Witham) v Lord Chancellor [1997] EWHC 237 (Admin), [1998] QB 575.

this chapter, two caveats need to be entered against over-celebration of this improved present, whether or not the Human Rights Act remains in being.

First, given their age when they reach their positions of power judges are often a generation behind society, fighting their war when the war is over (Lord Lane, etc), living the openness of the 1960s during the harsher 1990s, and in the first years of the 2000s driving forward with human rights just as their brief ascendancy in the political sphere is coming to an end. As of course we have already noted earlier in this book, almost from the moment of its enactment the Human Rights Act has been a source of criticism from government, and with David Cameron's elevation to leader of the Conservative Party in 2005 that critique has broadened to ensnare the Act within a world of other ills: political correctness; health and safety negativity; the nanny state gone mad; and so on. It may already be the case that as the leaders of the judiciary predisposed to human rights gradually leave the stage so they will be replaced by a new generation, less excited by the revolutionary potential of human rights, less keen to use the phrase to achieve change, less concerned by inequality and injustice, men from traditional schools and universities (as they still overwhelmingly are in the senior judiciary) who are harder and more contentedly privileged than their immediate predecessors.[33]

Second and linked to this is the concerted strategy by government, in reaction to the perception of increased judicial scrutiny, to deprive litigants of the opportunity of challenging government in court. Originally this was a reaction to the asylum cases that have been coming so regularly before the courts since the end of the Cold War, but it is by no means limited to these. Whereas in the past direct denial of access to justice has been sought, recent interventions have been subtler, erecting financial barriers to litigation by sharp reductions in access to state-supported legal aid. In the old days—those celebrated

---

[33] For a shift away from reliance on European Convention rights and towards common law rights approach that may not have quite the same progressive reach see Ch 12.

by John Finnis whose speech we discussed at the start of Chapter 2—the higher courts were like the Savoy, a beautifully luxurious service for all that was limited in practice only to those who could afford it. A new common law administering a fine British bill of rights, overseen by judges who no longer have the concern for equality and fairness shown by the Binghams, the Hales, and the Woolfs (though they disguise this from themselves with talk of freedom and liberty), is as easy as it is disturbing to imagine. Standing in its way is this idea of universal human rights. Surely there is truth there that is above all political and litigious fray, a given that cannot be altered. But where did the idea spring from? Why has it become so central to our global understanding of right conduct? Presenting as an inexorable given, human rights is anything but that; rather it is a success in our culture that is as fragile as it is important. We need to understand the origins of human rights if we are to grasp fully what is at stake in the effort to dismantle the UK's version of them. This is the topic of Chapter 4.

4

THE INEVITABILITY OF HUMAN RIGHTS

In the eighteenth and early nineteenth centuries, the Whigs were a political party in Britain whose supporters (both in the universities and in the higher reaches of journalism) became famous for an approach to history which saw everything that had gone before as having proceeded in neat, straight lines leading inexorably to good things, things they agreed with. In short, their own happy worlds. In a speech in August 2014, in Melbourne, Australia (a city that as it happens is called after that leading Whig, former British Prime Minister Lord Melbourne), the President of the UK Supreme Court Lord Neuberger took a highly 'Whiggish' approach to the emergence of human rights.[1] He thought that '[t]he history of Human Rights and the United Kingdom in the last 100 years can be divided into several periods.' First, there were 'the dark ages, the period before 1951, when the UK simply did not recognise human rights other than through the common law'. Since that old system of law 'developed such rights in a somewhat haphazard and leisurely way' there was a need for change. This began with the second phase, 'the middle ages, between 1951 and 1966' from the signing up of the country to the European Convention through to the year when 'UK citizens' were finally allowed by their government to 'go to the Strasbourg court and claim against the UK Government that their Convention rights were being infringed'. The

---

[1] 'The Role of Judges in Human Rights Jurisprudence: A Comparison of the Australian and UK experience' Supreme Court of Victoria, Melbourne, 8 August 2014: <https://www.supremecourt.uk/docs/speech-140808.pdf> [accessed 30 November 2015].

next phase of this happily inevitable history was merely an interlude. 'The years between 1966 and 2000 were the years of transition. UK citizens could complain to Strasbourg that their human rights were being infringed. However, they could not enforce, or even rely on, those rights in UK courts, as the Convention was not part of UK domestic law.' Then—wonderful news!—'[i]n 1998, Parliament fired the starting gun for the next period, the age of enlightenment, with the Human Rights Act, which formally brought the Convention into UK law. From 2 October 2000, judges throughout the UK were obliged to give effect to human rights under the Convention, and, indeed, all "public bodies" were generally under a duty not to infringe the Convention.' This is the age we have been in ever since, with human rights now having been able fully 'to leak into the judicial cerebellum' as had not been the case before the Human Rights Act—at this point indeed not so much a leak as an ethical deluge as the President might have said had he had more faith in his metaphor and slightly less in the old common law that was being superseded.

It is the fate of many modest men and women who do well in life (whether because of family, class, gender, education, talent, luck, or—more likely—a mix of all of these, and more) to treat not only as good but also as inevitable the structure of the society in which they find themselves and in which they have happened to thrive. But can Lord Neuberger seriously believe this story of the gradual movement of British law towards its current situation, one in which human rights are now assumed to flourish, and in the telling of which all political conflict and rival, defeated perspectives appear not so much to have been silenced as never even to have existed? If the President ever did truly hold this view, then the subsequent Conservative victory at the 2015 election, on, among other things, a mandate to repeal the Human Rights Act must have come as a terrible shock: was this to be the sudden end of a disconcertingly short 'Age of Enlightenment' that the Whiggish story demanded ought now to be here to stay? In fact Lord Neuberger's approach is typical of that taken by many—often otherwise perceptive—human rights commentators on the wider history of their own subject, both internationally (the UN) and regionally (the European Convention on Human Rights). We need now to look at both of these dimensions to human rights before we return to the domestic arena on which the President was commenting. Far from being just something good that can't help happening, 'human rights' have been part of a political story for as long as we have had this way of describing them, and even before that. Their ascent precedes the Second World War, albeit their ride to the top has been often rocky, marked by dips and dives along the way. There is nothing linear about the human rights story, whatever our contemporary Whigs might want us to believe. Understanding this in the round helps us to see how valuable was the enactment of the Human Rights Act in the shape that it took, and (as suggested right at the end of Chapter 3) also how precarious.

Our subject has previous history as a cuckoo.[2] Human rights have long been good at appropriating the best bits of the past, reconstructing selected episodes from history so as to give the impression of time-lines of Neuberger-like inevitability. The textbooks take us to the Hammurabi code[3] and even our hero of Chapter 3 Magna Carta when they seek to establish the roots of human rights as lying in that ancient respect for the independent authority of law that marks the start of the human rights story. The great religious leaders of the past are mustered in support of the idea of human dignity, or of compassion, or empathy, or altruism—or whatever we choose to call 'doing good' today. The Buddha, Jesus, Muhammad, and the rest come to the human rights historian wonderfully untouched by their relationship with ethereal otherness, or God (or even in the second of these cases by the fact of being God). Later waves of progress are similarly appropriated—democracy becomes a human rights achievement,

---

[2] What follows is drawn from my more detailed piece on this: C A Gearty, 'The State of Human Rights' (2014) 5 (4) *Global Politics* 391–400. Further references and developments of what I say here can be found there.

[3] Eg M R Ishay, *The Human Rights Reader* 2nd edn (New York: Routledge, 2007), at p 40.

reproduced in human rights form as 'civil and political rights'. Anti-colonial struggle gets renamed the right of a people to self-determination and forces itself into not one but both of the founding international covenants (otherwise primarily conceptualized in terms of individual rights) agreed in 1966. Anti-slavery, anti-racism, and the international movement to end discrimination against women have all enjoyed the same fate—it would not be fair to call it 'suffered' since these are rightly advances in our understanding of the opportunities that should be accorded the members of our species wherever they happen to be. All these stories are recast and retold in this contemporary vernacular. Human rights language is a discriminating plunderer, grabbing what it wants from what is encountered, invariably leaving the out-of-date stuff behind—and for sure achieving progress along the way.

The history-sensitive story is edgier, less conclusive. Writing in the thirteenth century Thomas Aquinas developed ideas about objective right which were to pave the way for the shift to the individual and his or her entitlements with which (via—depending on who you are reading—the later scholars of Grotius and/or Hobbes to the fore) it is fair to say the human rights idea truly begins. Our subject has always needed action as well as ideas, and the term's first great impact was rooted in its success as a foundational inspiration for late eighteenth-century revolution, in the shape both of the American Declaration of Independence in 1776 and, a little later, the celebrated French Declaration of the Rights of Man and of the Citizen in 1789, and—we should not forget to add—the remarkable Haitian constitution of 1805.[4] This phase was short-lived. Those who float to the top on the power of others risk perishing when their patron falls, and this is as much the case with ideas as it is with people. The collapse of the French empire on the defeat of Napoleon lost human rights their main national driver. Exposed and vulnerable as a result, the idea was duly hacked

---

[4] See <http://www2.webster.edu/~corbetre/haiti/history/earlyhaiti/1805-const.htm> [accessed 1 December 2015].

to near-death through the nineteenth century, the blows being delivered from Left (Marx), Right (Burkeans), and—some of the worst—the emerging proto-democratic centre (Bentham).[5] Haiti lost its constitutional leader first to despotism and shortly after to assassination. A now emancipated America provided no help, the new United States having turned sharply inwards, a fact reflected in a set of constitutional guarantees that spoke only to a domestic and legal (rather than any kind of putatively global) audience.[6]

Looked at from the outside, much of the human rights narrative that has since been rebuilt along the lines identified a paragraph ago has seemed to depend on support from ideas which were at this time its bitterest opponents. The big ideas of the nineteenth century—nationalism, socialism, democracy—had little time for individual rights, which they invariably saw as impediments to the sort of full life which could only be realized through community. True the European Christian hegemony of the period produced a new humanitarianism which found expression in a strong position on slaves, and a commitment to the 'loving of one's enemy' in the very tangible shape of rules for the better treatment of soldiers in war. But this was realized in the compassionate language of humanitarianism rather than the more robustly assertive voice of human rights. The human rights idea was nearly out for the count.

Just as revolution had made human rights in its first phase, so did human-made moral disaster create the platform for its second, the point at which Lord Neuberger's history begins. The aftermath of the First World War had seen a move towards global governance but it was really merely a loose vehicle for a deeper commitment to nationalism and to peoples' rights than had been possible in the colonial nineteenth century. However, this position became untenable after the carnage of the Second World War, with the new United Nations

[5] J Waldron, *Theories of Rights* (Oxford: Oxford University Press, 1984) is good on the details of the various critiques of the period.

[6] A Cox, *The Court and the Constitution* (Boston, Mass.: Houghton Mifflin, 1987).

charter now giving a share of the billing on the global stage to human rights as well as to state sovereignty.[7] With this came the beginnings of the idea's second golden age. Despite the 1948 Universal Declaration of Human Rights and the international agreements on rights that were to follow in the 1960s through to the 1980s, however, success was only properly to arrive with the end of the Cold War in 1989 and the embracing of human rights as a key organizing idea at what the victors confidently (albeit briefly) proclaimed in the best Whiggish fashion to be indeed 'the end of history'.[8]

Even now, in its supposed pomp, the universalism of international human rights law is less than it appears. The dysfunction was there even when the ground was being laid for its arrival. True the UN Charter does indeed set down human rights as a core value to be respected by all member states. Perhaps for a short while in the early 1940s there had been the possibility of the idea of human rights functioning in a constitutionally overarching kind of way with genuine global reach, effective and enforceable. But, by 1945 at least, national sovereignty had fought back and regained its primary position. Indeed it can be argued that in the UN's exemption of all internal state conduct from human rights scrutiny, the autonomous interests of member states achieved more an outright win than the mere score draw that the Charter might have seemed to suggest.[9] Not only has the UN tolerated human-rights-deriding states, it has brought them right into the core of the organization, embracing as key permanent members of its governing Security Council five states all of which have highly problematic records from a human rights point of view: the UK[10] and France for their treatment of colonial and post-colonial

[7] See UN Charter <http://www.un.org/en/documents/charter/> [accessed 4 December 2015].

[8] F Fukuyama, *The End of History and the Last Man* (London: Penguin, 1992).

[9] S Moyn, *The Last Utopia: Human Rights in History* (Cambridge, Mass.: Harvard University Press, 2010).

[10] On which see in particular A W B Simpson, *Human Rights and the End of Empire: Britain and the Genesis of the European Convention* (Oxford: Oxford University Press, 2001).

peoples, the USA for its military interventions abroad and its support for human rights abusing authoritarian regimes, and the Soviet Union (now Russia) and China for their brutal treatment of their own peoples and support for even worse governing elites elsewhere (eg in China's case, and infamously, North Korea). Much the same point can be made about the states that are added to the Security Council by way of election from time to time: these have recently included Pakistan, Azerbaijan, and Australia—all countries with what might fairly be called (at the very least) contemporary human rights records that fall some way short of perfection. The same jibe can be made about the main UN oversight body in the field, the Human Rights Council, which includes in its current or recent membership Saudi Arabia, China, Russia, the Maldives, Hungary, Cuba, and the United States. The institutional move a few years ago from a Human Rights Commission to a Human Rights Council was in part intended to address this problem, but it has failed to do so. The point here is not to make dramatic claims on behalf of human rights, to lament the current situation and call for reform. What we are seeing, rather, is a working through of that crucial first decision, to stick with sovereign states, a defeat for human rights that can hardly be re-presented as a victory, whatever our instinct for optimism might suggest.

The great flagship of international human rights, and forerunner of our European Convention, can be viewed in a similar vein. Though much celebrated today, the 1948 Universal Declaration of Human Rights agreed by the UN's General Assembly with no dissenting voices was heavily criticized at the time, not for its range (vast and ambitious) so much as for its utter failure to provide any mechanism for realization of any of the rights it so grandly proclaimed. Of course it was said that this was to come later, but only a very few over-scrupulous states took its content sufficiently seriously even to make the effort to abstain. The rest, finding no enforcement chapter, cheerfully agreed to everything. When 'later' finally came, in the shape of two international covenants agreed in 1966 and subsequently expanded, and covering (respectively) economic, social and cultural, and civil and political rights, there were further improvements over the course of time in that particular committees were tasked with periodic reviews and (latterly) some element of quasi-judicial accountability has been added. But the project of realization remains contaminated by a voluntarism that is made essential by a commitment to state autonomy that has remained fully in place as *the* cornerstone of UN activity.

The pattern is repeated into the post-Cold War age. Sometimes the model is the 1948 one of mere declaration, and on other occasions that of the hardly robust enforcement of 1966. True, there have been other, more effective means of addressing deficiencies in the old structures such as the development of special procedures and novel ways of challenging the supremacy of state power by placing human rights firmly back at the centre of the stage. (We had the example of Raquel Rolnik in Chapter 1.) In this regard we should note that the UN High Commissioner for Human Rights stands at the apex of an ethical bureaucracy of human rights advocates,[11] seeking to do good work directly under the loose cover of these otherwise sometimes rather anodyne international obligations, and engaging when the opportunity presents itself in a determinedly, activist diplomacy, throwing human rights into international political discussion if the circumstances require it. The story is not entirely or even mainly a bad one, but it is neither linear nor ethically inexorable.

And we cannot leave this international human rights canvas without asking a difficult question about the place on it of military aggression. Such violence is legitimized in international law in two ways: by the UN Charter itself, or alternatively in some way by the spirit of human rights itself, lurking with the UN and selectively available to be picked from and used whenever sovereign power demands. As far as the first of these is concerned, the declaration in

[11] See <http://www.ohchr.org/EN/Pages/WelcomePage.aspx> [accessed 1 December 2015].

article 51 that '[n]othing in the present Charter shall impair the inherent right of individual or collective self-defence if an armed attack occurs against a Member of the United Nations...' has been turned into a vehicle for the justification of international aggression which started with a US attack on Libya in 1986 and thereafter has received lip-service so increasingly perfunctory that the disguise of legality has been hard to maintain with a straight legal face, even for international lawyers gloomily familiar (as they all must be) with the need to accommodate legal norms to the situation on the unforgiving ground of national interest that is their main field of work. Where there is power, there will always be a lawyer tasked with delivering a legal justification, and this can usually be achieved with enough plausibility to provide some diversionary noise while force does its work.

As regards the second, human rights law has been similarly worked over by false friends who have sought to use its moral force as a cover to justify military aggression abroad and even a little bit of 'necessary evil' towards one's enemies wherever one finds them.[12] Successfully to counter this dangerously subversive assault, human rights idealists would need to transform the world away from its fixation on state power, to emphasize the primacy of the international text over state interest. But for all their fine language it is they, not the states, who are on the margins. On important, influential margins for sure, valuable and necessary too—but marginal nonetheless. Human rights is an important chapter in today's global story but it is not the whole novel, and even when it is prominently displayed on the page this military distortion reminds us that not all the shapes that it takes can be counted as benign.

Where does all this leave the European Convention on Human Rights, the source of Lord Neuberger's Whiggish dream and of the Human Rights Act that is the central focus of this book? Certainly it flows out of the international movement we have been discussing.

---

[12] The phrase is that of Michael Ignatieff: M Ignatieff, *The Lesser Evil: Political Ethics in an Age of Terror* (Edinburgh: Edinburgh University Press, 2004).

We can now see it as an early switch to the regional protection of human rights, a swerve in a more modest direction for sure but one which was probably rightly thought at the time to hold out the best hope of an authentic protection of these entitlements. It involves rights now being mediated through a regional framework sitting somewhere between the grandeur of the global and the insularity of the local. The American Declaration of the Rights and Duties of Man came even before the Convention, dating as it does from 1948,[13] and since the drafting of our European paradigm we have had regional initiatives of varying sorts in Africa and (more recently) Asia and the Middle East.[14] As with their international equivalents these are all in their different ways uneasy and unstable combinations of law, politics, and international relations. In a world of nation states and conflicting national interests it can hardly be otherwise.

The European Convention was and is not immune from exactly these pressures.[15] The capital fact that drove its creation was the need to protect western European states from further aggression after the conclusion of the Second World War. The document is itself a creature of the Council of Europe, set up after that conflict to bind together those nations, whether victorious or defeated, who, exhausted by war, now saw a voracious military power advancing from the east, picking off the weaker members of their continent, one by one. In their excellent study *Churchill's Legacy: The Conservative Case for the Human Rights Act*[16] Jesse Norman and Peter Oborne identify Britain's war leader as a driver

[13] See <https://www.cidh.oas.org/Basicos/English/Basic2.American%20Declaration.htm> [accessed 7 December 2015].

[14] For the African Court on Human and Peoples' Rights see <http://www.african-court.org/en/> [accessed 6 December 2015]. For the Arab world, see the decision made in early 2013 to establish an Arab Court of Human Rights. For a critical commentary see <https://www.fidh.org/IMG/pdf/20140320_arab_ct_pp_en.pdf> [accessed 6 December 2015].

[15] S Greer, *The European Convention on Human Rights: Achievements, Problems and Prospects* (Cambridge: Cambridge University Press, 2006).

[16] Jesse Norman and Peter Oborne, *Churchill's Legacy: The Conservative Case for the Human Rights Act* (Liberty: London, 2009).

behind this new Council, his seeing it (as early as in 1942) as '[w]ith Germany defeated ... the only realistic way to hold a dominant USSR at bay'.[17] Of course the intention was to defend the Council's members from all forms of totalitarianism but right from the start (or even before the start if we include Churchill in 1942), the primary goal was as an opening politico-legal shot in what we now know as the Cold War. Here are the Chiefs of Staff reporting on their post-war planning in July 1944:

> We realise that we must on no account antagonise Russia by giving the appearance of building up the Western bloc against her, and that for this reason the immediate object of a Western European Group must be the keeping down of Germany; but we feel that the more remote, but more dangerous possibility of a hostile Russia making use of the resources of Germany must not be lost sight of, and that any measures which we now take should be tested by whether or not they help to prevent that contingency ever arising.[18]

As the first author to explore this space fully, the thrust of the late Brian Simpson's great work on the subject was of a Convention which was fulfilling an important propaganda function at a critical time.[19] Following in this vein, the leading contemporary scholar of the period, Marco Duranti, sees in the motivation of those behind the Convention not so much a radical zeal drawing on past human rights revolutions as a mix of national as well as strategic intentions: resistance to totalitarianism from the east certainly, as Norman and Oborne and Simpson have suggested, but also the desire to obstruct radical politics closer to home. Duranti gives us two examples. First is that of the French Christian Democrats: these political actors 'looked to European human rights law as an international safeguard for the rights of the family in the domain of education, particularly as concerned private Catholic schooling', and in the case of those 'personalist intellectuals and Vichy theorists of corporatism' amongst them there

---

[17] Ibid at p 19.
[18] Simpson (n 10), at p 234.
[19] This was one of the central themes of his book (n 10).

was also the hope 'that the [Convention] would catalyze a radical restructuring of French society along medieval (corporatist) lines as well as protect the civil liberties of those accused of collaboration with the Axis enemy'.[20] The second of Duranti's examples echoes the argument of Norman and Oborne: not just Churchill's legacy, but also a Conservative one, a way of winning even when you are not succeeding at the ballot box:

> Marginalized right-wing advocates of free-market economics in the British Conservative Party...played a pivotal role in championing and framing European human rights law after 1945. This was a response to the momentary anxieties of a party in political opposition, some of whose members genuinely feared what they decried as the 'totalitarian' powers of the British Labour Government. The omission of economic and social rights from the ECHR reflected the hostility of leading Conservative politicians such as Winston Churchill and David Maxwell Fyfe towards Labour's economic and social policies.[21]

In its reactionary structure the Convention took its place among a range of European instruments that were popping up at this time— the new German and Italian constitutions among them—and that were assiduously going about the business of entrenching human rights as a bulwark against radical change, not a primary defence against Communism perhaps but prominent nevertheless.[22] And the Convention went on to do a very good ideological job, one for which many of us may indeed be grateful but which we can hardly describe as above the fray. In the mid-1950s, an effort by the German Communist Party to challenge its domestic ban as a breach of the Convention's guarantee of the right to political association proved unavailing, the case not even getting past the European Commission that in those

---

[20] See <http://ohrh.law.ox.ac.uk/the-human-rights-restoration-revolution/> [accessed 7 December 2015].

[21] Ibid.

[22] M Mandel, 'A Brief History of the New Constitutionalism or "How We Changed Everything so that Everything Would Remain the Same"' (1998) 32 (2) *Israel Law Review* 250–300.

days acted as a quasi-judicial gatekeeper to the European Court of Human Rights.[23] Later efforts to tackle strong laws against the employment of radicals in the public service in the same country (the *Berufsverbot*) proved similarly unavailing: these had their origins in a response to subversive violence from the Left in Germany but caught more than the proponents of such direct revolutionary engagements.[24] Of course, with the Cold War over greater risks could be taken,[25] but by then a new ideological opponent was hovering into view, in the shape of radical Islam, and here once again the Strasbourg Court has found itself wielding its Convention as a defender of pluralism and of 'human rights' values and not just guaranteeing the rights of those who, were they to succeed, might well threaten its destruction.[26] Excellent this may be, heartily we may approve of it—but dispassionate, supra-ideological end-of-history stuff it definitely is not.

And what, finally, of the British experience, the 'middle ages', the 'years of transition' and the (final?) 'age of enlightenment'? We have already seen how from the Conservative perspective politics helped shape the content as well as the very existence of the European Convention on Human Rights. This has always been true, too, of Labour's involvement. That party has invariably been constrained by its desire for electoral success into courting the British voter with a programme of government that frightens less than it promises. Human rights have played a role in this (self-)disciplining of Labour, from the UK being among the first to ratify the Convention in the last year of the Attlee administration (in March 1951), through to the decision to allow the right of individual petition to the European Court, a move which came in 1966, in the third year of the Wilson administration, the first Labour government since Attlee. This latter

---

[23] *German Communist Party v Federal Republic of Germany* app 250/57 (1957) 1 *Yearbook of the European Convention on Human Rights* 222 [in French].

[24] *Glasenapp v Germany* (1986) 9 EHRR 25.

[25] *Vogt v Germany* (1995) 21 EHRR 205 where earlier supportive decisions on the German ban were not followed.

[26] See generally *Refah Partisi (The Welfare Party) v Turkey* (2003) 37 EHRR 1.

act, at the time not a compulsory part of the Convention scheme for states, was especially important in light of the protocol that had been added to the Convention since 1950 specifically guaranteeing the protection of private property from aggressive governmental action.[27] It was as though Labour was saying that beneath the surface they were not as serious as their supporters claimed about truly radical change. Certainly it took off the table nationalization without the possibility of compensation, a point of which the sponsors of the initiative were not unaware.[28]

Such a framework was bound to look attractive to a Labour Party still bruised by its unexpected defeat in 1992 and out of power since the Wilson/Callaghan government had finally run out of steam in 1979. With the Thatcher administration having provoked widespread opposition on civil libertarian grounds, what better way to signal the novelty of the brand, the 'newness' of what was already beginning to be called 'New Labour', than by bringing the Convention right into the heart of British law, taking the final step resisted by earlier administrations, that of incorporating the Convention itself into UK domestic law? As we saw at the end of Chapter 3, leading judges were already arguing for just such a move, so the proposal could hardly lead to the party being mocked by its opponents as being exuberantly radical. On the other side of the political spectrum, a realization of the impotency of opposition (already thirteen years by 1992, with another five likely at very least) was making the trade unions more responsive to pragmatic judgments about the necessity for political concessions to the electorate, and anyway 'Europe' had lost its right-wing colour for many socialists, not least thanks to Conservative dislike of the social aspects of the EU's evolving agenda.

---

[27] Article 1 of the First Protocol.

[28] See Lord Lester of Herne Hill, 'UK Acceptance of the Strasbourg Jurisdiction: What Really Went on in Whitehall in 1965' [1998] *Public Law* 237–53. The acceptance was delayed until after a potential action had become time-barred: at pp 240–1 and 250–3, and see *Burmah Oil v Lord Advocate* [1967] AC 75.

First John Smith and then, after his unexpected death, his successor as Labour leader Tony Blair resolutely embraced the task of steering Labour closer to the middle ground of politics, from which it was believed elections were to be won. The rights initiative was crucial to this, a paper 'Bringing Rights Home' being issued at the end of 1996 promising to restore to the British the rights which they had generously bequeathed to others after the Second World War.[29] There was no Churchill but there was a bulldog, to help drive the point home. And broadly speaking, with a multiple of other factors as well of course, it worked. The Labour Party swept to power, in May 1997 on a mandate, among other things, to deliver the Convention into British law.[30] But what did this actually mean? How was incorporation realized in practice? In recent years four large-scale myths have been allowed to take centre stage: that the law enacted in 1998 subverts British parliamentary sovereignty; that it hands power to the judges; that it transfers supremacy over UK rights law to the European Court of Human Rights in Strasbourg; and that the law is a charter for villains. Each is false but in combination they have destabilized the measure to such an extent that repeal is now regarded by many as a desirable policy pathway. Only on a fantasy island could myths drive real-life decisions in this way. It is to each of these myths that we now turn.

---

[29] The Labour Party, *Bringing Rights Home* (1996).

[30] For an excellent account, see F M Klug, *Values for a Godless Age: The Story of the United Kingdom's New Bill of Rights* (London: Penguin, 2000).

5

THE SUPREMACY OF THE
HUMAN RIGHTS ACT

The proposed Sexual Offences Act (Remedial) Order 2013 may have been a humble piece of secondary legislation when it was introduced in the House of Commons, but despite this it warranted the attention of not one but two of the most senior members of the government. Introducing the order, the Home Secretary Theresa May declared the government to be 'appalled and disappointed' by why it was in her view necessary: a recent ruling of Britain's most senior court to the effect that the compulsory placing of sex offenders on a register for life without the possibility of review offended their rights under the Human Rights Act. The Home Secretary reported that the government was 'determined to do everything [it could] to protect the public from predatory sexual offences' and so it would 'make the minimum possible changes to the law in order to comply with the ruling'.[1] Hence the order being brought before the House of Commons—the law that had been found wanting by their lordships had been in an Act of Parliament. Shortly before Mrs May's remarks, the Prime Minister had gone even further, responding to a question on the matter from a backbench member of Parliament: 'My hon. Friend speaks for many people in saying how completely offensive it is, once again, to have a ruling by a court that flies in the face of common sense.... I am appalled by the Supreme Court ruling.' Like his Home Secretary, Mr Cameron painted himself as defiant in the face of this implacable judicial foe: 'We will take the minimum possible approach

[1] HC Debs, 16 February 2011, col 959.

On Fantasy Island: Britain, Europe, and Human Rights. First Edition. Conor Gearty.
© Conor Gearty 2016. Published 2016 by Oxford University Press.

to this ruling and use the opportunity to close some loopholes in the sex offenders register.' Not for long would he have to tolerate such wrong-headedness however: 'I can also tell my hon. Friend that a commission will be established imminently to look at a British Bill of Rights, because it is about time we ensured that decisions are made in this Parliament rather than in the courts.'[2]

We shall come to the facts of the case that caused all this fuss a little later. But first a simple point that appears to have escaped both Prime Minister and Home Secretary: as one of the judges in the case, Baroness Hale, was later to put it in the course of a public lecture, '[c]uriously, when introducing the order in Parliament, the Prime Minister was highly critical of our decision, but made no mention of the fact that the government could have chosen to do nothing about it'.[3] The truly 'minimum possible approach' would have been to ignore the case, something which would have been perfectly possible given the way that the Human Rights Act is constructed. Indeed being free not to do anything at all in a situation like this is at the core of what this legislation was about. To understand this—not a difficult point as we shall see and surely one you would have expected the Prime Minister (or at least his Home Secretary or her advisers) to have grasped—you do need a little recent history about the way in which this rights legislation came about; perhaps not knowing any of this is what led both of them into error.

At the end of Chapter 4, we left the Human Rights Act on the verge of being introduced by the triumphant new (and New) Labour administration of Tony Blair. There was a commitment, for sure, to the incorporation of the Convention into UK domestic law but no clarity about exactly how this was to be done: the paper promising the reform had been vague on detail, as of course had been the election

---

[2] Ibid, col 955.

[3] 'What's the Point of Human Rights?' Lady Hale, the Warwick Law Lecture 2013: <https://www.supremecourt.uk/docs/speech-131128.pdf> [accessed 11 December 2015].

manifesto.[4] During the summer of 1997, an old battle reignited between those factions in the party who wanted full-blooded socialism at some point in the (near?) future and those who had never been so keen on old school radicalism of this sort and who felt that Labour's electoral success had been largely down to forging a new, radical way of which meaningful human rights was a key part.[5] While the latter wanted strong judicially enforceable human rights, guaranteeing that individualism was at no risk from Labour's modern way of doing things, the former groups mistrusted anything which gave such a role to the judges, whom they saw as fervent enemies of progress in general and of the Labour movement in particular. (A not unreasonable view: we looked at some of the details of the courts' record on failing to protect the civil liberties of the Left in Chapter 2, and it is not pretty.) The question of how to embed a framework of rights in one's system had already come up in the many democratic countries that had embraced a rights code as the UK was getting to this question very late indeed, so there were plenty of precedents from which to choose.

No appetite was to be found across the Labour ranks for the Americanization of the British system. A supreme court with full judicial review on the Washington model was too much for any progressive of whatever hue; in the aftermath of contentious decisions (such as on abortion) and divisive nomination hearings (the failed candidacy of Robert Bork, for example) that route was universally seen as irredeemably politicized and partisan. The two favourites that emerged during those first summer months of government were the options offered by Canada and New Zealand. The first, favoured by the New Labourites, stood for strong judicial review—striking down legislation for rights violations—which however (and here was the difference from the USA) either the Federal or any of the provincial legislatures could then expressly refute by subsequently passing the

---

[4] The Labour Party, *Bringing Rights Home* (1996).
[5] The 'third' way: see A Giddens, *The Third Way: The Renewal of Social Democracy* (Cambridge: Polity Press, 1998).

law afresh in overt defiance of the court ruling. Indeed the Canadian system allowed for this to be done in advance, by the federal Parliament or any of the provincial legislatures, simply by passing a law 'notwithstanding' anything that might appear in their Charter of Rights.[6] In stark contrast to this the second approach—that of New Zealand—took minimalism to new lengths: there was a bill of rights there for sure but all it did was help with the interpretation of statutes and oversee executive discretion: no challenge to primary legislation was permitted, so Parliament (and in New Zealand's case a unicameral Parliament) continued to reign supreme.[7]

In the end, the new Labour government steered a clever route between these two possible solutions. The Human Rights Act provides in section 6(1) that all public authorities are henceforth required to act in a way that is 'compatible with the Convention rights' which are duly set out in schedule 1 of the Act (thereby delivering on the promise of incorporating the Convention into UK law). Furthermore, the Act also demands (in section 3) that all legislation must be interpreted 'as far as possible' in a way that accords with those rights, and this is applied to Acts of Parliament not only already passed but also to be passed in the future. So far, so reasonably straightforward, New-Zealand-like indeed. The novelty came in what to do about Acts of Parliament. The courts might encounter a piece of legislation which on its face breached one or more of the Convention rights but which could not be turned into something rights-compatible by any 'possible' interpretation, the words being too clear for that. In the US this would of course have exposed the law to being struck down. In Canada the same except that the Parliament there could then retaliate with one of their 'notwithstanding' laws. In New Zealand, nothing could be done at all. The Human Rights Act gave the judges the power in such circumstances to

---

[6] See the Canadian Charter of Rights and Freedoms 1982: <http://laws-lois.justice.gc.ca/eng/const/page-15.html> [accessed 20 March 2016]. The 'Notwithstanding Clause' is s 33(1) (and note there some limitations on the exercise of the right).

[7] New Zealand Bill of Rights Act 1990.

issue what the relevant provision section 4 called 'declarations of incompatibility', setting out the inconsistency between the law under scrutiny and the Convention rights and declaring the breaches that it found to be such in a new and highly particular kind of judicial order. Here is the rub: these declarations were specifically stated to have no legal effect. They are grand announcements of judicial distaste but no more than that—shouts of antipathy dressed up as legal remedies but without the usual enforceability that we take for granted comes with victory in court.

These pseudo-remedies in section 4 are the key way in which the Human Rights Act reconciles its commitment to human rights with its respect for parliamentary sovereignty. True, government has to make clear when introducing laws to Parliament the extent to which (if at all indeed) the proposed legislation fits with human rights,[8] and of course there is also the interpretative power (already mentioned) available to the judges which gives them some power to reinterpret parliamentary stuff they don't like. But that is it. Faced with implacable wording, the human rights norm must buckle before the parliamentary *Grundnorm* (to misuse a famous idea of a twentieth-century legal philosopher).[9] Much of the rest of the Act is a working through of this basic insight: only the senior courts are allowed to engage in such serious matters[10] and before they do they have to alert the government as to the possibility.[11] Public authorities that can point to legislation which gives them no alternative other than to act in a rights-conflicting way are liberated from their obligation to respect Convention rights.[12] Where a declaration of incompatibility is issued, both of the other branches of the state (the executive and the

---

[8] Human Rights Act 1998 s 19.

[9] H Kelsen, *Pure Theory of Law* 2nd edn translated from the German by M Knight (San Francisco: University of California Press, 1967).

[10] Human Rights Act s 4(5).

[11] Ibid s 4.

[12] Ibid s 6(2).

legislature) have the opportunity to respond if they so wish, with the executive being empowered to do so by ministerial order only if there are 'compelling reasons'[13] so to act without recourse to primary legislation. But these are options, not obligations. Parliamentary legislation stands unless Parliament (or exceptionally as we have just seen the executive) decides otherwise.

We can now see fully how wrong-headed the Prime Minister and his Home Secretary were in terms of the way they approached the remedial order regarding the sexual offences legislation that they brought to Parliament. Their comments made clear that they each felt there were 'compelling reasons' *not* to legislate rather than to legislate, yet imposing such amending legislation on the House is exactly what they chose to do when (to risk repetition ad nauseam to make the point) they could have determined—their consciences seemed to demand—that they should do nothing at all. So what was going on? Can Mr Cameron and Mrs May be simply this uninformed? This has been the suggestion at the start of this chapter but surely it cannot be the entire truth. Perhaps it all depends on what is meant by being wrong—error can take its colour from the response of the audience at which remarks are aimed. What is wrong in a seminar may be less wrong in a town hall meeting. You do not need to be avidly post-modern to see that error is in the eye of the beholder. Probing this point further takes us to the heart of the Human Rights Act, the very depths of how it set about seeking to protect individual rights from the vagaries of the (populist) political.

Let us take a look at the facts of the case that caused all the trouble, *R (F) v Secretary of State for the Home Department*.[14] Under the Sexual Offences Act 2003, those convicted of such offences and sentenced to thirty months' imprisonment or more incurred a lifelong duty to keep the police informed of where they were living and of any plan they had to travel abroad. As the President of the Supreme Court Lord

[13] Ibid s 10(2).
[14] [2010] UKSC 17, [2011] 1 AC 331.

Phillips put it, '[t]his duty persists until the day they die' as there is no 'right to a review of the notification requirement'.[15] After a two-day hearing, all five of the Supreme Court judges hearing the case found the absence of such an opportunity for review to be a breach of the Human Rights Act, in particular of article 8 of the European Convention (included in the Act with most of the other Convention rights of course). This is the provision guaranteeing a right to respect for a person's 'private and family life, his home and his correspondence' albeit with restrictions where these are for various legitimate reasons, are prescribed by law, and can be said to be 'necessary in a democratic society'. The 2003 Act failed the last of the tests here, the register-for-life approach being in the judges' eyes clearly a disproportionate way of achieving its safeguarding goal, causing far more individual human misery (to the individuals on it) than was either warranted or necessary. There were two claimants before the court: the first, F, was 11 years old when he committed his offences (rape and other crimes against a 6-year-old boy). The second, Mr T, had been convicted of the indecent assault of his daughter. True the obligation was burdensome and there was an inevitable risk of the notification requirement becoming public knowledge in an offender's community. But neither now disputed their convictions nor their initial placing on the register when it came into effect. They did not oppose the fact of a lifetime register, merely whether it was fair that 'an offender who can clearly demonstrate that he presents no risk, or no measurable risk of re-offending, should be precluded from obtaining a review of the notification requirements'.[16] They hoped to benefit from any such review but could not be sure of doing so. Close scrutiny of the data before the court revealed no basis in the government's argument that there was somehow or other an inherent propensity to offend in this way among this category of offender. In the wake of forensic scrutiny arguments about automatic dangerousness faded away.

---

[15] Ibid at para 1.

[16] Ibid at para 35 per Lord Phillips, quoting from Latham LJ in the Divisional Court.

The decision was hardly controversial among the judges who heard the case. The five Supreme Court judges were agreeing with no fewer than six of their colleagues—three in the Divisional Court and three in the Court of Appeal—who had heard the case on its way to this most senior of courts. The declaration of incompatibility made by the first of these courts was confirmed. Why the vast difference in perspective between the judicial and the executive branches, so large that, as we have seen, a sense (or at least a pretence) of coercion was played out by two of our most senior cabinet members? This is a point we will be coming back to time and again in the course of this book. Courts deal in fact and data. Their weapon is reason, their audience their own community of the legally informed. They do not need to get elected and have no obligation to court much less cave into the populist passions of the mass media. Real people appear before them, people on whom by definition the law has impacted in a severe, often devastating way (or they wouldn't have ended up in the courts in the first place in all likelihood). Politicians in contrast deal in the carelessly thrown together passing truths of the moment. Their careers depend on the sum of these producing a positive reaction in a polling booth every five years or so, and in opinion polls on an almost weekly basis apart from that. Solid argument is their enemy, worthiness and a devotion to accuracy two guarantors of failure. These are not criticisms necessarily, merely statements as obvious in their accuracy as the description a moment ago of the space the judges inhabit, two universes yoked together on a small island but light years apart.

If this were true then it is a fair question to ask why any government should suggest the Human Rights Act, still less any parliament enact it? The answer lies in the seductiveness of the general: human rights as an abstract idea echoes back to us all—and politicians particularly—a message about the ethical purity of the world in which we live. This is why even in its keenness to get rid of the Human Rights Act the government cannot bear to dispense with rights altogether—we are to have a new super-duper bill of rights, even better (we are told) than what has come before. The job of courts—and here John Finnis of whom we have earlier been so critical is absolutely right—is to particularize, to apply fine general language to specific fact situations. And politicians, the media, we ourselves may not like the implications on the ground of what we say we believe in.

So why didn't the executive simply ignore the declaration of incompatibility, tell the judges to get lost as the Human Rights Act went to such great pains (as we have seen) to allow them to do? The answer may lie somewhere deep within the structure of the British state—the political leadership staking out the public position, the civil servants advising them, the specialists in the area driving the response to the court, the lawyers interpreting the Supreme Court decision for them: all knew the truth of what the eleven judges had said and acted upon it, hidden in a disguise of duress and dressed up with further restrictions it is true (a point we have not elaborated here) but nevertheless delivering a chance of redemption for those stuck on a register for crimes long paid for and with no (measureable) chance of repetition. A word to describe this might be 'rational', another might even be 'civilized'. Perhaps the Prime Minister and his Home Secretary knew they didn't have to change the law; perhaps they didn't. Their knowledge was not essential; an ability to deliver the change to their own audiences was.

Nowhere does the mismatch between what we think we want—human rights for all—and what this means—human rights for *all?*—become clearer than when it extends to those who are not British but just happen to be here, sometimes we think with malicious (but unprovable) criminal intent. Surely Parliament can do what it wants to these malcontents? Once again the Human Rights Act says yes even if Parliament to its credit says no. After the attacks of 11 September 2001 (less than a year after the Human Rights Act was brought fully into force), the then Home Secretary David Blunkett introduced into the legislature a scheme for the detention of suspected international terrorists, men (and they were all men) who lived in Britain but who could not be expelled to their home countries because of a real risk that they would be tortured or killed there. (And no other countries would have them.[17]) The problem was that the case against the men in Mr Blunkett's sights could not be made in an open court of law following the usual criminal law rules—no offences could be confidently laid at their door. So they were simply detained, taken to a London prison (Belmarsh) and left there. Now while this is a little simplistically put—there were various procedures for checking the credibility of the suspicion about them and a court of sorts was engaged to deliver a degree of quasi-accountability—the fact remained that here was internment in all but name, not on Guantanamo's scale for sure (that pernicious system was just getting up and running in Cuba at the time) but significant still, involving a couple of handfuls to start with no one knowing where it might end.

This was the system that in a dramatic decision on 16 December 2004 the appellate committee of the House of Lords held to amount to a breach of the Convention rights set out in the Human Rights Act.[18] The details are not central to the issue of parliamentary sovereignty that we are discussing here—the right to liberty (article 5) was clearly in issue as was the discriminatory way in which the statute was deployed only against foreigners (article 14), with attempts that were made in court to defend the law by claiming it was necessary to protect the life of the nation at a time of public emergency (article 15) proving unavailing. The point here is that the ruling in the case on its face affected nothing. The men who were its beneficiaries and who had taken these proceedings remained in prison. The governor's authority to detain them remained intact. For all its explosive political implications, the decision amounted to nothing from a strictly legal point of view—the powers being explicitly set out in a (recent) Act of Parliament, the only 'remedy' available was that of a declaration of incompatibility, more (as we can now appreciate) an ethical than a court order. What next? The issue was one close to the government's heart, its security advice being (no doubt) that here were a bunch of

---

[17] The Anti-terrorism, Crime and Security Act 2001, part IV.

[18] *A v Secretary of State for the Home Department* [2004] UKHL 56, [2005] 2 AC 68.

dangerous malcontents whom it would be highly risky to release from detention. No doubt there were voices in government arguing for a retention of the Belmarsh system, perhaps with a re-enactment of the legislation in order to make the democratic will even more apparent. But as with the sex offenders case eight years later, wiser counsel prevailed. A new Home Secretary, Charles Clarke, decided to redesign the system so as to achieve the same security goals but without going so far as to intern and (crucially) without the discriminatory focus only on foreigners.

The Prevention of Terrorism Act 2005 was bitterly contested in Parliament in the way that the legislation it was replacing was not: unsurprisingly since the scheme of 'control orders' that it envisaged was specifically designed to reach British and non-British alike, and there is nothing more likely to concentrate the civil libertarian mind than the prospect of a law being deployed not just against the outsider but the local voter as well. Various human rights restrictions were built into the new law and these were in turn to attract judicial scrutiny in a way that fleshed out its overall goal of being human rights consistent as a framework. Shortly after its enactment, the London bombs of 7 July 2005 reminded everyone in the worst way possible that terrorism was not a problem that could be easily put in a box marked 'foreigners'. It was this Belmarsh decision of which in Chapter 2 we saw Professor Finnis being so sharply critical as having missed a point about possible deportation (which however none of the lawyers in the case had argued). A different view to Finnis's remains for now predominant, however. The Human Rights Act had passed an early and great test. And as with the sex offenders case, parliamentarians, cabinet Ministers, and civil servants proved themselves inclined to take human rights seriously even when the human rights law itself did not require that they should, and even when they had to pretend they were not doing so. The result is surely a better form of human rights protection, precisely because it is democratically entrenched. It is not imposed from the judicial clouds but grows from below in response to a prompt, not an instruction.

An effective Human Rights Act would see the declaration of incompatibility being used as a device to remind Parliament of what it had said in general terms it believed in, and to draw its attention to specific cases (as with the two just described) where for various reasons the legislators had felt driven to subvert its own ethical commitments. And because it takes fairly direct language to achieve this (or the interpretative power in section 3—the subject of Chapter 6—would kick in), it was not thought at the time of enactment that there would be many such declarations. So it has proved. A report issued by the Joint Parliamentary Committee on Human Rights early in 2015 noted that since the Human Rights Act came into force on 2 October 2000, UK courts have made a total of twenty-nine declarations of incompatibility, of which twenty have become final, having either not been appealed or survived appeal. The record of compliance with these politico-legal interventions has been as good as the stories emerging from the two cases we have studied in detail would suggest: only in respect of the extremely politicized issue of prisoner voting has neither the legislative nor the executive branch acted to bring the law into line with what human rights requires, and there the main antagonist (as we shall see in Chapter 7) is not the UK judiciary but rather the European Court of Human Rights itself.[19]

In analysing the trend in the making of these orders, the Joint Committee observed an interesting development: during the entire 2010–15 Parliament, only three declarations of incompatibility were made, with one of those still subject to appeal at the time of the publication of the report.[20] The two confirmed cases dealt, respectively, with the human rights demand for fair procedures in the inclusion of people on a barred list in the context of safeguarding

[19] *Smith v Scott* 2007, SC 345.
[20] Joint Committee on Human Rights 7th Report on Human Rights Judgments HL 130 HC 1088 11 March 2015: <http://www.publications.parliament.uk/pa/jt201415/jtselect/jtrights/130/13002.htm> [accessed 18 December 2015].

vulnerable people[21] and with a human rights insistence on not being too profligate in the disclosure of the past convictions and cautions of individuals even where the safeguarding of others was the goal.[22] The third concerned the Jobseekers (Back to Work Schemes) Act 2013 and the High Court's declaration in that instance was at the time the Committee reported subject to appeal to the Court of Appeal.[23] And that was it—very little news to report. The Committee merely drew 'to Parliament's attention the strikingly small number of declarations of incompatibility made by UK courts under the Human Rights Act during the lifetime of this Parliament', confirming as it did 'the significant downward trend in the number of such declarations since the Human Rights Act came into force in 2000'.[24] It did not offer any explanation as to what might lie behind the move. What is (not) going on?

The answer may lie in the fact that uncertainty about what is entailed in a declaration of incompatibility has spread from the executive branch to the bench itself. If they look like proper court orders, are received as such orders, and produce legal outcomes like ordinary remedies, then perhaps, after all, that is what they are, and we must therefore be cautious about their deployment. In the well-known 'right-to-die' cases of *R (Nicklinson) v Ministry of Justice; R (AM) and R (AP) v Director of Public Prosecutions*[25] three men (one through his widow after his death) challenged the legislation governing assisted suicide as it was interpreted at the time relevant to the men by the chief prosecutor in England and Wales, the Director of Public

---

[21] *Royal College of Nursing v Secretary of State for the Home Department* [2010] EWHC 2761 (Admin).

[22] *R (T, JB and AW) v Chief Constable of Greater Manchester Police, Secretary of State for the Home Department and Secretary of State for Justice* [2013] EWCA Civ 25, [2013] 1 WLR 2515. See further *R (T) v Secretary of State for the Home Department and Secretary of State for Justice* [2014] UKSC 35, [2015] AC 49.

[23] See *R (Reilly (No 2) and Hewstone) v Secretary of State for Work and Pensions* [2014] EWHC 2182.

[24] Joint Committee on Human Rights (n 20), para 4.2.

[25] [2014] UKSC 38, [2015] AC 657.

Prosecutions. No fewer than nine Supreme Court justices were involved. Two of them, Baroness Hale and Lord Kerr, approached the question in a conventional, even straightforward, manner. Having found the law to be a breach of the Convention, as Lady Hale put it, 'I see little to be gained, and much to be lost, by refraining from making a declaration of incompatibility.' Her ladyship then went on to explain the consequences of this in a way which it is hoped this chapter has now shown to be plainly correct:

> Parliament is then free to cure that incompatibility, either by a remedial order under section 10 of the Act or (more probably in a case of this importance and sensitivity) by Act of Parliament, or to do nothing. It may do nothing, either because it does not share our view that the present law is incompatible, or because, as a sovereign Parliament, it considers an incompatible law preferable to any alternative.[26]

The trouble is that her colleagues, Lord Kerr apart, did not agree with her. Led by the President of the Court Lord Neuberger, the justices managed to contrive a whole new jurisprudence about when to deploy the section 4 declarations even when the fact of the breach of the Convention and the inapplicability of section 3 are evident in a case before them. A new role for the jurisprudence of the European Court of Human Rights in resolving the question was staked out; a Strasbourg adjudicative technique known as the 'margin of appreciation' (on which more in Chapter 7) was drawn into the discussion; Parliament's view was suddenly something that should be waited for before the order could be made; and more along these lines. The overall sentiment was, as Lord Neuberger put it, one of being 'very cautious' about using the declaration.[27] The Court just about decided it had something it called 'constitutional authority' to make such a declaration (five votes to four) but only Baroness Hale and Lord Kerr would have done so in the case before them. None of the seven against a declaration seem to have remembered that all they were doing was

[26] Ibid at para 300.
[27] Ibid at para 103.

making an unenforceable order, more New Zealand than the United States. In the excitement of the occasion they seem to have forgotten their own relative unimportance, bought into the myth of human rights supremacy, and in so doing adding a new layer of complexity to a procedure that under the Human Rights Act was designed to be simple. The action was all supposed to be via section 3, mentioned once or twice here and to which we now turn, a site of one of the grandest fantasies of all. What potency the court has lies there.

6

THE SUPREMACY
OF THE JUDGES

In 2002, there was a rare outburst of judicial irritation from one of the most phlegmatic as well as influential of judges in the post-Human Rights Act era, Lord Bingham of Cornhill. Tom Bingham had made his fortune and his name at the commercial end of the Bar before becoming a judge so successful that he held the most senior positions in the judiciary as though they were naturally on rotation for his exceptional talent: Master of the Rolls, Lord Chief Justice, Senior Law Lord, and, almost, President of the newly formed Supreme Court (he was to retire just before the new court got going). We mentioned him briefly before as one of the key judges in the move to rights that the new, liberal dispensation among the leading judges in the 1990s had helped make possible. It was as Senior Law Lord that in the course of *R (Anderson) v Secretary of State for the Home Department* he indirectly chided a colleague on the bench in the House of Lords for adopting an approach to the Human Rights Act which, if followed by others, would amount to an act of 'judicial vandalism'.[1] What had irritated Lord Bingham was a particular reading of section 3, a provision mentioned at the end of Chapter 5 as the main source of the power which has meant that the judges have to engage in a fresh way under the Human Rights Act. For something so important—about which so many misconceptions have grown—it is surprisingly short; indeed we

---

[1] [2002] UKHL 46, [2003] 1 AC 837, at para 30.

On Fantasy Island: Britain, Europe, and Human Rights. First Edition. Conor Gearty.

were able to summarize it in a single clause towards the start of Chapter 5. Here it is in full:

(1) So far as it is possible to do so, primary legislation and subordinate legislation must be read and given effect in a way which is compatible with the Convention rights.

(2) This section
   (a) applies to primary legislation and subordinate legislation whenever enacted;
   (b) does not affect the validity, continuing operation or enforcement of any incompatible primary legislation; and
   (c) does not affect the validity, continuing operation or enforcement of any incompatible subordinate legislation if (disregarding any possibility of revocation) primary legislation prevents removal of the incompatibility.

The (b) and (c) parts of the second subsection here remind us of the impotency of the Human Rights Act in the face of parliamentary determination to flout its terms, the myth about which we discussed in Chapter 5. For present purposes the bits to concentrate on are s 3(1) and 3(2)(a) and since the second of these is a straightforward assertion of the reach of the provision (into the future as well as the past, a move which governs only until such a point in time as the legislature in its sovereign power determines that it should not), what we are really interested in is the first subsection. And that in turn leads to a focus on a single word, 'possible'. The judges are allowed to 'read' all legislation so as to make sure that it is 'given effect' to in a way that satisfies the Convention rights (all neatly set out in schedule 1) but only where this is 'possible'. Not where it is impossible then. But what are the limits of the possible?

The point exercised Parliament when the proposed law was put before it in 1997/8. The measure was drafted in this way as a compromise between the New Labour human rights ultras and the old school human rights sceptics in the party, the tension between whom gave birth to the Human Rights Act in this particular shape (a point we already mentioned in Chapter 5 and which need not be dwelt on further here). We know that 'possible' means more than 'reasonably possible' because an amendment to that effect was rejected by the Commons.[2] The then Lord Chancellor Lord Irvine—one of the primary parents of the measure and responsible for steering it through the Lords—was equally emphatic that 'possible' meant more than 'probable' though we might be forgiven here for thinking that he was merely stating the obvious.[3] Responding to the proposed amendment in the House of Commons the then Home Secretary Jack Straw said that it was the government's ambition to have 'the courts... strive to find an interpretation of legislation that is consistent with convention rights, so far as the plain words of the legislation allow, and only in the last resort to conclude that the legislation is simply incompatible with them'.[4] Beyond this rather flimsy guidance, the matter was simply left by the legislature to the courts to resolve. So at this very first stage of our enquiry into supposed judicial power under the Human Rights Act, we can be quite clear that the judges did not assert the interpretative responsibility we will be discussing; they had it thrust upon them by Parliament.

On the whole, subject to the 'judicial vandalism' that Lord Bingham saw off (and on which more in a moment), the judges have made an excellent fist of a difficult hand, working to discern what Parliament meant against a background of knowing (albeit never of course admitting) that Parliament did not itself (in any kind of collective way at least) know what it was doing, beyond simply deploying the word 'possible' in the way that it did. Early on, that other early advocate of human rights law in the 1990s, now elevated to Chief Justice, Lord Woolf of Barnes made some useful preliminary remarks, stressing that section 3 should only modify meaning to 'the extent... necessary to achieve compatibility'[5] and also reminding his colleagues on the bench that '[s]ection 3

---

[2] HC Debs, 3 June 1998, cols 415–37.

[3] HL Debs, 18 November 1997, col 535.

[4] HC Debs, 3 June 1998, cols 421–2.

[5] *Poplar Housing and Regeneration Community Association Ltd v Donoghue* [2001] EWCA Civ 595, [2002] QB 48, at para 75(b).

does not entitle the court to *legislate* (its task is still one of *interpretation*)'.[6] The background to this was that there had been some Scottish excitement in judicial and legal circles about having human rights law first when the law had been introduced there a year and more before the Human Rights Act itself came fully into force.[7] 'Don't go mad folks,' might have been a popular way of saying what was on Lord Woolf's mind. One judge could not help himself, however; one more senior in the judicial pecking order than even Lord Woolf, in a case that found its way to the House of Lords within a year of the measure coming fully into force across the United Kingdom (on 2 October 2000).

Despite its having been decided well before the cases began properly to flow, *R v A (No 2)*[8] remains one of the most controversial of all those decided under the Human Rights Act: it dealt with the issue of the extent to which we should in rape trials allow the jury to know of the previous sexual history of the person making the complaint of rape, relating (if a woman as was almost always the case in practice) not only to sexual relations with men generally but also with the accused specifically. Parliament took a certain view about the need to protect victims of such crimes and encapsulated it in legislation passed (as it happens) after the Human Rights Act but before that measure had come into force designed to protect complainants.[9] The courts took a different view; concerned with the fairness of the trial of the accused in such cases, and armed now with the Human Rights Act, they proceeded to use section 3 to 'read down' the legislation to ensure they got what they wanted.[10] It is a hard question about whose rights you

---

[6] Ibid at para 75(c) (emphasis in the original).

[7] See eg *County Properties Ltd v Scottish Ministers* 2000 SLT 965; *Brown v Stott* [2003] 1 AC 681.

[8] [2001] UKHL 25, [2002] 1 AC 45.

[9] Youth Justice and Criminal Evidence Act 1999, s 41.

[10] Not everyone in this field is as critical as this framing would suggest: see generally A Kavanagh, *Constitutional Review under the Human Rights Act* (Cambridge: Cambridge University Press, 2009) and specifically the same author's 'Unlocking the Human Rights Act: The "Radical" Approach to Section 3(1) Revisited' [2005] *European Human Rights Law Review* 259–75.

prefer: on the one hand those of the complainant not to have her case thrown out on the basis of prejudicial but irrelevant information; on the other, the right of the accused to have a fair trial which has (at very least it could be said) to involve a full picture of his past sexual relations with the person making the accusation. That is not the point of raising the case right now though, important though this dimension is. One of the judges in the Lords used this early opportunity to throw out a way of making sense of section 3 which he no doubt hoped would take off and become the routine way in which the courts did their section 3 job. Baron Steyn of Swaffield was born and brought up in South Africa where he practised law for a period before leaving in disgust at the system of apartheid under which he was required to operate.[11] He never lost his mistrust of legislative action and his belief in the courts as a bulwark against oppression. The Human Rights Act needed to be beefed up if it was to be any good. The route to this was via an invigorated assertion of the 'possible':

> [T]he interpretive obligation under section 3 of the 1998 Act is a strong one... In accordance with the will of Parliament as reflected in section 3 it will sometimes be necessary to adopt an interpretation which linguistically may appear strained. The techniques to be used will not only involve the reading down of express language in a statute but also the implication of provisions. A declaration of incompatibility is a measure of last resort. It must be avoided unless it is plainly impossible to do so. If a *clear* limitation on Convention rights is stated *in terms*, such an impossibility will arise.[12]

Now this was heady stuff indeed, going well beyond what this particular case needed. It seemed that Parliament would have to be totally clear it wanted to breach human rights and say so in terms if it did not want to fall foul of section 3. The 'possible' would seem to reach everything not specifically stated to be out of the question. If not going so far as the USA (where Congress can never fight back against rulings of the Supreme Court on the constitution) it was certainly matching the Canadian system

---

[11] See the sympathetic profile at <http://www.theguardian.com/politics/2005/oct/21/uk.humanrights> [accessed 8 January 2016].

[12] *R v A (No 2)* (n 8), at para 44 (emphasis in the original).

with its 'notwithstanding' clause and power of legislative retaliation that we mentioned in Chapter 5.

Attractive to the human rights believers though this was, it had the disadvantage of being manifestly not what the Human Rights Act had intended—we do not need to know exactly what section 3 was about to be clear that it was not this. His colleagues on the bench were not nearly so robust, perhaps recalling another of Lord Bingham's remarks, in one of those early Scottish cases, that '[j]udicial recognition and assertion of the human rights defined in the Convention is not a substitute for the processes of democratic government but a complement to them'.[13] The Steyn position did not take off. There was an almost immediate hostile reaction, and the final nail in this activist adventure was briskly nailed in with Lord Bingham's damning remarks about vandalism about nineteen months later. Even poor Lord Steyn had been dragged into line by then, rejecting an argument put by counsel but inspired by himself as amounting to not 'interpretation but interpolation inconsistent with the plain legislative intent', with the Steyn-reliant advocate now being told by Steyn Mark 2 that section 3(1) is simply 'not available where the suggested interpretation is contrary to express statutory words or is by implication necessarily contradicted by the statute'.[14]

In fairness to Lord Steyn, by the time of this climb-down, the lords had already begun to feel their way to what section 3 did mean in a way that had not been the case when the rape case had come up for decision. In his recanting in *Anderson*, his lordship referred to a decision that we can now see has claims to be perhaps among the handful of most important in the whole field, albeit not a frequently cited one, perhaps because of its mouthful of a title, *Re S (Minors) (Care Order: Implementation of Care Plan)*.[15] The leading speech (as judgments in the

---

[13] *Brown v Stott* (n 7), at p 703.

[14] *R (Anderson) v Secretary of State for the Home Department* (n 1), at para 59.

[15] [2002] UKHL 10, [2002] 2 AC 291. (I should admit to being involved in this case as a barrister so this may colour my view as to its importance.)

House of Lords used to be called) was made not by one of the large
personalities we have already encountered but by the rather less well-
known Lord Nicholls of Birkenhead. The neat solution this creative
judge found to the conundrum of section 3 was to throw the question
of the 'possible' back into the world of statutory construction—but
(and here was the neat move) construction this time not of the Human
Rights Act but rather of the Act to which the rights legislation was being
applied. Lord Nicholls's section 3 enquiry was set against a backdrop
of sensitivity to what courts were able and (more to the point) not able
or equipped to do. So, with regard to the work that can be done on a
statute under the regime of the 'possible' under section 3,

> a meaning which departs substantially from a fundamental feature of an
> Act of Parliament is likely to have crossed the boundary between inter-
> pretation and amendment. This is especially so where the departure has
> important practical repercussions which the court is not equipped to
> evaluate. In such a case the overall contextual setting may leave no scope
> for rendering the statutory provision Convention compliant by legitimate
> use of the process of interpretation.[16]

In this case, a Court of Appeal shocked by what it saw as legislative
gaps in the scheme of the Children Act 1989 had set about filling those
gaps with an ambitious new arrangement that entailed greater court
involvement in the care of children so as to ensure they were not
forgotten by the system after their initial care plans were put in place.
All laudable to be sure, and much of it bearing a close resemblance to
initiatives to change the 1989 Act that had been doing the conference
circuit, some sponsored by the judges themselves, but clearly drifting
into the realm of law-making, not law-discerning. Critically one of
the central thrusts of the Children Act had been to reduce the layers
of judicial engagement in these cases: as one of those involved in
drafting that Act (and now by a characteristically British constitutional
quirk sitting on *Re S* in the Lords as a former Lord Chancellor) Lord
Mackay of Clashfern put it, 'the fundamental change brought about by

---

[16] Ibid at para 40.

the Act' was the 'placing [of] the responsibility for looking after children who are the subject of care orders squarely on the local authorities' and that this was 'not in any way incompatible with the Convention'.[17] If there were problems, then these were for other branches of government to resolve; Lord Mackay ends his short speech in the case by saying that he 'would strongly urge that the Government and Parliament give urgent attention to the problems clearly described by the Court of Appeal [in this case] so that we do not continue failing some of our most vulnerable children'.[18] But section 3 of the Human Rights Act was not to be turned into some kind of ethical scaffold on which every public interest and law reform group was to be permitted to hang its new proposals and therefore, after a bit of litigation, call them laws. The Woolf line about interpretation not legislation was confirmed and fleshed out.

In the *Re S* case a big problem with the Court of Appeal's approach had been its failure to identify precisely which bit of the Children Act needed fixing and what exactly under section 3 it was proposed should be done. Nothing flushes out an inappropriate (and therefore not 'possible') reading of a section under human rights scrutiny more than looking at what needs to be added or taken away from the provision to make it Convention compatible. The more elaborate the additions or subtractions, the more they drifted beyond what the law in which they appeared was all about, then the more they were likely to be simply not tenable—or (in the language of section 3 again) not 'possible'. We can see from this, therefore, that far from imposing a judicial version of the law (as Lord Steyn in *Re A* and the Court of Appeal in *Re S* might be said to have been tempted to do), the right approach, and the one that is now routinely adopted, is to identify the purpose of the law under scrutiny and then see if the Convention changes proposed 'go with the grain' of that purpose, as the late Lord

---

[17] Ibid at para 109.
[18] Ibid at para 112.

Rodger of Earlsferry is said so felicitously to have put it.[19] The courts are not striking out on their own; they are squaring two statutory purposes, one in the Human Rights Act and the other in the law they have been called upon to examine for Convention compatibility, not so much masters of Parliament as servants striving to make sense of the multiple demands of their sovereign master.

A neat and important question remains, though, about what the purpose of an Act of Parliament might be said to be. When talking about section 3 itself earlier, the rather glib point was made that Parliament does not really know what it means when it legislates for the 'possible'. Legislation does not wear its object on its sleeve in this way. Of course purpose can be identified by having regard not just to the words used (in the Act viewed as a whole and with the preamble also taken into account) but also (in appropriate cases) to the supporting parliamentary paperwork as well, even on occasion the debates themselves. Much depends on the level of abstraction at which the judges chose to hone in on that purpose—the more broadly it is defined the easier will it be for section 3 to do its reforming work, the more narrowly, the more difficult as the conflict with purpose will be more likely to be exposed. We have to acknowledge that this zone of judicial discretion remains—and it can be a wide one. Take the case in which Lord Rodger's idea about going with 'the grain of the legislation' first came into play, *Ghaidan v Godin-Mendoza (FC)*.[20] A male couple had lived together in the same home for seventeen years, 'in a stable and monogamous homosexual relationship',[21] with one a protected tenant and the other not. The protected tenant died, on 5 January 2001 (shortly after the Human Rights Act had come into force). If the couple had been heterosexual whether married or living together, then the law was clear that the surviving spouse/partner

---

[19] Attributed to Lord Rodger by Lord Nicholls in *Ghaidan v Godin-Mendoza (FC)* (n 20), at para 33.

[20] [2004] UKHL 30, [2004] 2 AC 557.

[21] Ibid at para 33.

would become a statutory tenant by succession if still living in the house (as the survivor was in this case). As originally enacted, the relevant law—in the Rent Act 1977—had provided (following earlier laws) that a widow who was residing in the dwelling-house at the death of her husband should have a right to a statutory tenancy in priority over other members of her family. It was something the husband could not will away, however he might want to and however happy or unhappy the marriage might have been. This law had already undergone change over the years since 1977. Its gender-specific nature had not surprisingly become an issue for legislators: the husband in exactly the same position as the wife (a widower rather than widow) was originally not able to avail himself of the security offered by the law so that if other family members remained at the home and no agreement was possible he would have to throw himself on the mercy of the courts to secure anything at all. In 1980, Parliament substituted 'surviving spouse' for 'widow' in paragraph 2(1) of the relevant sched-ule so as to extend the protection to all spouses. Social change continued apace, however: what about the man and woman living together rather than married: why should not both the man and woman in such a relationship also be protected? So in 1988 Parliament added (via paragraph 2(2)) that 'For the purposes of this paragraph, a person who was living with the original tenant as his or her wife or husband shall be treated as the spouse of the original tenant'.

But what of homosexual relationships? As the law stood they did not qualify—indeed because of other changes if they were lucky enough to get anything, then it would now only be a less secure 'assured' rather than a statutory tenancy. In a major legal challenge before the Human Rights Act came into force, an attempt was made to expand the language to non-heterosexual couples but it failed.[22] When *Ghaidan* was being argued in the House of Lords, a bill was before Parliament which would, if enacted, establish a new scheme of

---

[22] *Fitzpatrick v Sterling Housing Association Ltd* [2001] 1 AC 27. The appeal was successful on other grounds.

civil partnerships and the effect of this would be, among other things, to extend protection to such surviving partners. Did the Human Rights Act make the difference anyway and so the legislation unnecessary? In *Ghaidan* there was no serious argument about whether the Convention rights were breached: case-law from Strasbourg and the wording of the rights on which this was based made fairly clear that the discrimination as between hetero- and homosexual couples contained within the Rent Act (as amended) amounted to a breach of the right not to be discriminated against in the enjoyment of one's Convention rights, article 14 operating in tandem with the right to respect for privacy in article 8.[23] But could the courts fiddle with the wording of paragraph 2(2) so as to bring the language into line with the Convention? Was such a reading 'possible'?

The matter reached the House of Lords. One of their number, Lord Millett, thought not. The 'legislative policy which Parliament has hitherto adopted [was] dependent on status and not merit'.[24] It was indelibly limited to couples of the opposite sex and it was up to Parliament—and Parliament alone—to change this, which (as has just been noted) at that very moment Parliament was considering doing. The matter under consideration had not been part of the legislative intention or purpose under the 1977 Act at any point, either originally or when the law was expanded in 1980 and again in 1988. To bring it within that scope now was, so far as Lord Millett was concerned, to usurp the legislative process since 'these questions [were] essentially questions of social policy which should be left to Parliament'.[25] None of the remaining four law lords sitting in the case agreed with him, however, and in its essence this was because they took a broader view of what the legislation had been really about. Far from being fixated on gender, it was concerned with relationships—its intention or purpose was to (in a way) reward couples whose life together had survived the exigencies of

---

[23] Principally *Karner v Austria* (2003) 38 EHRR 528.

[24] *Ghaidan v Godin-Mendoza* (n 20), at para 100.

[25] Ibid at para 101.

the everyday so that it had been only death that had brought their relationship to an end. The 1988 change showed this; Parliament had been willing to bust the marriage obligation to protect the survivor in a 'marriage' that had not so long before been condemned as merely 'living in sin'. The ruling in favour of the surviving partner was not removing 'the very core and essence, the "pith and substance" of the measure that Parliament had enacted'.[26] The extension being imposed 'would not contradict any cardinal principle of the Rent Act' but would rather 'simply be a modest development of the extension of the concept of "spouse" which Parliament itself made when it enacted para 2(2) in 1988'.[27] Maybe things would have been different if that change to encompass unmarried heterosexual couples had not been made and the law had still been stuck in the marital groove, but 'that bridge was crossed in 1988'.[28] As one of the judges in the case put it, '[s]ociety wants its intimate relationships, particularly but not only if there are children involved, to be stable, responsible and secure. It is the transient, irresponsible and insecure relationships which cause so much concern.'[29] This is what the statute was really about.

All well and good. But what did it mean for the precise wording of paragraph 2(2)? Lord Rodger thought that it could be revised so as really to read something along the lines of (changes in square brackets): 'For the purposes of this paragraph, a person [whether of the same or of the opposite sex] who was living with the original tenant [in a long-term relationship] [omitting 'as his or her wife or husband'] shall be treated as the spouse of the original tenant'.[30] This won't however be found by looking at the law in the statute book. There is a real issue here, which goes beyond the details of this case, about how

---

[26] Ibid at para 111, per Lord Rodger of Earlsferry, citing Lord Watson in (in a different context) *Union Colliery Co of British Columbia Ltd v Bryden* [1899] AC 580, at p 587.

[27] *Ghaidan* (n 20) at para 128 per Lord Rodger.

[28] Ibid at para 128 per Lord Rodger.

[29] Ibid at para 143 per Baroness Hale of Richmond.

[30] Ibid at para 129 per Lord Rodger. Square brackets added to assist understanding.

THE SUPREMACY OF THE JUDGES

far section 3 can be made to go, since its new drafts need to be learnt from the law reports not the statute book: it was mainly a concern about the implications of such an approach that had so exercised Lord Millett in dissent. Litigants and their advisers risk being positively misled by what they read in the legislation unless they are also keeping themselves up to date with the latest case-law (which might entail reading hundreds of pages to work out for themselves what a provision—once clear—now means).

Why did the lords push things as far as they did in this case? Surely they could easily have quickly agreed the declaration of incompatibility and let Parliament get on with changing the law, something it was considering doing anyway? After all this is what it had done when the question of the law on transsexual people had come before it, a couple of years before, in *Bellinger v Bellinger*.[31] All sides involved in that case (including the government which intervened in the House of Lords through the Lord Chancellor) accepted that there was an incompatibility with the Convention so far as the failure to give legal recognition to the acquired gender of transsexual persons was concerned (the right to privacy in article 8 and here also as it happens the right to marry in article 12). Despite this, fiddling about with the pre-existing law under section 3 was not on. In the words of Lord Nicholls once more giving the lead judgment, it would 'represent a major change in the law, having far reaching ramifications' and so was 'pre-eminently a matter for Parliament' which was all the more the case because the government had 'already announced its intention to introduce comprehensive primary legislation on this difficult and sensitive subject'.[32] A declaration of incompatibility was the right way to go. Mrs Bellinger could wait for changes in the law. In contrast of course Juan Godin-Mendoza could not: if the lords had found against him he would have no home to return to if and when Parliament finally got round to changing the law. The landlord Mr Ghaidan would have secured a new

---

[31] [2003] UKHL 21, [2003] 2 AC 467.
[32] Ibid at para 37.

tenant. Aileen Kavanagh has pointed out how much seeing the facts as the judges saw them helps understand their reasoning, and this is a prime example.[33] The declaration of incompatibility would have been total defeat for Godin-Mendoza; for Bellinger it was a likely delayed victory.

The cases that we have been discussing here are fairly old by the standards of the Human Rights Act. In truth the issue has been largely sorted out and rarely gives rise to controversy. Every now and again a set of facts comes along where the judges are tempted to wave their interpretative wands in a *Ghaidan v Godin-Mendoza* way to secure justice. A touching example is surely *R (Baiai) v Secretary of State for the Home Department*[34] where an unpleasant law required all those subject to immigration control to get the written permission of the Home Secretary before they could marry, for which the authorities had the temerity to charge £295 (£590 if both partners were caught by the provision). The instructions issued under the relevant legislation were very broad, going way beyond the ostensible purpose of checking whether a marriage was genuine. So the subsection requiring the Secretary of State's permission was gaily rewritten by their lordships to mean, as before, 'has the written permission of the Secretary of State to marry in the United Kingdom' but now adding 'such permission not to be withheld in the case of a qualified applicant seeking to enter into a marriage which is not one of convenience and the application for, and grant of, such permission not to be subject to conditions which unreasonably inhibit exercise of the applicant's right under article 12 of the European Convention'.[35] This was quite a mouthful. Three years later the provision was finally removed, but during that whole intervening period no lawyer would have had a clue about what the law required by looking only at how it appeared in the statute books. We can guess that the lords were not so sure that the legislature would

---

[33] Kavanagh (n 10), at p 120.
[34] [2008] UKHL 53, [2009] 1 AC 287.
[35] Ibid at para 32 per Lord Bingham of Cornhill.

have made the necessary change if it had been left up to them through use of the declaration process, the litigants here being non-nationals. This feel for individuated justice is one of the driving forces of the Human Rights Act as we shall see when in Chapter 9 we look in the round at who it has protected. We end this chapter by repeating a point we made in Chapter 5, about the courts being concerned with real people, with actually making abstract language about equality work in practice, in a way that legislators often fight shy of, wanting both to hold the ethical position and to depart from it when they feel like it. Because of the Human Rights Act, courts are not able to be as pragmatic (hypocritical) as this. But nor are they sovereign in the way that critics—not least the Prime Minister himself—have affected to believe.

7

THE SUPREMACY OF
STRASBOURG

The cases we have been focusing on in Chapters 5 and 6 were of course British and our discussion of sections 3 and 4 was very domestic, concentrating on how the judges here have interpreted what is, after all, a highly unusual Act of Parliament. As we were concerned on the whole with the mechanics of the judicial capability under the Act, it was natural to gloss over how the judges were approaching the substance of the matter before them, the Convention rights set out in the first schedule to the Act. Had we done so, we would have immediately appreciated how all of them have drawn their inspiration (and guidance on how to resolve the questions of interpretation before them) from the European Court of Human Rights at Strasbourg. We came across this court towards the end of Chapter 3 and again briefly in Chapter 4. It is the multinational bench of judges whose job it is both to hear applications from member states of the Council of Europe alleging breaches of the 1950 European Convention on Human Rights by other member states and also to adjudicate in cases brought by individuals against one or other of the states. There are hardly any of the first category of cases but literally hundreds of thousands of the second. The individual (whether natural or legal, national or non-national, it does not matter) claims that he or she (or it) has been a victim of a human rights violation for which the state in which he or she lives (or it is based) is said to be responsible.[1]

---

[1] See art 34 of the European Convention on Human Rights and Fundamental Freedoms: <http://www.echr.coe.int/Documents/Convention_ENG.pdf> [accessed 27 March 2016].

On Fantasy Island: Britain, Europe, and Human Rights. First Edition. Conor Gearty.

Initially a kind of add-on for purist human-rights-respecting nations, this right of individual petition is now obligatory across all the forty-seven European states that are part of the Council and who as a result automatically submit themselves to Strasbourg's jurisdiction. In the early days there were hardly any cases of this (or any) sort at all but as the Council expanded, the Cold War ended, and yet more states joined, more and more people became aware of its reach. The litigants poured in. The Court has toiled to get through its backlog of cases, to cope with its popularity as a *deus ex machina* serving up justice for its hundreds of millions of potential users, from Lisbon to Vladivostok, Iceland to Istanbul.[2]

Needless to say there has been some pushback from the countries concerned: no nation likes to be told it is not as sovereign as it seemed. Various declarations have been made about the need for Strasbourg to respect the court rulings of member states more, about being less intrusive, and so on,[3] and the Court itself has developed restraining principles that it imposes on itself from time to time: 'the margin of appreciation' is one,[4] the 'principle of subsidiarity'[5] another. In the end, though, it has been generally acknowledged that the Court has to act where it finds a breach of a Convention right in a case that finds its way to it: its legal character gives it no other option. The enforcement of its decisions is not simple. There is a convoluted system of oversight by the Council of Europe through its political Committee of Ministers but the main job of making the Strasbourg Court's decisions bite lies with the member states themselves. These European Court of

[2] Things have improved of late though: A Donald, 'The remarkable shrinking backlog at the European Court of Human Rights' UK Human Rights Blog 1 October 2014: <http://ukhumanrightsblog.com/2014/10/01/the-remarkable-shrinking-backlog-at-the-european-court-of-human-rights/> [accessed 19 January 2016].
[3] Eg the Brighton Declaration on ECHR adopted in Spring 2012: see <http://www.echr.coe.int/Documents/2012_Brighton_FinalDeclaration_ENG.pdf> [accessed 19 January 2016].
[4] See *Handyside v United Kingdom* (1976) 1 EHRR 737.
[5] See *Von Hannover v Germany (No 2)* (2012) 55 EHRR 388.

Human Rights decisions don't invariably reach automatically into the domestic legal order the way European Union law often can and does. Here is where the states could have foiled the Court if they had really wanted to, dragged their heels so much that the place became a noisy irrelevance, its grand pronouncements signifying nothing. But viewed overall and give or take a few bad patches, the record of obedience across Europe is not bad at all.[6]

Despite all the hostile energy generated by the issue (some already noticed with more to come in a moment), the UK has a record to match, indeed better, any state as a 'good' pupil when it comes to following the dictates of Strasbourg. Not that there has been much aggravation from that Court to worry the government: Parliament's Joint Committee on Human Rights looked into the whole question of implementation of British judgments very carefully in the spring of 2015,[7] finding that the proportion of cases in which the UK actually lost was remarkably low, not much more than 1 per cent.[8] Even this puny success rate has been 'steadily reducing in recent years: it was approximately 1.3% in 2010, 1% in 2011 and .6% in both 2012 and 2013'.[9] Now if this were a court in Belarus or Kazakhstan a very obvious rat would no doubt long have been smelt and human rights groups would be (surely rightly) up in arms about the government's routine 99.5 per cent success rate before its judges. Not only is that not the case with the Strasbourg Court—advocates strongly support it and

[6] See Council of Europe, *Execution of Judgments of the European Court of Human Rights* at <http://www.coe.int/t/dghl/monitoring/execution/default_en.asp> [accessed 19 January 2016] for a sense of the way this system works.

[7] Joint Committee on Human Rights, *Human Rights Judgments* Seventh Report of Session 2014–15. HL 130, HC 1088 (11 March 2015). There is a very good recent study: K S Ziegler, E Wicks, and L Hodson (eds), *The UK and European Human Rights: A Strained Relationship* (Oxford: Hart Publishing, 2015).

[8] Ibid para 2.2. The exact figure is 1.34% and is achieved by comparing the number of applications made with the number of violations finally found: see further the government's own *Responding to Human Rights Judgments: Report to the Joint Committee on Human Rights on the Government Response to Human Rights Judgments 2013–14* Cm 8962 (December 2014).

[9] *Human Rights Judgments* (n 7), para 2.2.

certainly no one treats it as a comic camouflage for state power—but the main point of discussion in Britain is—amazingly it might be thought—about how Strasbourg is *exceeding* its remit, pushing the UK too far, forcing its continental laws on us, and so on. It has been Britain that has been in the van of 'reining in' Strasbourg with various declarations and summits and so on, behaving a bit like a football team that reacts hysterically to a referee after a match in which only one foul was given against them, a hundred appeals from the other side being ignored. To an extent this is a straightforward misunderstanding of how the Court's caseload gets handled. A *Daily Mail* headline on 'Europe's war on British justice' was rooted in the assertion that the 'UK loses 3 out of 4 human rights cases'[10] but this was based on ignoring all the cases that had been rejected out of hand early on (inadmissible applications), a convenient temptation towards the sensational to which the *Telegraph* and the *Sun* have also in their time succumbed.[11]

Nor has Britain been at all tardy when it comes to implementing those few cases that go against it. Leaving aside one particular issue (on prison voting: more on this shortly) the story is a positive one. The Joint Committee felt moved to 'commend the Government for its generally very good record on implementing' the few Court judgments that find a violation.[12] This is true. The UK has historically been very good here, taking the Committee of Ministers seriously and doing its best to address Court concerns where it has been the losing party, a trend of compliance that has seen the number of cases concerning Britain on file in the Committee's implementation folder decline year on year.[13]

[10] *Daily Mail* 11 January 2012: <http://www.dailymail.co.uk/news/article-2085420/Europes-war-British-justice-UK-loses-human-rights-cases-damning-report-reveals.html> [accessed 19 January 2016].
[11] See *Human Rights Judgments* (n 7), para 2.2 for the references to the exact newspaper headlines.
[12] Ibid para 2.12.
[13] Ibid para 2.10.

Nowhere is the mismatch between fantasy and fact clearer than in how the media presents the Strasbourg Court to British audiences and what that body in fact actually does. This goes beyond the sorts of headlines about Strasbourg victories that we have just noted, those screams of rage beloved of sub-editors that are inevitably rooted in misrepresentation (more about this in Chapter 8). Nor is it simply down to Ministers who do not like implementing Strasbourg decisions lashing out at a requirement which is, after all, imposed on them by a wider governmental commitment to law but which happens in this particular case to work against what they perceive to be the national interest. It would have been very odd, for example, if the then Secretary of State for the Home Department Michael Howard had not been cross about having to implement (through paying legal costs and expenses to the applicant families) the Strasbourg decision that the security forces had breached the right to life of three members of the IRA whom they had killed in Gibraltar when it had been common ground that their intention had been to detonate a bomb on the island in a way that was certain to cause extensive casualties.[14] But the moneys got paid over and Britain quietly chose to remain in the system at a time when the individual petition was not compulsory and they could have dumped it without at that time having also to leave the Council of Europe.

The issues here go much deeper. As we have seen, one of our main political organizations, the Conservative Party, has found itself taking an approach to all things European which has over the years been growing ever more hostile, culminating in the recently held referendum on EU membership itself. A subset of this anti-European drift in the Tory Party has seen the Strasbourg Court come increasingly to the fore as (yet another) example of (bad) Europe. Now we do need to mention the prisoners' cases which have had such a huge impact. In *Hirst v United Kingdom (no 2)*,[15] the Court offered its

---

[14] *McCann v United Kingdom* (1996) 21 EHRR 97.
[15] (2005) 42 EHRR 849.

opponents an open goal in the shape of a particularly egregious client (a man who killed his landlady with an axe) who managed successfully to argue that the UK's blanket ban on prisoners voting offended the third of the articles of the First Protocol to the Convention, designed to secure effective representative government. The point was in some ways as dodgy as the client; all the relevant right requires is 'free elections at reasonable intervals by secret ballot, under conditions which will ensure the free expression of the opinion of the people in the choice of the legislature'.[16] Maybe if *Hirst* hadn't been decided the way it was the Euro rights-sceptics would have found another target, but this was one not to be missed. On the back of *Hirst* and the many cases it has generated (both in Strasbourg and at home[17]) the Conservatives have found themselves becoming ever more angry about Strasbourg. As the fervour of the sceptics increased, warnings by politicians like Dominic Grieve QC about needing to see the big picture and taking the rough with the smooth began to get routinely ignored, such messengers even being sacked for their temerity as truth-sayers (as Grieve was in 2014, from the post of Attorney General).

During their 2010–15 period in office the Tories were forced by their political partnership with the Liberal Democratic Party to be restrained about the Convention: as we noted right at the start of this book the 'Lib Dems' have long been huge fans of things European in general and human rights in particular. This impotence ended with the 2015 election, fought on a manifesto pledge to 'break the formal link between British courts and the European Court of Human Rights, and make our own Supreme Court the ultimate arbiter of human rights matters in the UK'.[18] A short strategy document had already

[16] Art 3, First Protocol.
[17] For a good summary see House of Commons Library Briefing Paper, *Prisoners' Voting Rights: Developments Since May 2015* (CPB 7461, 12 January 2016) with the pre-May 2015 story also covered: <http://researchbriefings.parliament.uk/ResearchBriefing/Summary/CBP-7461> [accessed 19 January 2016].
[18] The Conservative Party Manifesto 2015 p 60: <https://www.conservatives.com/manifesto> [accessed 19 January 2016].

made clear how much the party hated the Strasbourg Court, how its 'mission creep' had to be restrained.[19] The recently retired Chief Justice Lord Judge joined in, giving an interview to the lawyers' magazine *Counsel* which was sufficiently forthright to be headlined by the *Daily Mail* as 'Human rights court "is a threat to democracy": Ex-Lord Chief Justice blasts unelected Strasbourg judges'.[20] Even a serving Supreme Court judge, Lord Sumption, could not resist using a speech in Malaysia to knock the Court, drawing an approving comment from the *Mail* under the headline, 'Human rights court is dictating law like east Germany, warns leading judge'.[21]

So what exactly does the Human Rights Act have to say about Strasbourg? Of course when making the Convention part of UK law it was necessary to think about what to do with all that Strasbourg stuff which told you more about what each right meant. We have already anticipated the answer to this in the opening remark in this chapter about the extent to which the courts here do as a matter of practice rely heavily on that case-law. But the law is less East German than might be supposed. This is what the relevant bits of the section dealing with this issue (section 2) say:

(1) A court or tribunal determining a question which has arisen in connection with a Convention right must take into account any—
   (a) Judgment, decision, declaration or advisory opinion of the European Court of Human Rights
   ... whenever made or given, so far as, in the opinion of the court or tribunal, it is relevant to the proceedings in which that question has arisen.

---

[19] *Protecting Human Rights in the UK: The Conservatives' Proposals for Changing Britain's Human Rights Laws* (undated): <https://www.conservatives.com/~/media/files/download able%20Files/human_rights.pdf> [accessed 19 January 2016].

[20] *Daily Mail* 1 October 2014: <http://www.dailymail.co.uk/news/article-2775796/Human-rights-court-threat-democracy-Ex-Lord-Chief-Justice-blasts-unelected-Strasbourg-judges.html> [accessed 19 January 2016].

[21] *Daily Mail* 28 November 2013. (Lord Sumption): <http://www.dailymail.co.uk/news/article-2515284/Judge-warns-Human-Rights-Court-dictating-law-like-East-Germany.html> [accessed 19 January 2016].

And that's it. The bits left out relate to other Council of Europe bodies that are or were involved with the Convention's interpretation but none of that has proved controversial. The focus has been on the Court. The intention is clearly to take into account in the sense of *have regard to* rather than *automatically to follow* all Strasbourg decisions. When the Bill was before the Lords an amendment was tabled by (of all people!) the Shadow Conservative Lord Chancellor, Lord Kingsland, to the effect that the Strasbourg case-law should be turned into binding precedent.[22] As the noble lord reasonably pointed out, 'if our judges only take account of the jurisprudence of the European Court of Human Rights, we cast them adrift from their international moorings'.[23] Expressing himself 'intrigued to hear the noble Lord, Lord Kingsland, move the amendment and be more European than the Europeans',[24] the then Labour Lord Chancellor Lord Irvine argued for rejection—the clause as drafted got the balance 'right in requiring domestic courts to take into account judgments of the European Court, but not making them binding'.[25] The Bill 'would of course permit United Kingdom courts to depart from existing Strasbourg decisions and upon occasion it might well be appropriate to do so'.[26] With his face saved by the Lord Chancellor's empty promise to reflect on the contents of the amendment, and not wishing to rally his troops to defeat a major part of the government's manifesto-approved agenda, Lord Kingsland withdrew his amendment.[27]

The fuss that section 2 has caused ever since has been the result not of its drafting but of how the courts initially approached it. There was a lot to be said for Lord Kingsland's remark about the inadvisability of letting the UK and Strasbourg versions of rights drift in different

---

[22] HL Debs, 18 November 1997, cols 511–16.
[23] Ibid col 512.
[24] Ibid col 513.
[25] Ibid col 514.
[26] Ibid col 515.
[27] Ibid col 514.

directions. And this was not just any international law, of course; the rulings of the European Court of Human Rights needed to be implemented by the government insofar as they involved this country. As it stood, section 2 gave rise to a real risk of conflict between the two legal regimes, the courts here saying one thing, Strasbourg another with the government embarrassed by having to enforce both. Now Lord Irvine may have been relaxed about this, but the senior judges in charge of interpreting the law were not. In a very early case, Lord Bingham of Cornhill made an important intervention, declaring that the 'duty of national courts is to keep pace with the Strasbourg jurisprudence as it evolves over time: no more, but certainly no less'.[28] This particular judge's overwhelming authority and importance has already been noted. His judicial colleagues tended to fall in with him, and here was no exception. Over the years the judges allowed the permissive language of section 2 to harden into an unavoidable obligation. Counsel got into the habit of treating the Strasbourg case-law as they would a major decision from the House of Lords, trying to distinguish the ones they didn't like, celebrate the ones they did, but never seriously suggesting all they needed to do was mention ('take into account') them and then carry on regardless. Even the lords were prepared (sometimes grumpily it has to be admitted) to change their minds after a Strasbourg decision or not to develop a line of argument because the European Court has already predetermined the outcome: in the dramatic phraseology of Lord Rodger of Earlsferry in an important terrorism case in 2009, 'Argentoratum locutum: iudicium finitum—Strasbourg has spoken, the case is closed.'[29]

Now well-meaning though all this was, it simply did not accord with the intention of section 2, as evidenced not only by its words but by the clear statements in Parliament explaining its intention (not that the judges were supposed to look at the latter, of course). Towards the

---

[28] R (Ullah) v Special Adjudicator [2004] UKHL 26, [2004] 2 AC 323, at para 20.
[29] Secretary of State for the Home Department v AF (No 3) [2009] UKHL 28, [2010] 2 AC 269, at para 98.

end of the first decade of the Human Rights Act's active life, the UK got itself a new Supreme Court with its first decisions being handed down in the autumn of 2009. The lords' judicial role was consigned to history. The judges might still be able to call themselves lords but they were mainly now 'Justices' and occupants of a fine new building, across the road from Parliament. Here were not the sort of people to regard themselves as the servants of a higher judicial power. In only their fourteenth case, an opportunity came along to redefine the relationship with Strasbourg along the lines originally intended. The facts of *R v Horncastle and others*[30] threw the point into the sharpest of sharp relief. The accused persons were four men who on the evidence of their victims (if believed) had committed two very serious crimes: two of them causing grievous bodily harm to one person, the other two kidnapping a young woman. There was corroborative evidence pointing to their guilt but in each case the evidence of the alleged victims was central to their convictions. The problem was that neither was available to appear at the trial of their alleged wrongdoers: the first had died (in a way not attributable to the attack) after he had given a detailed witness statement but before the trial while the second (the young woman) had run away just before the proceedings involving her started, too scared to give evidence but also leaving a full statement about what she said had happened. Each statement was admitted, the men were convicted, and their appeals to the Court of Appeal dismissed. But was this fair under the Human Rights Act?

Article 6(1) of the Convention guarantees everyone a right to a fair trial in 'the determination ... of any criminal charge against him', with paragraph 3(d) of the same article going on to say quite specifically that this includes the 'minimum' right 'to examine or have examined witnesses against him ...'. In a series of cases decided over a number of years, the Strasbourg Court has interpreted this as meaning that where a statement was 'the sole or, at least, the decisive basis' for a conviction then achieving such an outcome without the opportunity to cross-

---

[30] [2009] UKSC 14, [2010] 2 AC 373.

examine such witnesses breached the accused's article 6 rights. The matter had been fully ventilated in a very recent Chambers decision of the Court involving this country, in *Al-Khawaja and Tahery v United Kingdom*,[31] where this approach had been reiterated and confirmed. But the *Horncastle* convictions made sense in British terms: UK statute law allowed statements in these exceptional circumstances: but did these provisions now have to be 'read and given effect' under section 3(1) in a way that meant that these men must now go free?

The Supreme Court mustered an unusually large bench—seven of their number—to speak with one voice through its President, Lord Phillips, declaring the answer to be a definite no. Strasbourg should not be allowed to rule the roost on such a sensitive matter, whatever Lord Bingham (now of course departed from the bench) might once have said:

> The requirement to 'take into account' the Strasbourg jurisprudence will normally result in the domestic court applying principles that are clearly established by the Strasbourg court. There will, however, be rare occasions where the domestic court has concerns as to whether a decision of the Strasbourg court sufficiently appreciates or accommodates particular aspects of our domestic process. In such circumstances it is open to the domestic court to decline to follow the Strasbourg decision, giving reasons for adopting this course. This is likely to give the Strasbourg court the opportunity to reconsider the particular aspect of the decision that is in issue, so that there takes place what may prove to be a valuable dialogue between this court and the Strasbourg Court. This is such a case.[32]

Lord Phillips then went on to explain exactly why this was the case here: the law on hearsay evidence was very well developed, its exceptions ('required in the interests of justice'[33]) carefully drawn in a way that compensated for the absence of direct evidence with numerous safeguards designed to give the accused person against whom such statements were being entered a fair trial notwithstanding the exceptional

---

[31] (2009) 49 EHRR 1.

[32] *Horncastle* (n 30), at para 11.

[33] Ibid at para 14(2).

circumstances in which the evidence was being admitted. This being the case 'the sole or decisive rule [was] unnecessary'.[34] Its introduction had 'resulted in a jurisprudence that lacked clarity'[35] and had been imposed 'without discussion of the principle underlying it or full consideration of whether there was justification for imposing the rule as an overriding principle applicable equally to the continental and common law juris-dictions'.[36] Quite an indictment of their colleagues on the European Court of Human Rights, and the declaration of a new, more equal partnership with its judges. Strasbourg did not inflame things when the *Al Khawaja and Tahery* case came before its Grand Chamber after these rebellious pronouncements in *Horncastle*, finding that, actually, when you looked very closely at the right, there was—surprise, surprise, and contra the earlier cases—no automatic breach of article 6 in circumstances like those before the Court.[37] In vain did the two dissen-tients (ranged against fifteen in favour) declare that this important protection of the right of defence was 'being abandoned in the name of an overall examination of fairness'.[38] The British judge on the Court, who we might well speculate was the behind-the-scenes broker of the compromise between these two august tribunals, observed in his short concurring opinion that the case afforded 'a good example of the judicial dialogue between national courts and the European Court on the application of the Convention to which Lord Phillips was referring' in *Horncastle*.[39] And true to form, when Horncastle and his fellow-appellants took their cases to Strasbourg, they found the door now firmly closed to them, not even getting past the Chamber stage in their search for a breach.[40]

[34] Ibid.
[35] Ibid at para 14(5).
[36] Ibid at para 14(6).
[37] (2011) 54 EHRR 807.
[38] Judges Sajó and Karakaş, at p 870.
[39] Judge Bratza at p 862.
[40] European Court of Human Rights 16 December 2014.

The politicians may not quite have kept up with it but since *Horn-castle* there has indeed been a new mood of—not defiance exactly—but more calm co-responsibility so far as the UK courts have been concerned. In *R (Haney, Kaiyam, Massey) v Secretary of State for Justice; R (Robinson) v Governor of Her Majesty's Prison Whatton and the Secretary of State for Justice*,[41] the authority of a Strasbourg decision was almost casually swatted aside.[42] The norm remains that of the regarding of Strasbourg rulings as presumptively correct, especially if these are pronounced by its 'Grand Chamber' in which as many as seventeen of the judges gather for cases they regard as particularly important. These are to be followed more or less as a matter of course, even where the judges might not like the consequences. But the mood changes when a case like *Vinter v UK*[43] comes along. Here the Grand Chamber found that whole life orders of imprisonment violated article 3's prohibition on 'inhuman and degrading treatment or punishment' because the prisoners in jail for life (including those before it in this case) had no real prospect of ever being released: this could occur only at the discretion of the Secretary of State and then solely on 'compassionate grounds', such as, for example, a terminal illness or a serious incapacity. In *R v Newell; R v McLoughlin*[44] a troupe of the most senior judges in the land (the Lord Chief Justice; the President of the Queen's Bench Division, the Vice-President of the Court of Appeal (Criminal Division); and two others, from the Court of Appeal and the High Court respectively) gathered to lay waste to the Strasbourg decision in *Vinter*. The Lord Chief himself pronounced the burial rights: the law in the UK was fine by article 3 and the view in *Vinter* that it was not proceeded from a faulty understanding of what the relevant legislative scheme entailed. Properly explained (as the judges were now doing) the national law was not at all uncertain or unclear, and life prisoners did have a chance to

[41] [2014] UKSC 66, [2015] AC 1344.
[42] *James v United Kingdom* (2012) 56 EHRR 399.
[43] European Court of Human Rights (Grand Chamber) 9 July 2013.
[44] [2014] EWCA Crim 188, [2014] 1 WLR 3964.

get out which was wider than had been supposed and so in practice Convention compatible: this was because the Secretary of State was 'bound to exercise' the relevant power of exceptional release 'in a manner compatible with principles of domestic administrative law and with article 3'.[45] True there was this (unattractively named) 'Lifer Manual' which had not been revised to reflect what the judges now said was the right approach, but this was a mere reflection of (out-of-date) policy and not a legal document.

Once again Strasbourg raised a white flag in response to London's aggression. In a judgment delivered on 3 February 2015, *Hutchinson v UK*,[46] the Court's fourth section (beneath the Grand Chamber, being just seven judges and not seventeen) blamed the 'Lifer Manual' for having caused all the trouble and, recalling 'that it is primarily for the national authorities, notably the courts, to resolve problems of interpretation of domestic legislation',[47] went on to find exactly the same law which had been previously castigated as clear after all. *Newell and McLoughlin* made the difference, it being the case that 'in the United Kingdom, as in the other Convention States, the progressive development of the law through judicial interpretation is a well-entrenched and necessary part of legal tradition'.[48] Of the seven judges only one (Judge Kalaydjieva) dissented, concluding his brief remarks by suggesting that when 'the Court of Appeal's part in the admirable post-*Vinter* judicial dialogue said "Repent!", he wondered "whom it meant?"'. The matter is now with the Grand Chamber, with argument having been heard on 21 October 2015, so it will be interesting to see if this larger body has a different reply from the one delivered by the majority in *Hutchinson*.

There is a large potential consequence in this *Horncastle* turn in UK law. 'If so august a body as the UK Supreme Court can dispense at will

---

[45] Ibid at para 29 citing *R v Bieber* [2009] 1 WLR 223.
[46] 3 February 2015. Referred to Grand Chamber on 1 June 2015.
[47] Ibid at para 24.
[48] Ibid.

with Strasbourg decisions then why should not we do the same?' is a question that can now be asked across Europe's other constitutional tribunals. The earlier *Hirst* prisoner-voting case had already offered governments everywhere another tempting query: 'if the UK cannot be bothered to implement Strasbourg judgments why should we?' The result of both has been a double assault on the integrity of the Strasbourg-based system of human rights, driven not by a recalcitrant outsider but by the land of the Mother of Parliaments, of Magna Carta, etc, etc. Highlighting the prisoners' cases, the Council of Europe Human Rights Commissioner Nils Muižnieks has already warned a Westminster parliamentary committee that if other countries follow the UK lead in claiming that 'compliance with certain judgments is not possible, necessary or expedient' then this 'would probably be the beginning of the end of the ECHR system'.[49] In the spirit of *Horncastle* (as well as *Hirst*) a new Russian law now enables the Russian Constitutional Court to declare rulings of international bodies 'impossible to implement': the bill entered into force when it was signed off by President Putin on 14 December 2015.[50] The vote in the Duma (lower house) came the same day as a Strasbourg ruling against Russia on a matter related to state spying.[51] True, the story remains the broadly positive one with which this chapter started, with there being many examples of Strasbourg's continuing influence, a point nicely attested to by the recent work of the newly appointed Council of Europe

[49] P Leach and A Donald, 'Russia defies Strasbourg: is contagion spreading?' *Blog of the European Journal of International Law* 19 December 2015: <http://www.ejiltalk.org/russia-defies-strasbourg-is-contagion-spreading/> [accessed 19 January 2016].

[50] 'Russia passes law to overrule European Human Rights Court' BBC News 4 December 2015: <https://www.google.co.uk/webhp?sourceid=chrome-instant&rlz=1C5CHFA_enGB56 4GB565&ion=1&espv=2&ie=UTF-8#q=bbc+%E2%80%98Russia+passes+law+to+overrule+ European+Human+Rights+Court%E2%80%99> [accessed 19 January 2016].

[51] *Zakharov v Russia* European Court of Human Rights 4 December 2015 (Grand Chamber). There is a wider dimension to the case: see P De Hert and P Cristobal Bocos, 'Case of Roman Zakharov v Russia: The Strasbourg follow up to the Luxembourg Court's Schrems judgment' *Strasbourg Observers* 23 December 2015: <http:// strasbourgobservers.com/2015/12/23/case-of-roman-zakharov-v-russia-the-strasbourg-follow-up-to-the-luxembourg-courts-schrems-judgment/> [accessed 19 January 2016].

rapporteur on 'The implementation of judgments of the European Court of Human Rights'.[52] But for how long? If fictions about Strasbourg influence at home only serve to stimulate or ease the introduction of much harsher conditions for human rights abroad, then here is an export from fantasy island that collides in a most unfortunate way with brutal realities elsewhere.

---

[52] *Impact of the European Convention on Human Rights in States Parties: Selected Examples* AS/Jur/Inf (2016) 04 (8 January 2016): <http://website-pace.net/documents/19838/419003/AS-JUR-INF-2016-04-EN.pdf/12d802b0-5f09-463f-8145-b084a095e895> [accessed 19 January 2016].

8

A CHARTER FOR THE BAD

Received opinion has become so familiar with the idea of the Human Rights Act as a protector of villains that the perception has become normalized within our culture, assertion becoming truth in the absence of speedy refutation. It is the Act that kept 'notorious terrorist' Abu Qatada in the UK years after he should have been sent back to Jordan to face terrorism charges. The Italian 15-year-old killer of head teacher Philip Lawrence outside the gates of his own school in north London in 1995 was able to stay in Britain after serving his sentence because he could rely on his 'human right to family life' in the UK. Imprisoned mass murderers have a right to access pornography under the Human Rights Act just as axe killers like John Hirst (whom we met briefly in Chapter 7) have won the right to vote in prison. The examples are legion; of those mentioned above, some are inaccurate (Abu Qatada was not convicted due to insufficient evidence in Jordan when he was finally sent there[1]), incomplete (the Lawrence killer's main crutch against expulsion was EU law[2]), or downright inaccurate (Dennis Nilsen's efforts to access pornography in prison and to publish his own book have been unsuccessful,[3] and when one looks at the

[1] See <http://www.independent.co.uk/news/world/middle-east/abu-qatada-to-walk-free-after-being-cleared-of-terrorism-plot-charges-by-jordan-court-9752346.html> [accessed 20 January 2016].

[2] 'Court rejects challenge over Chindamo deportation' *Guardian* 31 October 2007: <http://www.theguardian.com/uk/2007/oct/31/humanrights.immigrationpolicy> [accessed 20 January 2016].

[3] Department of Constitutional Affairs, *Review of the Implementation of the Human Rights Act* (July 2006), at p 30. For the effort to publish the autobiography see *Nilsen v Governor of HMP Full Sutton* [2004] EWCA Civ 1540, [2005] 1 WLR 1028.

On Fantasy Island: Britain, Europe, and Human Rights. First Edition. Conor Gearty.
© Conor Gearty 2016. Published 2016 by Oxford University Press.

Hirst judgment closely it becomes clear that under no Strasbourg-imposed scheme would murderers be entitled to the vote, as opposed to some less serious offenders).

None of these caveats inhibits politicians from parading their hostility to the Human Rights Act off the back of some tragedy or other for which blame can be, however implausibly, attributed to the measure. The shadow Home Secretary David Davis deployed the Nilsen application as a weapon in his attack on the Act as early as 2004.[4] As leader of the opposition, David Cameron found the occasion of the non-deportation of Mr Lawrence's killer a convenient one for his declaration that the Human Rights Act 'has to go'.[5] On one later occasion, with the Conservatives now in government, the Home Secretary Theresa May made a self-evidently absurd case—about a Bolivian student whose cat saved him from deportation—the centre of her speech to the Conservative conference in 2011 about the stupidity of the Human Rights Act. 'I am not making this up,' she said—except she just had, or at least grossly exaggerated a small part of a case into its core ruling.[6] The furious nonsense surrounding the legislation might best be summed up by a short correction that appeared in the *Daily Mail* on 28 September 2014: 'A comment article on 13 August about the European Court of Human Rights said that the supply of heroin and gay porn to prisoners was now a "right". We are happy to clarify that this was not meant to be taken seriously and

---

[4] *The Telegraph*, 'Tory review of human rights law is attacked' 24 August 2004: <http://www.telegraph.co.uk/news/uknews/1470064/Tory-review-of-human-rights-law-is-attacked.html> [accessed 20 January 2016].

[5] *The Telegraph*, 'David Cameron: scrap the Human Rights Act' 22 August 2007: <http://www.telegraph.co.uk/news/uknews/1560975/David-Cameron-Scrap-the-Human-Rights-Act.html>.

[6] 'Theresa May under fire over deportation cat claim' BBC News: <http://www.bbc.co.uk/news/uk-politics-15160326> [accessed 20 January 2016]. See also C Gearty, 'Theresa May's human rights stunt' *Guardian* 4 March 2013: <http://www.theguardian.com/commentisfree/2013/mar/04/theresa-may-human-rights-stunt> [accessed 20 January 2016].

is not the case.'[7] The barrister Adam Wagner has written an excellent short paper with many of the worst excesses of press and political hostility laid bare, calling it (entirely appropriately) 'The Monstering of Human Rights'.[8]

We will be coming back in Chapter 9 (when we turn to facts) to the way in which the Human Rights Act has operated for those at the margins of our society, whether they be asylum seekers, prisoners, or other vulnerable persons, such as those with mental health problems, children, or defendants in criminal trials. It certainly does all this, and very often does it very well indeed. As we shall see the story is rather more nuanced than the orthodox view summarized above suggests, that what the judges (and other public officials of course) have been trying to do is to connect Parliament's clear intention to guarantee rights equally to everyone within our jurisdiction (the aim of the Human Rights Act as stated in its express wording) with the ugly fact that—whatever our legislature may have said—many politicians and opinion-formers do not want this ethical insight to be worked through onto any difficult front lines. That is for later, a recovery of what is good and worthwhile about the Human Rights Act. Here we are still in the realm of fantasy and this idea of the Act as a 'villains' charter'[9] is one of the most entrenched of all.

In truth, and leaving aside the work it has been doing in protecting the vulnerable, the measure could be altogether more plausibly described as supportive rather than subversive of state power. This is not to say the Act has not been doing the good just ascribed to it; rather it is to remind us that no story about a law as influential as the

---

[7] See A Wagner, 'Is this the best human rights correction ever? Or the worst?' *UK Human Rights Blog* 29 September 2014: <http://ukhumanrightsblog.com/2014/09/29/is-this-the-best-human-rights-correction-ever-or-the-worst/> [accessed 20 January 2016].

[8] 19 September 2014: <https://adam1cor.files.wordpress.com/2014/09/the-monstering-of-human-rights-adam-wagner-2014.pdf> [accessed 20 January 2016].

[9] L Gies, 'A Villains' Charter? The Press and the Human Rights Act' (2011) 7 (2) *Crime Media Culture* 167–83.

Human Rights Act has been can be tied to a single, simplified sound bite. Take first the sorts of rights it protects and then the fact that it must rely on judges to give it life. We should recall what we saw in Chapter 3, namely that the Left had in the 1980s and 1990s generated quite a head of steam *against* any proposed human rights law on the basis that far from protecting equality and dignity it would entrench privilege and unfairness. Old socialists like Professor John Griffith at the London School of Economics knew well that to have such a measure was to rely on judges to enforce it, and to depend on the unelected elite branch of the constitution to protect the people was asking for trouble[10]—and having reviewed the judicial record before the Act (as we did in Chapters 2 and 3) who can blame him? Worse still, to Griffith and his ilk, would be a situation where these conservative privileged white men (with the very occasional privileged white woman) would be handed a rights document as conservative as the European Convention to play with and with which to oversee democratic activity.[11]

The idea of the Convention as at least in part a 'conservative' document should not, by now, be a surprise. We have seen how an argument along these lines held sufficient sway over the New Labour architects of the Human Rights Act that they (perhaps reluctantly?) designed the measure in a way that preserved the sovereignty of parliament (the loss of which being another myth that we have critically scrutinized, in Chapter 5). Even in its current shape, though, the imprint on the Human Rights Act of its conservative origins is clear for all those who want to see. To start with there is the modesty of the rights protected: a collection of civil and political rights that were rightly thought central to the rebuilding of Europe after the Second World War but which now look spectacularly unambitious, at least when viewed from the perspective of the vibrant international human rights jurisprudence that is these days to be found in other fora (some of

---

[10] J A G Griffith, 'The Political Constitution' (1979) 42 (1) *Modern Law Review* 1–21.
[11] J A G Griffith, 'The Rights Stuff' (1993) 29 *The Socialist Register* 106–24.

which we glanced at in Chapter 4). There are hardly any social and economic rights, nothing on cultural rights, precious little involving any robust impact on equality (beyond the enjoyment of the civil and political rights already set out), and pressing issues such as indigenous, environmental, and disability rights pass the document by completely. To put it in this bald way is not being entirely fair on the Strasbourg or (since 2000) British courts that have had the job of making the rights set out work in specific situations. The judges—both here and in Strasbourg—have not been averse to imaginative reinterpretations so as to give this legacy document from 1950 a more modern voice. Strasbourg has stretched the right to respect for privacy to improve the situation of gay and transgender men and women, for example,[12] and has also tried its best to bring scandalous neglect of environmental and planning enforcement within the range of the Convention.[13] In 2015, the UK Supreme Court was able to point to the right to education in the first of the Convention's Protocols (also included in the Human Rights Act) to secure access to student loans for young people who were being denied them on account of an insecure immigration status that could not be changed before the moment for university entry had come and gone.[14] There are other examples. But the central point is that these extrapolations are outriders, that, as the distinguished South African judge Kate O'Regan put it in a lecture in London on the South African constitution, 'text matters'[15] and so judges are—if not hidebound exactly—then at least constrained by the terms of the document they have before them and so not able to go on ethical frolics at will.

[12] Eg *Norris v Ireland* (1988) 13 EHRR 186; *Goodwin v United Kingdom* (2002) 35 EHRR 447.

[13] *Lopez Ostra v Spain* (1994) 20 EHRR 277; *Guerra v Italy* (1998) 26 EHRR 357.

[14] *R (Tigere) v Secretary of State for Business, Innovation and Skills* [2015] UKSC 57, [2015] 1 WLR 3820. See further *R (Nyoni) v Secretary of State for Business, Innovation and Skills and Students Loan Company* [2015] EWHC 3533 (Admin).

[15] K O'Regan, 'Text Matters: Some Reflections on the Forging of a New Constitutional Jurisprudence in South Africa' (2012) 75 (1) *Modern Law Review* 1–32.

The result has been many defeats in court for those who seek to force the Convention into a more contemporary social democratic shape, especially in the field of socio-economic rights. Such defeats are not merely neutral; they are valuable to government, equipping it with a simple sound-bite defence of this or that regressive measure, namely that it 'complies with human rights' and so (it is implied or sometimes stated explicitly) cannot be a source of criticism on this score. Many such cases have, unsurprisingly, been tried out in the British courts since the turn to austerity that came with the election of the Conservative-led coalition government in 2010, and they have over-whelmingly ended in defeat. Two examples may be given here. In *R (Reilly) v Secretary of State for Work and Pensions*,[16] a government scheme that required work for no pay was unanimously held to be 'nowhere close' to the problem that the Convention's prohibition on 'forced or compulsory labour' (in article 4(2)) was intended to address.[17] The following year, an ambitious frontal assault on benefit caps on account of their discriminatory impact was seen off by the same court, albeit on this occasion by the narrow vote of three to two.[18] What made the difference here, as so often in cases like these, was Strasbourg's own insistence, often repeated, that where 'high level social/economic policy' was involved in a case, the test for a violation was ratcheted up so that the impugned provisions had to be 'mani-festly without reasonable foundation' insofar as the justification for infringing the right was concerned before judicial intervention could be warranted.[19]

---

[16] [2013] UKSC 68, [2014] AC 453.

[17] Ibid at para 83 (Lord Neuberger and Lord Toulson).

[18] *R (SG and others) v Secretary of State for Work and Pensions* [2015] UKSC 16, [2015] 1 WLR 1449 (Lords Reed, Carnwath, and Hughes; Baroness Hale and Lord Kerr dissenting).

[19] The case most often cited on this is *Stec v United Kingdom* (2006) 43 EHRR 1017: see eg *R (SG) v Secretary of State for Work and Pensions* (n 18), at para 135iii per Lord Hughes (from which the direct quotes in the text are taken); *Humphreys v Commissioners of Her Majesty's Customs and Revenue* [2012] UKSC 18, [2012] 1 WLR 1545.

This point about human rights law as absolution for the exercise of state power extends also into the arena of civil and political rights where it might have been expected that the Strasbourg Court would have been more confident in its determination to resist apparent rights violations. While it is true the courts are more robust here, with the winning cases coming along more frequently, there are occasional examples in this field as well of an old-fashioned supportiveness of executive power returning to centre stage from time to time. Thus in *Brannigan and McBride*[20] the European Court of Human Rights backed a dilution of the right to liberty enacted in reaction to political violence in Northern Ireland by agreeing with the UK submission that the emergency emanating from that corner of the country 'threatened the life of the nation' and so legitimized the challenged law (made under the derogation power contained in article 15 of the Convention). The Conservative government of the day made great hay with the decision, just as had the opposition with the earlier ruling which had given rise to the need for the derogation in the first place, *Brogan v United Kingdom*.[21] The issue was a really important one in the Thatcher/ Major period; though it might be thought almost quaint from today's more brutal perspective, seven-day detention without charge was the focus of much public protest and tension between the British and Irish governments. So the court ruling really mattered. A more contemporary example of a Strasbourg intervention helpful to government— and once again on a topical issue—would be that Court's decision on 10 April 2012 to approve the extradition of Babar Ahmad to the United States.[22] The argument by Ahmad and three of the four other men in the case (all facing terrorism charges in America) was that the long sentences likely to be imposed and likely also to be served in perpetual isolation at a brutal 'Supermax' facility amounted to a breach of each of their rights not to be subjected to inhuman or degrading treatment

[20] (1993) 17 EHRR 539.
[21] (1988) 11 EHRR 117.
[22] *Ahmad v United Kingdom* (2013) 56 EHRR 1.

or punishment. Controversially accepting assertions about conditions at these prisons from US authorities, the Court rejected the applicants' claims as to how bad they were, thus missing a chance to grow its jurisprudence on prison conditions and in the course of doing so giving 'the first green light for US top-security prisons'[23]—a green light marked, 'no human rights problems here'. The Prime Minister expressed himself 'very pleased' with the outcome.[24]

Mr Cameron might well say the same about the more recent *Sher and others v United Kingdom*.[25] Here the Strasbourg Court held that the right of suspected terrorists to take proceedings to challenge the lawfulness of their detention did not preclude the use of closed court hearings, at which neither the detainee nor his lawyer was present, where the purpose of these occasions was the submission of confidential information supporting the authorities' line of investigation. As the Court put it in that case, 'terrorist crime falls into a special category' with the Convention not being applied 'in such a manner as to put disproportionate difficulties in the way of the police authorities in taking effective measures to counter organised terrorism...'.[26] Since the Human Rights Act came into force there have been similar cases in the UK, such as for example *Austin v United Kingdom*,[27] where the Court supported a reading of the law by the House of Lords which had allowed the 'kettling' of protestors for long periods. Following the British judges, the Court saw the police intervention as implicitly sanctioned by the right to liberty in article 5. Despite not having included any allowance for such action in its

---

[23] *Independent* 10 April 2012.

[24] Ibid. Babar Ahmad was jailed for twelve-and-a-half years for helping to support terrorist groups online but was reportedly returned to Britain in the summer of 2015: 'Babar Ahmad returns to UK after being sentenced for supporting terror groups' *Guardian* 19 July 2015: <http://www.theguardian.com/uk-news/2015/jul/19/babar-ahmad-returns-after-jail-sentence-in-us-for-supporting-terrorist-groups> [accessed 20 March 2016].

[25] European Court of Human Rights (Fourth Section) 20 October 2015.

[26] Ibid para 149.

[27] (2012) 55 EHRR 359 (GC).

(longish) list of exceptions, that article only applied to true 'deprivations' of liberty of which this was not one—a rather contrived analysis which can only serve to copper-fasten a controversial means of crowd control which has wide ramifications for the ease with which legitimate public protest can be conducted: you don't often go on a march if you might end up being cordoned in a tight public space for hours on end.

It is important not to draw too strong a series of conclusions from these cases at Strasbourg. On a number of important occasions since the Human Rights Act came into force, Strasbourg has indeed stepped in to act as a brake on our judges' tendency to support the authorities, the retention of DNA samples being one such example,[28] and the deployment of wide stop and search anti-terrorism powers another.[29] Nor should the impression be drawn from this that the House of Lords and its successor body the Supreme Court have been invariable defenders of the status quo, protestors needing always to rely on the European Court to bail them out. The local judges have produced their own fair share of positive decisions on political liberty.[30]

Viewed in the round, what these various cases on social and economic as well as political rights show are benches of judges—both here and in Strasbourg—seeking on a case-by-case basis to make the correct call, often asserting the rights of the individual against the state it is true,

---

[28] *S v United Kingdom* (2008) 48 EHRR 1169 (GC).

[29] *Gillan and Quinton v UK* (2010) 50 EHRR 1105.

[30] *A v Secretary of State for the Home Department* [2004] UKHL 56, [2005] 2 AC 68 (on detention without trial) and *R (Laporte) v Chief Constable of Gloucestershire Constabulary* [2006] UKHL 55, [2007] 2 AC 105 (on the right of protest) are two of the most impressive. The backward steps that there have also been may in retrospect have been pushing beyond the limit of what could be done to protect freedom of assembly under the Human Rights Act: *R (Gallastegui) v Westminster City Council and others* [2013] EWCA Civ 28, where a statute 'carefully targeted only at those few who wish to set up camp in Parliament Square' was found not to breach articles 10 or 11 (Lord Dyson MR at para 60); *R (Barda) v Mayor of London* [2015] EWHC 3584 (Admin) where the fencing off of parts of Parliament Square Gardens was judged to be permitted within the terms of the Human Rights Act. Cf *City of London v Samede* [2012] EWHC 34 (QB).

but also (especially in the former field) coming down on the other side, in the process of doing so fortifying a controversial state action with a veneer of human rights protection. We might like some of these outcomes and dislike others, but we cannot deny that they flow out of rational argument and a bona fide effort to ensure that right outcomes are reached. Of course none of the cases favourable to government get the airtime in politics or the media that is accorded to decisions on controversial matters that go the other way. Strasbourg is only noticed when it can be made into a source of righteous indignation by sceptical politicians and their cheerleading newspapers.

Thus far, the cases making our point about the Convention's supporting role in relation to power have focused on the legitimization offered by judicial readings of the rights contained in it which support what might otherwise have been thought to have been anti-libertarian action by government: 'kettling', detaining, expelling, and so on. We have been drawing attention to (broadly speaking) 'illiberal' actions by the authorities that have been given clean bills of health by their human rights judicial overseers. What about private power? There is an important, different way in which the Convention can do conservative work, when it is deployed by powerful actors so as to resist radical efforts by government to control their activities. Here is the main reason why the old Left regarded human rights with such distaste. To understand this dimension to the Convention these days we need to be doubly imaginative. First we must recall that private power can also be against the public good; that it is not just governments who can do wrong. (Our neo-liberal assumptions are becoming so entrenched that this point is often forgotten.) And second (this is the really fresh move against the background of New Labour and Conservative hegemony) we must try to envisage a government intent upon doing something seriously to tackle the damaging implications of the exercise of such private power. If all this sounds a trifle abstract perhaps a few concrete examples will serve to make the point: the housing crisis in the UK is caused largely by the refusal of private companies to build on the land banks they have secured as the easiest routes to the profits demanded by their shareholders; the unfairness at the core of education in England and Wales lies in the separate provision of 'independent' schools which have insulated generations of the elite from the (less materially fortunate) people around them; the chaotic transport infrastructure that the privatization of the railways brought about and the effects of which are still being strongly felt. One could go on—but this is a sufficient taste. Another way of focusing this point would be to note that we have at the moment a leader of the opposition intent on radical change which, were he to achieve power and be able to wield it effectively, might well produce legislative interventions of this kind. Where should Jeremy Corbyn stand on the Human Rights Act?[31]

Not unequivocally in favour, that is for sure. There can be little doubt that the Act would function as a strong shield *against* state intervention of this sort, returning to its founding Convention's origins as a hedge against 'extremism' from the Left more than the Right (on which see Chapter 4). To pick some of the examples mentioned above, the private school system would be most likely able to resist change through reliance on the same education right (in the first protocol) that we earlier saw delivering (with article 14) access to student loans for a particular needy class of potential student. Even something so modest as the withdrawal of the tax advantages enjoyed by such elite schools (based on their being charities) which surfaces as an option every now and again in the political sphere has been seen off in the past on, among other grounds, the human rights problems that it would cause.[32] In a similar vein, the right to property in article 1 of the first protocol may be heavily qualified but it is not so attenuated that it does not prevent the taking without compensation of the assets

---

[31] Note, though, that the current Labour leader Jeremy Corbyn did vote for the Human Rights Act on its second reading in the Commons.

[32] Independent Schools Information Service, *Independent Schools: The Legal Case*. A joint opinion by Anthony Lester QC and David Pannick with a foreword by Lord Scarman (ISIS, 1991).

of an individual.[33] We need to recall in saying this that 'individual' here might be a high net worth person such as the Duke of Westminster[34] or a former ruler asserting compensation via his historic right to confiscated land,[35] or even a corporate entity with assets that it seeks to protect.[36] It was the fear of compensation that inhibited Labour from undoing in full the privatization of the railways which had been achieved by the Conservative government—even offering some compensation led to a human rights-based challenge from those natural and (mainly it can be imagined) purely legal 'persons' who asserted they were not getting back enough.[37]

One can imagine how frustrating it would be for any future Corbyn (or Corbyn-like) administration to find its room for manoeuvre so hemmed in by a law that during the barren years of neo-liberal certainty it had grown used to believing was always on its side. Tempting might be a push for repeal but it would not be easy to undo the liberal/left assumptions about the progressiveness of human rights at a single stroke of the legislative pen. Leaving the Act in place and treating the inevitable declarations of incompatibility that would result with radically infused contempt would be another option, though how this would go down within its own constituency of soft

---

[33] *James v United Kingdom* (1986) 8 EHRR 123. See *Salvesen v Riddell* [2013] UKSC 22 where Lord Hope spoke critically in the context of an art 1 of the first protocol case of the Scottish Deputy Minister having 'displayed a marked bias against landlords...As a minority group landlords, however unpopular, are as much entitled to the protection of Convention rights as anyone else,' at para 38.

[34] *James v United Kingdom* (1986) 8 EHRR 123.

[35] *The Former King of Greece v Greece* (2000) 33 EHRR 516, (2002) 36 EHRR CD 43. 'Ex-king of Greece is paid £7m for seized royal homes' *The Telegraph* 29 November 2002: <http://www.telegraph.co.uk/news/worldnews/europe/greece/1414727/Ex-king-of-Greece-is-paid-7m-for-seized-royal-homes.html> [accessed 10 May 2016].

[36] *Olympic Delivery Authority v Persons Unknown* [2012] EWCA Civ 1012; *Manchester Ship Canal Developments v Persons Unknown* [2014] EWHC 645 (Ch).

[37] They lost: *Weir v Secretary of State for Transport* [2005] EWHC 2192 (Ch). 'Shareholders lose Railtrack case' *The Telegraph* 14 October 2005: <http://www.telegraph.co.uk/news/1500623/Shareholders-lose-Railtrack-case.html> [accessed 10 May 2016]. S Jenkins, 'Railtrack shares trial exposes ministers with a license to steal' *The Times* 17 July 2005.

left support would be likely to present complications. It is worth repeating that these human rights litigants would not be the usual suspects, the radical environmentalists, welfare recipients, asylum seekers, and so on; they would be the big companies, the banks and individuals funded by others to disrupt such a government's progressive agenda. We have had a taste of this with one of the few above-the-radar acts of New Labour radicalism: the ban on hunting with dogs. This relatively minor piece of progressive legislation drew from its opponents not one but two legal challenges, each rooted in (among other arguments) human rights and each reaching the Supreme Court not once but twice.[38] All in all seeing off its opponents *after* it had secured the legislation took the government eight days in the Supreme Court, tying up no fewer than nine Supreme Court judges in the first hearing and five in the second with as many as sixteen counsel involved over the two hearings. And this is not to take into account the litigation in the lower courts. Defending radical action can be a costly business when open to well-funded challenge on human rights grounds.

The first of these hunting cases concentrated on procedure—the strongest point for those seeking to destroy the legislation lay in undermining the way it had been passed (via the Parliament Acts, thus obviating the need for the House of Lords' agreement). Procedural fairness is very important for the powerless—we see that clearly in Chapter 9. But the term is not as politically neutral as it sounds. When the administrative state first geared up to deliver services for the masses in the new democratic environment of twentieth-century Britain, cries of indignation went up from those who thought that the result was the collapse of the rule of law into a 'new despotism' (as Lord Hewart called it in his famous book in 1929 (mentioned in Chapter 2)). Lawyers love procedure and of course it needs to be acknowledged that good procedure ensures that a decision is fairly

---

[38] R (Jackson) v Attorney General [2005] UKHL 56, [2006] 1 AC 262; R (Countryside Alliance and others) v Attorney General and another [2007] UKHL 52, [2008] AC 719.

made. The Convention case-law is full of strong procedural interventions, but while this can do good for sure it can also undeniably slow down public interest decision-making, and serve as a rod with which the powerful—those resisting change—can exhaust the energies of progressives. So for those inclined to believe in a strong state, the turn of UK law towards greater and greater procedural fairness which began in the 1960s,[39] and which has gathered pace since then, has been more of a mixed blessing than its lawyerly and liberal supporters have seemed to suggest.

Exactly the same move has taken place in the Strasbourg Court where—amid much controversy—the first generation of judges on that bench turned the article 6(1) guarantee of fairness in civil cases into a due process requirement for all administrative decision-making that 'determined' the 'civil rights' of applicants (both terms broadly defined).[40] This mattered enormously in those countries (in Scandinavia mainly) where social democratic administrations had deliberately steered public decision-making away from the courts. In Britain, too, the judicial review oversight of such matters has been found to be wanting. This is all now old history: we have become familiar with the idea that procedural fairness is an unqualified human good. The direct duty on public authorities to act consistently with the Convention (section 6(1)) has also meant that the many procedural aspects of articles other than article 6 have also been imported into our jurisprudence, thereby handing those who would defy public power another set of tools with which to resist change. The potential for reactionary obstructionism might not matter so much if it were thought a price worth paying to ensure that the socially deprived also have a say before decisions inimical to their interests are made by remote public servants—an important strand to our discussion in Chapter 9. But

---

[39] Often dated to *Ridge v Baldwin* [1964] AC 40.

[40] See D J Harris, M O'Boyle, and C Warbrick, *Law of the European Convention on Human Rights* 3rd edn by D J Harris, M O'Boyle, E P Bates, and C M Buckley (Oxford: Oxford University Press, 2014), at pp 389–98.

have we entered a period in our culture where the provision of legal aid for the poor has become something which government feels under no obligation to provide? The savings for human right that are to be found in the legislation are not convincing to many.[41] Since the vulnerable client is not likely to be able to represent him- or herself, it means that—in the absence of some *pro bono* intervention—these cases may simply disappear off the lists. We are left only with the powerful. What price due process then?

And casting its large shadow over this question of fairness is the whole issue of damages. The drafters of the Human Rights Act tried to be very careful here, circumscribing the potential of damages so as to avoid ratcheting up the cost to the state of human rights litigation.[42] They did so reasonably confident that the remedy would not be overused, not least because the Strasbourg record on damages as a source of 'just satisfaction' (the formula for a remedy in the Convention[43]) was, by comparison with the UK courts, pretty stingy. That is how it played out at first,[44] but recently there has been a change of tack. Of great importance in this regard might prove to be the High Court decision in *R (Infinis Plc) v Ofgem*.[45] In this case, the applicant had no private law claim for the failure to accredit it under a particular statutory scheme, the defendant regulator having misapplied the law, not out of any sense of deliberate badness but just by getting the legal requirements wrong. Framing this as a breach of Infinis's property rights under the first protocol opened the door for a damages award that reflected the clear calculable loss to the company from the

---

[41] Legal Aid, Sentencing and Punishment of Offenders Act 2012, s 10(3)(a)(i). For a survey of the law on legal aid and the litigation it has stimulated see Legal Action Group, *Litigating to Save Legal Aid* (February 2016) <http://www.lag.org.uk/magazine/2016/02/litigating-to-save-legal-aid.aspx> [accessed 31 March 2016].

[42] By linking such awards to what it hoped would continue to be a parsimonious Strasbourg standard rooted in 'just satisfaction': Human Rights Act s 8.

[43] See art 41 of the Convention.

[44] See *Anufrijeva v Southwark London Borough Council* [2003] EWCA Civ 1406, [2004] QB 1124.

[45] [2011] EWHC 1873.

mistake, a whacking £2.5 million plus. This was the award the judge made, the ruling being later upheld in the Court of Appeal.[46] As a leading law firm's *Administrative and Public Law E-Bulletin* wryly put it, '[t]his is an outcome which should be of interest to anyone operating within a regulated industry', while '[c]onversely, regulators applying complicated schemes will need to ensure a robust decision making process to avoid the finding of a Convention violation and a potentially large damages award.'[47] Company directors should think carefully about where their own interests genuinely lie before believing everything that they read in their *Mail* and *Telegraph* about this iniquitous 'Charter for the Bad'.

[46] [2013] EWCA Civ 70. Cf *Williams v Hackney London Borough Council* [2015] EWHC 2629 (QB), a case involving successful reliance on art 8 which produced damages of £10,000 for each claimant, the judge '[r]eminding [himself] that awards of this type should be fairly modest' (Sir Robert Francis QC at para 122).

[47] Herbert Smith Freehills, 'Misapplication of statutory scheme leads to damages award under European Convention on Human Rights' *Administrative and Public Law E-Bulletin* 15 March 2013. And the Act as a whole is being used with increased frequency by business: J Croft, 'Human Rights Act cited in increasing number of UK legal cases' *Financial Times* 9 November 2015: <http://www.ft.com/cms/s/0/e35ef2ee-84a7-11e5-8095-ed1a37d1e096. html> [accessed 18 March 2016].

PART III
THE FACTS

THE FACTS

9

PROTECTING THE EXPOSED

We ended our section on the fantasies that surround the Human Rights Act by straying into some facts about the measure's usefulness to the powerful, and it is to the full range of the facts about the Act that we turn properly in this part of the book. If the Human Rights Act does not do all the dreadful things that are claimed for it by its enemies—subvert Parliament; hand power over to Strasbourg; turn our judges into legislators; support the wicked—then what on earth does it do? Of course we have already been feeling our way towards the right answer to this question as we have worked our way through the fantasies that we have been encountering, but the time has now come to confront the question directly. We saw in Chapter 8 how the Act can support executive authority and also how it can be deployed by those with resources in society so as to get their way or to defend themselves from unwelcome state intrusion. This is a part of but not the whole picture. While the hostile caricature is overdrawn, there is lurking within it a nugget of ethical truth. The Human Rights Act has enabled a range of individuals to secure legal remedies that in the pre-Act days would never have been achieved, perhaps even contemplated. While often this has worked for reasonably well-supported people and their families (a point we consider in Chapter 10), it has been particularly valuable for those whose grip on society is fragile, whose hold on their lives is precarious, whose disadvantage has robbed them of means of adequate engagement with adversity.

Of whom are we speaking? These are the people whose tenuous connection with the mainstream has left them vulnerable to being passed over by conventional legal frameworks of support—the asylum seekers; the prisoners; the homeless; people with mental disabilities;

On Fantasy Island: Britain, Europe, and Human Rights. First Edition. Conor Gearty.
© Conor Gearty 2016. Published 2016 by Oxford University Press.

those with criminal convictions for sexual offences; and others. 'Villains' many are not but some may be; likeable they are not guaranteed to be; exposed they all certainly are. The Act reaches the maligned and ignored in this new way, giving a voice to the previously voiceless, dragging on to the centre stage of civilized behaviour those who have long been marooned in the wings, on the margins of visibility. If the Human Rights Act is best viewed as an ethical project, then it is one aimed at a new inclusivity of this sort. This does not mean transforming the lives of the previously ignored—the Act is limited (as we have seen in Chapter 8) in its capacity to impact positively on the substance of a person's economic situation. But it does mean treating them the same as the rest of us, an insight about equality that sounds bland but the working through of which can often be dramatic. It is this shift to universality that is one of the main factors explaining the animosity shown to the Act that we have discussed, particularly in Chapter 1, and to which this book is intended as a kind of antidote. The public claim is that 'the Act protects the bad guys'. The private thought is 'how dare this law treat everybody as though they were the same as us'.

In this extended chapter our job is to make sense of the Act's engagement with these individuals and communities in our society by exploring the ways in which it has fleshed out its universalist mandate. The difference the Human Rights Act has made has come about sometimes directly through litigation involving specific claimants, but more often through case-law generated by others that has required the state to change the way it relates to them and thenceforth to people like them. There are three broad dimensions to this, and we move now to each in turn so as better to understand what this remarkable piece of legislation is truly about, and (therefore) its importance. If we were bound to give them abstract descriptions then these would be 'fairness', 'justice', and 'inclusivity', but the dryness of such terms fails to capture the very human stories that are at the core of the Act and through which generalizations of this sort are given life and warmth. Litigation ensures that the Human Rights Act is not only a code of philosophy but a manual for practical action as well.

Fairness for All

A clue to the first of these universalist principles, fairness, lies in the way we ended Chapter 8, reflecting on the pros and cons of due process in the administration of the public sphere. Of course 'red tape' of this sort can be a way of tying progressive initiatives up in knots, forcing hearings and other forms of interactions with people and entities affected by proposed decisions which are burdensome on the decision-maker while lacking any social utility. If this were all procedural fairness amounted to, then certainly it would quickly end up as little more than a shield preventing good things happening rather than as a way of guaranteeing that public decisions are taken properly. As we have seen this has long been a social democratic concern about the availability of judicial review of administrative action, and was, in a nutshell, what drove one of the main anxieties in Chapter 8, about the vulnerability of the Human Rights Act to manipulation by the rich and powerful, their reliance on arguments based on the Act to avoid or complicate proper regulation of their activities. But there is another side to procedure.

What about all those decisions that the state routinely takes which impact in a huge way on particular individuals but about which they invariably have had no say whatsoever? I am not thinking now about Acts of Parliament—we cannot expect to be individually consulted when general rules are being framed in the legislature in a way that we anticipate might impact on us negatively (though of course corporations and trade unions try exactly this all the time, as do others rich enough to hire lobbyists). What concerns us here is more the effect on individuals of discretionary rulings by public officials, and, putting our interest more specifically, the decisions of this sort that impact negatively on those individuals (and their families) who have limited financial, social, or political capital with which to fight such determinations before they are made, or to resist their consequences afterwards—dreadful though these might often be. These vulnerable people have rarely if ever been able to insist on their views being heard before the life-changing moment hits them: they lose their house because of alleged bad behaviour; they are separated from their newborn babies because they are in prison; they are expelled from the country without their being able to explain they face death at home; they are denied their liberty because they are suspected (on secret evidence) of being terrorists; they are refused discharge from a mental home without being given the chance to prove they are well; and so on. Now whether these people are likeable or honest or have led blameless lives or are none of these things is entirely beside the point. What links all of them is that they are vulnerable. Historically these categories of individuals have rarely if ever been given a chance to put their point of view. For these people due process—more to the point its absence—matters a great deal indeed.

It is worth taking a moment to flesh this point out, since the connection between rights and procedural fairness may not be so obvious, and yet we are saying it is one of the three core features underpinning human rights litigation on behalf of the vulnerable. Of course there are some absolute rights for which the point is by the by: the ban on torture is not one which can be obviated by a fair hearing before the brutality starts, and no state authority is allowed to enslave you after it has briskly asked you, at gunpoint, for your point of view on what is about to happen. On the other end of the spectrum, though, and here we make our first explicit connection between rights and process, there are rights' guarantees where the entitlement to be heard is core. Article 5 is one, setting out the right to challenge the deprivation of one's liberty; article 6 is another with its insistence on fair procedures when a civil right is being determined or a criminal charge being brought. Before taking fairness into less obvious territory let us look first at how it operates in this familiar landscape for the people with which this chapter is concerned.

So far as article 5 on the right to liberty is concerned, two outstanding examples come to mind from the Convention case-law, each of which was very controversial when first decided but both of which are now embedded in our framework of legal protection (albeit that the second is still making waves in the politics surrounding human rights law). The first raised the question of the detention of persons found to be suffering from mental illness. The old legal regime here gave even patients held under compulsory powers precious little opportunity to reassert their mental health and so secure their liberty. Starting with the leading case of *Winterwerp v The Netherlands*,[1] the Strasbourg Court went about insisting on various procedural safeguards and these have led directly to a framework of tribunals set out in our mental health legislation at which hearings are accorded to those who wish to escape their incarceration. The UK-specific addition to this case-law came in *HL v United Kingdom*,[2] in which a large, remaining gap in domestic mental health law was exposed by Strasbourg and closed. HL was an adult male with autism and also profound learning disabilities. Having lived in care for some thirty years (from the age of 13) he was discharged into the community to live with a married couple who went on to act as his carers. However, after HL became agitated at the day centre he attended, he was taken back to hospital (not under duress as he had been sedated and so did not resist) and simply left there. His condition declined. His carers were initially unable to visit him. They mustered the energy and showed the determination to have recourse to the courts, but lost in the House of Lords where a majority held that he was not being formally detained and so no wrong (or 'tort' of false imprisonment) had been committed, and that even if the judges were wrong about this, the defence of necessity was available to the authorities.[3] The result was that where patients were informally admitted in this way no safeguards existed at all so far as their right to liberty was concerned, in stark contrast with the post-*Winterwerp* regime of compulsory admission under the Mental Health Act. It took the European Court of Human Rights to explode the idea that HL was a free agent in the hospital, and to impose some procedural

---

[1] (1979) 2 EHRR 387.

[2] (2004) 40 EHRR 761.

[3] *R (L) v Bournewood Community and Mental Health NHS Trust* [1998] UKHL 24, [1999] 1 AC 458.

safeguards on what had been in truth a 'deprivation of liberty' under article 5. As so often, starting from the fact of the right (to which exceptions had to be made) produced a different result from when the primary focus was on the conduct of the defendant (as was invariably the case with the common law).

The second celebrated (or notorious, depending on one's taste) article 5 case concerns the sensitive issue of the expulsion of suspected terrorists. Before *Chahal v United Kingdom*,[4] such deportees had no practical say over their expulsion or the country to which they might be sent, even if it was one in which there was a strong likelihood that they would be killed and/or tortured. In *Chahal*, which concerned a suspected Sikh 'terrorist' wanted by the Indian authorities, the European Court of Human Rights imposed a set of procedural constraints which gave such individuals a strong input into the decision to deport them and as to the destination that was being arranged for them—and if no place could be found where they would not be likely to be ill treated the only option was to keep them where they were, in the United Kingdom, however distasteful this might be. This was a torture case under article 3 it is true (to which we return shortly when discussing equality), but also a procedural one with article 5(4)'s promise of state provision of a means of challenging such detention being found by the judges to have been breached (unanimously, whereas the article 3 finding was by twelve votes to seven). The *Chahal* procedure is now firmly entrenched in statute and case-law but, the decision on prison voting aside,[5] there is probably no single case which has driven the present government's animosity to human rights more than it, not helped by the fact that an aide to the Home Secretary who had to deal with the fall-out from it was a young special adviser called David Cameron.[6] Even a Labour Party Home Secretary was early

---

[4] (1996) 23 EHRR 413.

[5] *Hirst v United Kingdom (No 2)* (2005) 42 EHRR 849.

[6] Carl Gardner, 'David Davis: "Cameron in opposition 'really wanted to leave the Convention'"' HEADOFLEGAL 29 October 2014: <http://www.headoflegal.com/

on expressing an inclination to redraw the balance in the Convention and to repeal the Human Rights Act in order freely to be able to do so; shortly after retiring from the government he said that as a result of the Human Rights Act, the government was fighting crime and terror with 'one hand behind our back'.[7]

Turning now to the second right in the Convention (and therefore the Human Rights Act) aimed specifically at fairness, we can glide over the criminal side of this (replicatory on the whole of already existing safeguards, the occasional *Horncastle* aside[8]) and concentrate on the civil side. We have already noted in Chapter 8 the insistence in article 6(1) that the 'determination' of all 'civil rights' should require the engagement of independent judicial or judicial-style authorities, and when we were doing so we expressed our concern about the deployment of this right as a defensive shield against progressive state intrusion on property rights. Now embedded in the domestic case-law, this article has however done its judicializing job well in circumstances where the vulnerable have found their civil rights being determined by bureaucratic authority. Mainly Strasbourg has been to thank for this, with cases such as *Tsfayo v United Kingdom* applying article 6 safeguards to the processing of claims for housing and council tax benefit,[9] a route down which the British courts have been more reluctant to go,[10] albeit they have accepted that if a public

2014/10/29/david-davis-cameron-in-opposition-really-wanted-to-leave-the-convention/> [accessed 12 February 2016].

[7] Interview with John Reid former Secretary of State for the Home Department 16 September 2007 in the *News of the World* reported in the *Telegraph*: 'John Reid calls for human rights law reform' 17 September 2007: <http://www.telegraph.co.uk/news/uknews/1563347/John-Reid-calls-for-human-rights-law-reform.html> [accessed 12 February 2016].

[8] See Ch 7.

[9] (2006) 48 EHRR 457.

[10] See *Tomlinson, Ali and Ibrahim v Birmingham City Council* [2010] UKSC 8, [2010] 2 AC 39; *R (G) v Governors of X School* [2011] UKSC 30, [2012] 1 AC 167.

137

decision is 'directly decisive' for a civil right then article 6 applies.[11] In *Fazia Ali v United Kingdom*[12] the right to a home of a person not intentionally homeless was judged a 'civil right' under article 6, although the facts of the case revealed no breach. In contrast to this the case-law on article 6 makes clear that tax matters are outside the reach of the article.[13]

Fairness as a fundamental Convention value goes further than these explicitly procedural rights. Most rights in the Convention (and therefore in the Human Rights Act) are neither absolutist in their insistence on the right (such as article 3, mentioned above) nor explicit in their demand for a fair hearing (the articles we have just been discussing). Rather they are qualified, permitting exceptions in certain circumstances, and it is through the operation of these exceptions that an indirect right to a hearing, to express your point of view, makes its appearance. We need to dig a little more deeply to find this but find it we can, and without too much archaeological excavation either. The key is to conceptualize fairness more broadly than we have been doing up to now. There are two criteria governing exceptionality to these 'mainstream' rights that crop up time and again, one insisting that any departure from the rights be regulated by law and the other requiring that these limitations be proportionate in their deleterious impact on the right affected. The first is set out in the Convention while the second has been hewn out of it by a process of judicial interpretation but both are fundamental. Each opens the door to new levels of fairness in public decision-making. We need to explain now how, so far as both of these are concerned, this can be the case.

First is the need for law. An essential requirement before a departure from a right will be sanctioned—evident in all the articles setting out qualified rights in some shape or form—is that the limitation on a

---

[11] See Lord Dyson in *R (G) v Governors of X School* (n 10), at paras 63–9. Cf *R (King) v Secretary of State for Justice* [2015] UKSC 54, [2015] 3 WLR 457 (no civil right of association which would entail decisions about solitary confinement in prison attracting art 6 safeguards).

[12] 20 October 2015 (app 40378/10).

[13] *R (APVC 19 Ltd and others) v Her Majesty's Treasury* [2015] EWCA Civ 648.

given right must be 'prescribed by' or 'in accordance with' law. Looked at from the angle we are now taking, we can see that this is a due process test writ large: don't go after us for merely exercising our rights without telling us beforehand that you were planning to do this, the message preferably taking the shape of a settled rule we were able to consult before we went about our business. A prime example of how this works is *Malone v United Kingdom*,[14] a leading Strasbourg decision which has long since fed through into our domestic law. In the course of his trial for handling stolen goods, Malone discovered (through a revelation during the giving of police evidence) that his phone had been tapped without (as it turned out) any statutory or common law authority. Relying on his right to respect for privacy in article 8, he was able later to establish in Strasbourg a breach of this Convention right. The government's argument, supported in earlier proceedings in the national courts,[15] had been that the authorities could do that which no law prohibited (and so should be able to get on with tapping, it not being banned) but this submission was given short shift by the Strasbourg judges. Doing things behind the scenes on the basis of ministerial sanction had failed to play fair with the public in that no one could regulate their conduct with any kind of knowledge of what the state might be able to get up to. Now of course there was no suggestion of the authorities being required to seek Malone's opinion before they tapped his phone: such an insistence on process would have been as laughable as it would have been counter-productive. It was a broader, democratic kind of fairness, about a citizen's knowledge of the potential power of the state over him or her, that the European Court was concerned about. Since this pioneering finding in *Malone v United Kingdom*, the whole of our national security apparatus has been put on a statutory footing, most recently evidenced in the Investigatory Powers Bill introduced into Parliament in November 2015. There is a decent argument that the post-*Malone*

---

[14] (1984) 7 EHRR 14.
[15] *Malone v Metropolitan Police Commissioner* [1979] 1 Ch 344.

framework of security legislation has secured the secret services the benefits of legal legitimacy without having compelled too much in the way of a change of practices: that is a discussion for another day, not about the achieving of this sort of parliamentary engagement but rather about its consequences.

How far does this requirement for prior awareness of the law go? In times of early Strasbourg-related tension in the UK, one transformation which might well have brought an early end to the country's relationship with the European Convention was peremptorily rejected, albeit (it has to be admitted) on slightly dubious grounds. The argument was that the common law was itself inherently unfair in that it was capable of springing surprises (in the shape of new developments in the law) on litigants who had had no way of knowing these changes were about to occur. The submission was resisted, with the common law of contempt (which produced a new rule out of what the applicants in Strasbourg said was thin air) surviving in one case,[16] and the extension of the crime of rape to cover married partners being allowed in another.[17] The Court avoided the undoubted uproar that would have followed abolition of the ancient Anglo-Saxon system of law in favour of continental codification by the clever ruse of saying that such changes as had occurred in the cases before them would have been 'reasonably foreseeable' (perhaps with legal advice),[18] a sleight of hand designed to save a system of law the Strasbourg judges had no desire to accidently destroy.[19]

If a kind of large-scale due process is served by the 'prescribed by law'/'in accordance with law' criterion, then the fairness achieved by the second control on departing from the non-absolute rights in the

[16] *The Sunday Times v United Kingdom (No 1)* (1979) 2 EHRR 245.

[17] *SW v United Kingdom; CR v United Kingdom* (1995) 21 EHRR 363.

[18] *CR v United Kingdom* (n 17), at para 41; *SW v United Kingdom* (n 17), at para 43. For the reference to legal advice see the Opinion of the European Commission on Human Rights, *CR v United Kingdom*, at para 49; *SW v United Kingdom*, at para 48.

[19] A juror punished under the contempt law for having researched the history of the accused in the case in which she was sitting could not rely on the prohibition on retrospective laws in art 7 to avoid punishment: *Dallas v United Kingdom* European Court of Human Rights 11 February 2016.

Convention, proportionality, is more individually tailored, closer to the articles 5 and 6 case-law than the *Malone*-type jurisprudence we have just discussed. This is the insistence that appears in many of the articles setting out these qualified rights that the departure from the right is warranted not only if 'prescribed by/in accordance with law' but also where this is 'necessary in a democratic society'. As has already been anticipated, more often than not this boils down to a judgment about whether the proposed interference is proportionate, with the Strasbourg and British courts having developed various tests as to what this means; crudely put, disproportionate equals unnecessary while proportionate equals necessary. This test of proportionality has spread through the Convention, often finding its way into articles which do not have this direct route in via the 'necessary in a democratic society' formula, article 5 (on the meaning of a 'deprivation' of liberty) for example, article 6 (where the 'implied right' of access to the courts is concerned), and article 14 (on discrimination) as well. We will have much to say about proportionality as we deepen our discussion of the protection of the marginalized in this chapter—it is the engine at the heart of the whole human rights project. For now though what we need to note is that a major factor in assessing the proportionality of an intrusion into a right will often be whether or not the individual affected has been treated properly as an individual, his or her situation properly understood—and the best way to do this will often be to hear what they have to say.

Not being explicit in an article 5 and article 6 way, the role of fairness in the case-law on proportionality can take many different shapes. The leading case on the application of the Human Rights Act to executive discretion, *R (Daly) v Secretary of State for the Home Department*,[20] was in many ways if not a 'right to be heard' then 'a right to be involved' case, driven by a broad reading of fairness and an awareness of human fallibility. The policy the judges in the House of Lords were striking down was one which mandated the search of prison cells in

---

[20] [2001] UKHL 26, [2001] 2 AC 532.

the absence of affected inmates. The point of objection was that legally privileged documents could be scrutinized in the course of such searches even though the relevant policy guidance ostensibly controlled such prying. The major objection taken by the law lords when the case reached them was to the absolute nature of the absence requirement. While this made sense for the 'core of dangerous, disruptive and manipulative prisoners, hostile to authority and ready to exploit for their own advantage any concession granted to them',[21] other means for achieving the end of such searches should be found for the ordinary prisoner not intent upon disruption, such as—for example—already pertained in Scotland. Here is a fresh kind of fairness-in-action, with the prisoner assisting in, even invigilating, the search of his or her own possessions, not so much a 'have you a view on whether I should search you' so much as 'please help me to do it properly, preventing me from succumbing to the temptation of disproportionality'. While Lord Bingham rooted his reasoning in the common law he made clear that—as Lord Steyn demonstrated in his speech in the same case—the outcome could also be firmly rooted in proportionality via the 'necessary in a democratic society' limb of article 8(2).

There are many illustrative cases of this general point. In *R (Tracey) v Cambridge University NHS Hospital Foundation Trust*,[22] the Court of Appeal ruled that an NHS Trust had a legal duty to tell a patient with mental capacity that a 'Do Not Resuscitate' notice had been placed in his or her records, not least in order for them to be able to access a second opinion on such a vital matter if they so wished.[23] In the shocking case of *ZH v Metropolitan Police Commissioner*, it was the failure to talk with the carers of a severely disabled 16-year-old boy before deploying restraint techniques against him that was a key

---

[21] Ibid per Lord Bingham, at para 19.
[22] [2014] EWCA Civ 822.
[23] See ibid per Lord Dyson MR, at para 55.

reason behind the police being found in breach of both article 5 and (on these exceptional facts) article 3.[24] Another couple of prison cases make the consultation point in a more orthodox fashion. In *R (P and Q) v Secretary of State for the Home Department* the question was the difficult one of how long should newborn babies be left with their mothers after having been born in prison.[25] The policy was that they be prohibited from remaining with their mother after they reached the age of 18 months. The issue clearly engaged the right to respect for family life in article 8 and equally clearly there was a legal basis for the policy and also a legitimate aim for the separation that the policy forced. But was it to be applied rigorously without regard to individual situations, where for example the separation might be particularly awful for both parties or where alternative placements outside prison were likely to be highly unsatisfactory? The Court of Appeal thought not; the policy needed to admit of 'greater flexibility'.[26] Most cases would go the way the policy demanded, it was true, but 'there may be very rare exceptions where the interests of the mother and child coincide and outweigh any other considerations'.[27] Then the crucial remark: 'The mother must be given a fair opportunity to argue that that is so.'[28] Contrast this outcome with *R (Mellor) v Secretary of State for the Home Department*,[29] which concerned a prisoner's desire to be given access to artificial insemination facilities to start a family. The relevant access asserted that '[e]ach case [was to be] considered on its own facts'[30] and this was enough for the Court of Appeal. In rejecting the claimant's arguments, the appeal judges stressed that it did 'not follow

---

[24] [2013] EWCA Civ 69.

[25] [2001] EWCA Civ 1151, [2001] 1 WLR 2002.

[26] Ibid at para 101, per Lord Phillips of Worth Matravers MR giving the judgment of the court.

[27] Ibid at para 106.

[28] Ibid.

[29] [2001] EWCA Civ 472, [2002] QB 13.

[30] Ibid at para 17 per Lord Phillips.

from [the ruling] that it will always be justifiable to prevent a prisoner from inseminating his wife artificially, or indeed naturally'.[31]

Administrative convenience will frequently point in the direction of general and invariable policies, with however the inclination of the courts pointing firmly in the opposite direction, towards rules qualified by an openness to exceptions. The availability of special cases in turn demands that a framework be put in place where the argument for such exceptions can be made, a presumption of some kind of hearing in other words. This is easier where there are few cases—babies in prison; a prisoner who wants a child—than when what is required necessitates a change in a routine affecting thousands—prison cell searches stand out as an obvious example. This tension is echoed in a controversial line of cases which have gone back and forth between Strasbourg and the senior appellate courts here. These have been concerned with the extent to which supposedly disruptive or vulnerable tenants should be able to argue their individual cases in front of an independent judicial authority before being evicted. The leading decisions in England and Wales are now *Manchester City Council v Pinnock*[32] and *London Borough of Hounslow v Powell*.[33] The relevant social housing scheme distinguished between secure tenants on the one hand and, on the other, all those who were either new to their property ('introductory tenants'), licensees under homeless legislation, or whose antisocial behaviour had lost them their secure status, leaving them on effective probation for a set period of time ('demoted tenants'). In search of more decisiveness in housing policy (less 'red tape') Parliament had wanted these latter three categories of tenants to be more exposed to immediate eviction than secure tenants and to that end had quite deliberately sought to deprive them of any judicial forum in which to assert that their eviction was in their very particular

---

[31] Ibid at para 45 per Lord Phillips.
[32] [2010] UKSC 45, [2011] 2 AC 104.
[33] [2011] UKSC 8, [2011] 2 AC 186 decided with *Leeds City Council v Hall* and *Birmingham City Council v Frisby*.

and individual circumstances disproportionate (and therefore in human rights language a breach of article 8 which was not saved by being 'necessary in a democratic society' under article 8(2)). Prodded by the Strasbourg Court, and it has to be said somewhat grumpily, the Supreme Court has now allowed that such particular appeals can be made, that the County Court proceedings built into the legislation should not be solely about ensuring that the right procedures have been followed (and so reversing the view that earlier English decisions had been inclined to take). A seven-judge Supreme Court felt able to deploy the interpretive power in section 3 of the Human Rights Act to achieve this end. Restricted though it might be, and with a narrower test of proportionality than is usual, these cases have nevertheless now given occupiers a chance to argue their case to remain at home when previously no such opportunity would have been available. Like the new mothers in *R (P and Q) v The Secretary of State for the Home Department*, the Human Rights Act has delivered a right to be heard.

We end this section with an outstanding example of how the Human Rights Act has broadened our understanding of fairness in a way that reaches groups whose unpopularity is such that the natural majoritarian instinct is to refuse to have anything to do them. Inevitably these cases are controversial. In *R (Wright) v Secretary of State for Health*[34] the defendant Minister kept a list of those considered unsuitable to work with vulnerable adults. Once on the list, no new care posting could be offered by any employer and any care position already held had to be given up. Working with children was also ruled out. These controls all kicked in even if the listing was provisional, in other words was made pending a final determination by the Secretary of State. Inevitably this confirmatory process could take months, during which those listed (if they worked in the sector, which was highly likely) faced the collapse of their professional lives. The House of Lords unanimously condemned the absence of any opportunity to make representations before a name was included in the list as

---

[34] [2009] UKHL 3, [2009] AC 739.

incompatible with the article 6(1) right to have the determination of a 'civil right' done only after a fair hearing, and issued a declaration of incompatibility. This stands therefore as another example of the operation of that important procedural safeguard in article 6(1) that we have already examined. Giving the main speech in the case, Baroness Hale also found article 8 to be engaged so that to be compliant under paragraph 2 'procedures must be fair in the light of the importance of the interests at stake'.[35]

It was the second of these points that was to the fore in *R (L) v Metropolitan Police Commissioner*.[36] L had once been accused of neglecting her child and failing to cooperate with social services. She later got a job as a playground assistant, but when her employer secured an Enhanced Criminal Records Certificate (ECRC) this past situation was revealed and she was promptly dismissed. L was unsuccessful in both the High Court and the Court of Appeal and her final appeal was unanimously dismissed by the Supreme Court. However the judges there took the opportunity to say some very challenging things about the way the scheme as then constructed operated in practice. Giving the main judgment, Lord Hope was clear that article 8 was engaged as privacy encompassed the sphere of employment, and extended to embrace exclusion from it.[37] This being the case, 'the issue [was] essentially one of proportionality'.[38] Of course there will always be a public interest in sharing data about past criminal behaviour but as time elapses since the occurrence of such misbehaviour so the privacy interest must be allowed to grow. And the breadth of the data-sharing in the scheme—going beyond the criminal and charges of the criminal to embrace cautions and (even) allegations in local police records that had never been tested at trial (much less led to a conviction)—was

---

[35] Ibid at para 37 per Baroness Hale.
[36] [2009] UKSC 3, [2010] 1 AC 410.
[37] See *Sidabras v Lithuania* (2004) 42 EHRR 104. Art 6 was not argued.
[38] (n 36), at para 42.

extreme here. A new balancing was required, one which considered not only the risk to the vulnerable group of non-disclosure but also the likely disruption to the private life of those being considered for listing. The individual principally concerned might well have a role to play in this.

> In cases of doubt, especially where it is unclear whether the position for which the applicant is applying really does require the disclosure of sensitive information, where there is room for doubt as to whether an allegation of a sensitive kind could be substantiated or where the information may indicate a state of affairs that is out of date or no longer true, chief constables should offer the applicant an opportunity of making representations before the information is released.[39]

And to the police likely to throw their hands up in horror at such a new hurdle? '[I]t will not be necessary for this procedure to be undertaken in every case' but where it has to be the 'risks in such cases of causing disproportionate harm to the applicant outweigh the inconvenience to the chief constable'.[40]

Justice

Hearing the other side will often be enough to get human rights law on side with whatever process it is that the executive (in one of its many guises) is seeking to effect: we have seen many such examples in the discussion we have just had on fairness. The assumption behind this is worth reminding ourselves of lest its obviousness pass us by: once we have heard the potentially affected person (the prison mother; the care-worker; the tenant facing eviction), it is thought that we are much more likely to make a fair decision on the substance of their case. If seeing is not necessarily believing, then at least it is empathizing. Already embedded to some extent in administrative

---

[39] Ibid at para 46 per Lord Hope. Only Lord Scott took a different, more restrictive line on this issue of consultation: see para 60.
[40] Ibid at para 46 per Lord Hope.

law,[41] by deepening this right to be heard the Human Rights Act is doing here exactly one of those things it is principally designed for—throwing light on a vulnerable individual, giving him or her space before a life-changing decision is taken about him or her. Being able to speak up and being listened to is one of the most important human rights of all.

There will be situations, however, where a hearing will not be enough, where the law points in the direction of a harsh outcome, one that cannot be redeemed by a consultation before it takes effect. What then? Courts are reluctant to do too much re-engineering of the substance of a legislative mandate in order to dilute the impact of provisions of which they might happen to disapprove. For a judge to ask for a hearing for the other side is more judicial and less combative than for him or her simply to decide the matter in a different way. This is especially the case when to achieve the second of these a rereading of the legislative mandate for the challenged decision will be required, something that can then easily take us to the outer margins of the 'possible' under section 3. This is the issue we discussed at some length in Chapter 6 when we considered the fantasy of supposed judicial supremacy under the Human Rights Act. But as we saw there as well, one powerful motive can very occasionally trump even the natural hesitancy of the judges to push too ambitiously at the limits of the possible. That motive is the desire to do justice. It is very particular, rooted in the facts before them, and can spring into action where the fair proceedings option is not available. We saw two excellent examples of exactly this in Chapter 6: *Ghaidan v Godin-Mendoza (FC)*[42] and *R (Baiai) v Secretary of State for the Home Department*.[43] The first was the case where a gay man was enabled by a very ambitious reworking of the relevant provision to remain in the home which he had shared

---

[41] See eg *R (Osborn and Booth) v Parole Board; in re Reilly* [2013] UKSC 61, [2014] AC 1115.

[42] [2004] UKHL 30, [2004] 2 AC 557.

[43] [2008] UKHL 53, [2009] AC 287. To similar effect is *R (Aquilar Quila and Bibi) v Secretary of State for the Home Department* [2011] UKSC 45, [2012] 1 AC 621.

with his late partner, and the second was the ruling which alleviated the financial payments required of those subject to immigration control who wanted to marry and were being opportunistically charged a fortune by the authorities for their romantic temerity. Of interest at this point is not the cleverness of the section 3 analysis but rather the kind of litigants that were before the court: a gay man and a couple subject to immigration control. Here were litigants who would not be at the forefront of legislative concern and for whom the Human Rights Act functioned as a guarantor of justice where none would otherwise have been forthcoming and direct harm would have been caused as a result, in the form of either eviction or a failure to conclude a marriage without large-scale financial loss. The same was true of the litigants in R (MM, GY and TY) v Secretary of State for the Home Department, the refusal of whose citizenship on the basis of a member of the family being an Islamic extremist was judged unlawful—the coerced severance of their relationship with the family member would have engaged the Human Rights Act's right to respect for family life and the decision itself was beyond the scope of its parent Act and consequently unlawful.[44]

The small stable of justice cases shows the Human Rights Act at its pioneering best. The court wants to do right by the litigant and finds that human rights law enables it to do so, not so much 'hard cases making bad law' as 'hard cases being enabled to produce good law'. In EM (Lebanon) v Secretary of State for the Home Department,[45] the House of Lords unanimously overturned decisions in the lower courts in order to prevent the removal under immigration law of a mother and her son to Lebanon, there being a 'real risk of a flagrant denial of the right to respect for their family life'[46] if they were to be sent there. The problem arose from the effect of Shari'a law in Lebanon (from which place and law the mother had long been a fugitive). This would have

---

[44] [2015] EWHC 3513 (Admin).

[45] [2008] UKHL 64, [2009] AC 1198.

[46] Ibid at para 2 per Lord Hope.

removed all her custody rights had she been compelled to return; the boy, now 12, would have been handed to a father he had never met and whose violence towards his mother had been the cause of their divorce in that country many years before. Hard though these facts are, it is not the norm to protect non-citizens from the effect of their own countries' rules, however terrible they may be in the eyes of the host European state. The judges were keen to stress that here was a 'very exceptional case'[47] which warranted this dramatic pushing beyond even Strasbourg's then current boundaries (so far as the extra-jurisdictional reach of article 8 as opposed to, say, the ban on torture was concerned).

An early case from the criminal sphere makes the same point. In R v Offen,[48] the defendant had wholly ineffectually and as a clear result of mental deficiencies twice robbed building societies with an imitation firearm. The first time he gave himself up to the police. On the second, a customer had simply gone out and taken the money back from him, with his friends later telephoning the police to tell them of his failed efforts at robbery. Despite such obvious extenuation, Offen was jailed for life—legislators were going through one of their 'tough on crime' phases and had instituted a regime of (to use the sporting analogy frequently deployed at the time) 'two strikes and you are out' so far as serious crimes were concerned. This caught Offen—the law deliberately made no allowance for the facts, other than in a clause allowing leniency in 'exceptional circumstances'. It was via this proviso that Lord Woolf and his colleagues forced through a more proportionate (and therefore Convention-compatible) sentence, for Offen and for a number of others convicted under the same law that the judges had insisted on also bringing before them. Judges guard their discretion in sentencing with great vigilance, for this is where the individual finally becomes visible behind that haze of generalized legislative aggression towards all wrongdoers (which only the absence both of specific cases

---

[47] Ibid at para 18 Lord Hope; Lord Carswell at para 58.
[48] [2001] 1 WLR 253.

and of any obligations of implementation has made possible in any event).

Very occasionally, the urge to do justice breaks the barriers erected against socio-economic readings of the rights in the Convention, barriers that we identified and discussed in Chapter 8. Legislation enacted in 2002 meant that late claimants for asylum (as the Secretary of State judged it) had no claim against the state to be prevented from drifting into destitution while their applications were considered, while also being prevented by law from working, 'paid or unpaid, or engag[ing] in any business or profession'.[49] Three men whose asylum claims were rejected found their way to the House of Lords, where the dreadful consequences for them personally were set out—rough sleeping; begging; eating from bins; medical ailments that went untreated. Their lordships unanimously found a breach of article 3's prohibition on inhuman and degrading treatment towards the men and used a provision which explicitly referenced the need to comply with the Convention in the relevant legislation to insist that they be provided with support. As Baroness Hale put it, 'we are respecting, rather than challenging, the will of Parliament'.[50] Certainly there was something of a contradiction here: 'be nasty to asylum seekers while respecting their rights' was the odd, mixed message that the court had to unravel. Parliament had wanted it both ways: to be tough and tender simultaneously. Faced with a choice, and the facts laid out before them, the law lords unhesitatingly chose the latter.

Will the Supreme Court do the same in the remarkable cases of *R (Rutherford and A) v Secretary of State for Work and Pensions*?[51] In Chapter 8

---

[49] *R (Limbuela, Adam and Tesema) v Secretary of State for the Home Department* [2005] UKHL 66, [2006] 1 AC 396, at para 34 per Lord Hope.

[50] Ibid at para 75.

[51] [2016] EWCA Civ 29. An earlier case on the scheme, *R (MA and others) v Secretary of State for Work and Pensions* [2014] EWCA Civ 13, [2014] PTSR 584, was heard by the Supreme Court in March 2016. Judgment is awaited. Cf *Hurley v Secretary of State for Work and Pensions* [2015] EWHC 3382 (Admin); *R (A) v Secretary of State for Work and Pensions* [2015] EWCA Civ 772.

we saw how reluctant the courts are to engage with the human rights impact of welfare legislation: in R (Reilly) v Secretary of State for Work and Pensions,[52] a challenge to a work for no pay scheme got nowhere close to success in the Supreme Court while in R (SG and others) v Secretary of State for Work and Pensions[53] a challenge to benefit caps was seen off in the same arena, albeit on this occasion by the narrowest possible majority of three justices to two. Perhaps there was a straw in the wind here because in the Rutherford case the judges' fortitude in deferring to brutal welfare legislation crumbled in the wake of the facts. There were two sets of appellants. The first, Susan and Paul Rutherford, cared for Susan's disabled grandson, relying on twice weekly relief from carers who stayed over in the couple's third bedroom when they were present. The second, known in the case only as A, was a female victim of violence living in housing protected under a government sanctuary scheme, designed to mitigate the effects and continued threat of violence. Each set of applicants had need of an additional bedroom in the relevant properties but this incurred them an extra charge (popularly known as a 'bedroom tax'), payable because they lived in public sector accommodation and could not establish their need under new rules limiting the size of the property they rented. In each case the Court of Appeal issued a declaration that the appellants had suffered discrimination contra to article 14 taken together with article 8. So far as the Rutherfords were concerned, the rules allowed an additional bedroom where the caring was of a disabled adult but not of a child. And in relation to A, it could be shown that the overwhelming majority of those in these sanctuary schemes were women. Here were two clear statuses concerning which discrimination could only be allowed under settled Strasbourg case-law if there were an objective and reasonable justification. The Court was unequivocal in finding neither explanation here. A's child had been conceived because her violent partner had raped her, and now out of

[52] [2013] UKSC 68, [2014] AC 453.
[53] [2015] UKSC 16, [2015] 1 WLR 1449.

jail after serving a sentence of attempted murder (of someone else) he was on the prowl for her again. The scheme allowed victims of such violence to remain in their homes and a secure ('extra') bedroom was a vital part of this. The Rutherfords worked together to care for Susan's grandson, whose 'profound mental and physical disability caused by a very serious and rare genetic disorder' required 'round the clock care from at least two people'.[54] The designation of the carer's bedroom as surplus led to a reduction of their housing benefit by 14 per cent. It is hard to imagine a more harrowing set of facts with which to draw into full view the impact of such legislation. Changes to the benefit system which make sense against the background of an imaginary, feckless sponger enjoying a life of luxury on the state look less sensible, vicious even, when confronted with the risks incurred by one woman in the course of everyday life, and the heroism shown by two others in the case of crippling bad fortune. Can the Supreme Court avert its eyes from such predicaments so as to avoid doing justice? Or will a democratic hostility that depends on abstracted reasoning and hypothetical wrongdoers prove to be persuasive?

Inclusivity

We turn now to the last of our deep explanations of the Human Rights Act, why its rights function as they do and attract the controversy that so often surrounds them. The 1998 Act is clear in following the European Convention's lead in extending its rights to all those within its remit regardless of nationality or country of origin. In this regard the Human Rights Act is truly a *human* (not a *British* or a *European*) bill of rights. Parliament is on the whole content with such an abstract claim of ethical universality; few are prepared to go as far as Martin Howe QC did in his contribution to a 2012 Coalition-

---

[54] R (Rutherford) v Secretary of State for Work and Pensions (n 51), at para 16 per Thomas LCJ giving the judgment of the Court.

inspired commission on bills of rights in dividing up and doling out rights to people on the basis of their nationality, as UK citizens (grade 1), EU citizens (grade 2), and the rest.[55] While equality is all fine in theory, it is its practice that has proved particularly controversial. In taking this human rights claim seriously, the judges have incurred the wrath of many in the political and media worlds responsible for the fantasies which we discussed in Part II. Not content like Martin Howe QC to change the message, consistent efforts have been made to shoot the messenger.

There are four different ways in which the Human Right Act has forged ahead in its extension of ordinary life guarantees to those whose status as outsiders has traditionally left them very vulnerable. Let us look at each in turn, starting with what may be the most surprising, and certainly one that is among the most dramatic: the genuinely outside outsiders. On 20 January 2016, Mr Justice Bernard McCloskey and Judge Mark Ockleton sitting in the Upper Tribunal of the Immigration and Asylum Chamber ordered that three unaccompanied boys and a dependent adult should be allowed to live with their family in Britain while their asylum claims were being examined.[56] The four had fled Syria in September and arrived at the Calais 'jungle' camp in October where expert evidence testified to conditions being akin to a 'living hell',[57] with unaccompanied children particularly vulnerable to violence. The individual plights of each of them were particularly bad, but not more so than many in the same situation in the camp. The judges sought to control the precedent value of their remarkable intervention by referring to the 'intensely fact sensitive' nature of the cases[58] albeit at the same time acknowledging 'the innate capacity of humankind to shock and abhor' so that 'the possibility of

---

[55] Commission on a Bill of Rights, *A UK Bill of Rights: The Choice Before Us* (December 2012) art 26 of his draft bill of rights: vol 1, p 215.

[56] R (*ZAT and others*) v *Secretary of State for the Home Department* [2016] UKUT 61.

[57] Ibid at para 5.

[58] Ibid at para 52.

still stronger cases [could] not be discounted'.[59] Welcoming the decision Judith Dennis, policy manager at the Refugee Council, said, 'Everyone has the right to live in safety with their loved ones.'[60] But do they?

The judges based their ruling on the Human Rights Act, and in particular article 8's guarantee of a right to respect for family life, so there was a definite grounding for this aspiration in UK law. Here was a decision taken at home (in this case the Home Secretary's refusal to admit the applicants) which had ramifications abroad, the effect of which attracted the attentions of the Human Rights Act. It is unusual but not impossible for those outside the jurisdiction adversely affected by such domestic decisions to get to the UK's domestic courts; in this case the four had the Migrants' Law Project of Islington Law Centre to thank for getting as far as they did. The Strasbourg Court has set out the principles which are to guide decision-making in such circumstances, specifically on whether a state is under a positive duty (usually imposed by article 8 on the right to respect for family life) to admit those seeking to enter it.[61] It was by relying upon these that Mr Justice McCloskey and Judge Ockleton were able to navigate their way through a thicket of EU and asylum law to arrive at what they clearly felt was in the circumstances before them the only decision they could morally reach. Will the idea survive in our law? Much will depend on the way it reaches our most senior courts. The Calais camp case has the most riveting of facts, reminding us once again of what we have been discussing just a moment ago, the importance of the demands of justice revealed by the specific facts of any given case. In another immigration case with powerful facts, *Chikwamba v Secretary of State*

---

[59] Ibid at para 52.

[60] 'Four Syrian refugees must be brought from Calais camp to Britain, judges rule' *Guardian* 20 January 2016.

[61] *Sen v Netherlands* (2001) 36 EHRR 81; *Tuquabo-Tekle v The Netherlands* European Court of Human Rights, 1 December 2005; *Mayeka and Mitunga v Belgium* (2006) 46 EHRR 449. See also *AS (Somalia) and another v Secretary of State for the Home Department* [2009] UKHL 32.

for the Home Department,[62] the House of Lords emphasized the capacity of article 8 in suitable cases to outweigh the public interest in the maintenance and enforcement of immigration control, but there the individual affected was within the jurisdiction rather than outside. It is a humane leap to move from solicitude to the foreigner within to embracing also the stranger without (even the one with relations already upstairs).

Not that we should think for a moment that this second category, the foreigner already within the UK (of which *Chikwamba* is an example), has been unproblematic. In the case itself the required removal of a woman settled in the UK with her family was as Lord Scott remarked 'elevating policy to dogma' in a way so impenetrably absurd that 'Kafka would have enjoyed it.'[63] The Home Office did try it though and had won at the then first appellate stage, before an adjudicator. It took this and other cases at the highest level before the importance of family life for those resident in the UK but subject to immigration controls started to (paraphrasing a speech of Lord Neuberger to which we referred in Chapter 4) 'leak into the administrators' cerebellum'.[64] How far does this human rights protective umbrella extend? In *D v United Kingdom*[65] a person suffering from AIDS successfully argued that the 'conditions which would confront [him] in the receiving country [were] themselves a breach of the standards of Article 3' such that 'his removal would expose him to a real risk of dying under the most distressing circumstances and would thus amount to inhuman treatment'.[66] This compassionate intervention has not spawned the cases that might have been imagined, the decision being more often cited to be distinguished than followed.

---

[62] [2008] UKHL 40, [2008] 1 WLR 1420.

[63] Ibid at para 6.

[64] Other cases include *EM (Lebanon) v Secretary of State for the Home Department* (n 45); *EB (Kosovo) v Secretary of State for the Home Department* [2008] UKHL 41, [2009] AC 1159 and *Beoku-Betts v Secretary of State for the Home Department* [2008] UKHL 39, [2009] AC 115.

[65] (1997) 24 EHRR 423.

[66] Ibid at para 53.

PROTECTING THE EXPOSED

Seeking to avoid life-destroying medical neglect or dodging immigration law while family ties naturally establish themselves in the UK
are one thing, but alleged criminals, suspected terrorists even, wanted
abroad for crimes committed or for terrorist activities allegedly
engaged in, are surely quite another? Unsurprisingly here is a field
that has remained highly controversial. In *Soering v United Kingdom*[67]
the Strasbourg Court intervened to prevent the return to the United
States of a man facing charges there which could have led, if successfully proved, to the death penalty. Given how long executions took to
be finalized and then to take place, it followed that a stay on 'death
row' would be inevitable and it was this which the judges found would
have involved a serious risk of a breach of article 3. It was only after
assurances that the death penalty would not be sought that Soering
was returned (and subsequently convicted and sentenced to life
imprisonment). *Chahal v United Kingdom*[68] is a case we have already
encountered in this chapter as an exemplar of the fairness dimension
to human rights litigation, but it also deploys the principle of equality
with impressive lack of equivocation: do to others as you would do to
your own. Here the *Soering* principle was applied to suspected terrorists from India whose plausible claim was that they would be ill treated
and/or killed on their return to their home state. The line of authorities
to which it has given rise have not exactly been cheerleader decisions
for human rights, however right they might be in principle. In *RB
(Algeria) and another v Secretary of State for the Home Department*[69] the Abu
Qatada case produced an outcome largely favourable to the authorities but not before great strides had been made in fleshing out the
breadth and range of obligations under articles 3 and 6 so far as the
removal of suspected foreign terrorists was concerned. These were
then further developed in a subsequent Strasbourg intervention,

[67] (1989) 11 EHRR 439.

[68] (n 4).

[69] [2009] UKHL 10, [2010] 2 AC 110. Cf *Kapri v The Lord Advocate (Government of Albania)*
[2013] UKSC 48, [2013] 1 WLR 2324.

asserting a breach of article 6 on the facts before it on account of the 'real risk' of a 'flagrant denial of justice' in the tainting of the applicant's retrial in Jordan through the use of evidence obtained by torture.[70] As already observed, the human rights safeguards put in place were so successful that Abu Qatada was eventually acquitted.[71] It is unlikely that when legislators agreed the term 'everyone' in the Human Rights Act in 1998 they had had Abu Qatada or people like Abu Qatada at the forefront of their minds. It is left to judges to flesh out what grand parliamentary language means in concrete situations.

Our third category of case is closely connected to what we have just been discussing, but in some ways even more morally serious, engaging as it does our own bad conduct rather than that of other states. The concern here is with poor treatment of foreigners within the jurisdiction solely on account of their outsider status; not their removal it is true but rather the deployment of special rules within the country, operated to their disadvantage. We saw an example in R (Baiai) v Secretary of State for the Home Department[72] where a lavish fee was imposed on those subject to immigration control who desired to marry. Another example, also discussed in this chapter, was Limbuela[73] where the law lords reinterpreted a provision of the asylum law so as to avoid a category of asylum seeker falling into impoverishment as a deliberate consequence of government policy. But the most outstanding example of all is one of the most famous cases under the Human Rights Act, the Belmarsh decision of 16 December 2004.[74] We looked at its wider political context in Chapter 5. Here we want to highlight the dramatic way in which the House of Lords fought back against a detention regime, introduced in the aftermath of the attacks on 11 September 2001, that targeted for indefinite incarceration only suspected *international* terrorists rather than

---

[70] Othman (Abu Qatada) v United Kingdom (2012) 55 EHRR 1.
[71] See Ch 8.
[72] (n 43).
[73] (n 49).
[74] A v Secretary of State for the Home Department [2004] UKHL 56, [2005] 2 AC 68.

others of the local variety.[75] Were there no other sort? Even before the attacks on London by UK nationals on 7 July 2005, it was patently absurd to claim that there were not. The truth was that being an easy target, the (non-voting) foreigner could be offered up as a sacrifice to media and public outrage. Their lordships were having none of it, brushing aside a claim of emergency necessity to find that the discrimination at the core of the law rendered it incompatible with Convention rights. Baroness Hale put her finger on why the Human Rights Act had to object to such an invidious approach:

> No one has the right to be an international terrorist. But substitute 'black', 'disabled', 'female', 'gay', or any other similar adjective for 'foreign' before 'suspected international terrorist' and ask whether it would be justifiable to take power to lock up that group but not the 'white', 'able-bodied', 'male' or 'straight' suspected international terrorists. The answer is clear.[76]

The fourth and final category of outsider-protection afforded the Human Rights Act takes us into territory which will also be occupied in Chapter 10 when we turn to the positive, protective impact of the Convention on members of the 'ordinary' public as well as the outsiders we are discussing here. After a fair bit of uncertainty the Strasbourg Court has recently clarified that the Convention follows the troops of member states abroad, that if a country decides to engage militarily outside the jurisdiction then it must do so in the knowledge that it has taken its human rights obligations as well as its weapons along for the ride.[77] The issue disproportionately affects the British, whose armed forces are more inclined than most to be deployed abroad, and it was the behaviour of some of its soldiers in Basrah in southern Iraq in 2003 that produced the leading case of *Al-Skeini and others v United Kingdom*: the killing of civilians in various incidents in the area and the death in custody of the hotel receptionist Baha Mousa, his 'body and face ... covered in blood and bruises; his

---

[75] Anti-terrorism, Crime and Security Act 2001, s 21(1).

[76] (n 74), at para 238.

[77] *Al-Skeini and others v United Kingdom* (2011) 53 EHRR 589.

nose ... broken and part of the skin of his face ... torn away' after three days in detention.[78] The Strasbourg Court has been the leader here drawing the British judges away from a tendency towards a narrow reading of jurisdiction.[79] It may be that the majority of these European judges share the view of their colleague Judge Bonello, whose concurring opinion in *Al Skeini* asserted that it 'ill behoves a state that imposed its military imperialism over another sovereign state without the frailest imprimatur from the international community, to resent the charge of having exported human-rights imperialism to the vanquished enemy', likening this to 'wearing with conceit your badge of international law banditry, but then recoiling in shock at being suspected of human-rights promotion'.[80] Whether this is the case or not, as we shall very shortly see, the reach of the Convention into military conduct abroad has drawn the ire of the generals and their supporters in government and the press, with changes being proposed in the new bill of rights to be brought before Parliament.

The beneficiaries of the extension of the Human Rights Act remit that we have been considering in this chapter have been those not normally first in the queue for legal protection. This legislation puts flesh on the bare bones of what we say we believe in—fairness; justice; and inclusivity—testing our claims against very specific, and often heart-rending facts. Which of the winning litigants in any of these cases deserved to lose? Critics of rights legislation are much more comfortable keeping their strong views at arm's length from the facts. But the Act's strengths go beyond its reach into these dark unprotected corners of our world. One of the least regarded or publicized aspects of the Human Rights Act has been how it has also engaged with the mainstream of the everyday as well as the lives of our precarious outsiders. The facts speak for themselves here as well; we turn to these in Chapter 10.

---

[78] Ibid at para 64.

[79] *Al Skeini and others v Secretary of State for the Defence* [2007] UKHL 26, [2008] 1 AC 153.

[80] (n 77), at para 37 of the concurring opinion of Judge Bonello. See further on this issue *Al-Saadoon v Secretary of State for Defence* [2015] EWHC 1769.

10

MAKING A DIFFERENCE

The British army's Chief of Staff General Sir Nicholas Carter warned in an interview in *The Telegraph* at the end of January 2016 that legal actions against soldiers 'could undermine Britain on the battlefield'.[1] The ostensible context of his remarks was the prospect of processing some 1,500 allegations of abuse that had been made to the government-funded Iraq Historic Allegations Team. It was, he thought, 'something that would, over time, undermine our ability to take the sorts of risks that are necessary to be able to prevail on the battlefield'. The military and Ministers have certainly been unhappy about the extension of the reach of human rights law to British forces abroad, with junior Defence Minister Penny Mordaunt having also observed that 'parasitic lawyers' have been using European human rights legislation that was 'not written for conflict situations' so as to bring claims against British troops.[2] This is the subject with which we ended Chapter 9, an example of the controversy the Convention can generate when it reaches out to those vulnerable to state power wherever they happen to be. But Sir Nicholas did not only have Iraqi and Afghani victims of soldier excess (whether real or imagined) in mind: he also observed that 'If our soldiers are forever worrying that

---

[1] 'Legal actions against soldiers "could undermine Britain on the battlefield" warns chief of general staff' *The Telegraph* 29 January 2016: <http://www.telegraph.co.uk/news/uknews/defence/12130929/Legal-action-against-soldiers-could-undermine-Britain-on-the-battlefield-warns-chief-of-general-staff.html> [accessed 10 February 2016].

[2] '"Parasitic law firms" blamed for legal actions against UK troops' *Daily Mail* 27 January 2016: <http://www.dailymail.co.uk/wires/pa/article-3419783/Parasitic-law-firms-blamed-legal-actions-against-UK-troops.html> [accessed 10 February 2016].

On Fantasy Island: Britain, Europe, and Human Rights. First Edition. Conor Gearty.

they might be sued because the piece of equipment that they're using is not the best piece of equipment in the world, then that is clearly a potential risk to the freedom of action which we need to encourage in order to be able to beat our opponent.'[3] It is unlikely that the enemy will sue a military opponent for having chosen to send its troops out in poorly protected transport vehicles or with vulnerable defensive clothing. The fear here is of the Ministry of Defence being sued by ordinary soldiers. This is where the Human Rights Act has certainly made a difference, one that has been unwanted by those in charge of battle-zones (as opposed to at least some of the junior officers and privates that have to enter them).

Three incidents of this sort have given rise to the leading case. On 25 March 2003 Corporal Stephen Allbutt, Lance Corporal Daniel Twiddy, and Trooper Andrew Julien were serving with the Queen's Royal Lancers as part of a Royal Regiment of Fusiliers battle group during the fourth day of an offensive by British forces to take Basrah. They were in one of a number of Challenger II tanks which had been placed at a dam in hull down positions to minimize visibility to the enemy. Unable to see the tank properly and mistaking it for a bunker containing hostile personnel, another regiment's tank shelled it, killing Allbutt (and another trooper David Clarke) and injuring Twiddy and Julien. In the second incident, in 2005, Private Phillip Hewett was deployed to a battle group near Al Amarah in Iraq. His unit was made up of three Land Rovers none of which was equipped to provide protection against improvised explosive devices (IEDs). Left unescorted in the town and without electronic counter-measures to protect against such devices, the Land Rover was blown up, killing three, including Private Hewett. The following year a similar IED killed Private Lee Ellis, the driver of a Land Rover in the same region, this time one with electronic protection albeit without a vital extra element fitted to it at the time. Allbutt's widow, and both the injured men (Twiddy and Julien), brought actions against the army, alleging negligence

---

[3] *The Telegraph* (n 1).

in provision of the poor equipment with which Allbutt and the two claimants had been sent into battle and also in the poor quality of the training they had been given, both before deployment and in theatre. The second and third claims arising out of the poorly protected Land Rovers were taken by the mother of Hewett and the son and brother of Ellis. They alleged that the Ministry of Defence had 'breached article 2 of the European Convention on Human Rights and Fundamental Freedoms by failing to take measures within the scope of its powers which, judged reasonably, it might have been expected to take in the light of the real and immediate risk to life of soldiers who were required to patrol' in these lightly armed vehicles.[4] The Ministry of Defence contended that none of the proceedings should be allowed to proceed, arguing that it was protected from litigation by the long-entrenched principle of 'combat immunity'—in effect that war protected it from ordinary liability. This argument enjoyed some success in the lower courts before the Supreme Court, sitting as a panel of seven judges, ruled unanimously that the Convention applied and by a bare majority of four to three that the cases should be permitted to proceed to trial.

The decision is an important one for the guidance it gives on how far the Convention can be productive of effects outside the state's own territory. Here our interest lies in its extension not to the vulnerable outsider far away but to the serving soldier in the theatre of conflict, and in particular to the application to him or her of article 2's positive obligation on the state to protect life. Giving the lead judgment for the majority, Lord Hope considered his finding that the obligation did apply fortified by a report from the Parliamentary Assembly of the Council of Europe of some years before which had observed that 'members of the armed forces are citizens in uniform who must enjoy the same fundamental freedoms and the same protection of

---

[4] *Smith, Ellis, Allbutt and others v The Ministry of Defence* [2013] UKSC 41, [2014] AC 52, at para 10 per Lord Hope. Ellis's son also sued in negligence arising out of the same set of facts.

their rights and dignity as any other citizen, within the limits imposed by the specific exigencies of military duties'.[5] The same report had 'emphasised that members of the armed forces cannot be expected to respect humanitarian law and human rights in their operation unless respect for human rights is guaranteed within the army ranks'.[6] Speaking for the majority, Lord Hope allowed that a 'very wide measure of discretion... must be accorded to those who were responsible on the ground for the planning and conduct of the operations during which these soldiers lost their lives and also to the way issues as to procurement too should be approached'[7] but this did not mean that the matter was entirely outside the law.

How did article 2 and the common law of negligence find themselves being extended to the battlefield in this way, protecting soldiers for sure but creating the difficulties concerning which we have seen the Chief of Staff of the army being so critical? Without the Human Rights Act we can be quite certain that neither article 2 nor the law of negligence would have even been thought of as having any kind of bite in the circumstances surrounding the deaths of these three men. But nor would either have reached the myriad of 'ordinary people' closer to home whose lives have been blighted by official error and for the protection of whom the Human Rights Act has done valiant work. In Chapter 9 we looked at what were in many ways the predictable claimants under human rights law, arguing that their vulnerability (as criminal suspects; prisoners; suspected antisocial individuals; people with mental disabilities; etc) was what made the application of this law to them all the more important (and also, it is true, all the more controversial). But vulnerability is not an immutable category of person: it can strike at any time. The 1998 Act has been important here too.

---

[5] Ibid para 54, per Lord Hope citing recommendation 1742 (2006) of the Parliamentary Assembly, on the human rights of members of the armed forces made in the light of a report on this issue by the Parliament's committee on legal affairs and human rights (doc 10861).

[6] Ibid per Lord Hope.

[7] Ibid para 81.

These headline-making Iraqi cases drew their energy from decisions under the Human Rights Act situated far closer to home: here are the litigants you don't read about in the *Mail* and the *Telegraph*, or hear about in Conservative Party speeches.

The story of the Convention's application to such persons starts with an important Strasbourg decision, *Osman v United Kingdom*.[8] The father of the former school student was killed (and the boy himself seriously injured) by one of the pupil's past teachers, a man whose behaviour had earlier revealed him to have had an unhealthy obsession with the pupil. His conduct had been brought to the attention of the police in the period leading up to the attacks, but they had done nothing. English law as it then was guaranteed the police immunity for any negligent decisions they might make in the course of their operational duties,[9] so efforts to bring the authorities to account in the domestic courts proved unavailing. The European Court of Human Rights took a different view, holding that the absolute rule denying the right to sue in such circumstances was disproportionate and so a breach of the implied right of access to the courts to be found in article 6(1). Now this ruling immediately proved very controversial, with much criticism being directed at the way the Court analysed the English law on strike out.[10] Indeed it did not long survive as a precedent in Strasbourg, being effectively dismantled in a case that reached the Court just three years later.[11] By then, however, for all the ridicule heaped on it, the case had exposed to critical scrutiny not just the police immunity in English law but the insulation from liability that was also enjoyed by a myriad other public authorities engaged in various functions scattered across the law. Under the critical gaze of a more determinedly litigious climate, the local courts themselves set about dismantling or at least diluting many of these previously solid

---

[8] (1998) 29 EHRR 245.

[9] *Hill v Chief Constable of West Yorkshire* [1989] AC 53.

[10] C A Gearty, 'Unravelling *Osman*' (2001) 64 (2) *Modern Law Review* 159–90.

[11] *Z and others v United Kingdom* (2001) 34 EHRR 97.

protective rules.[12] Though the Strasbourg intervention was loudly asserted not to be the driver of the changes, it can hardly not have had some kind of role as director of the litigious traffic.

Another aspect of the *Osman* ruling has proved more enduring even if it did not avail the Osman family itself on the facts of the case. The Strasbourg Court took this opportunity to lay down authoritative guidance on when article 2 could be said to import a duty on the part of the authorities to act so as to prevent loss of life, the very issue on which the litigants in the Iraqi case just discussed were later to rely. A breach of the article occurs if it is established 'that the authorities knew or ought to have known at the time of the existence of a real and immediate risk to the life of an identified individual or individuals from the criminal acts of a third party and that they failed to take measures within the scope of their powers which, judged reasonably, might have been expected to avoid that risk'.[13] In *Osman* the European judges voted by seventeen votes to three that this high standard had not been met on the facts before them. The test has since been applied in English law[14] and now serves as an important discipline for the police and other authorities when considering how to react to the threats of violence against third parties that regularly cross their desks. In *Keenan v United Kingdom*[15] the principle was extended to protect detainees from suicide as well as from being attacked by fellow prisoners.[16] In *Savage v South Essex Partnership NHS Foundation Trust*[17] the daughter of a woman detained as a mental patient who had absconded and then thrown herself in front of a train was allowed to take a civil action for breach of article 2. While 'the threshold (real and immediate risk to life) for

---

[12] See eg *Barrett v Enfield London Borough Council* [2001] 2 AC 550.

[13] *Osman* (n 8), at para 116.

[14] In *Chief Constable of the Hertfordshire Police v Van Colle; Smith v Chief Constable of Sussex Police* [2008] UKHL 50, [2009] AC 225.

[15] (2001) 33 EHRR 913.

[16] On which see *Edwards v United Kingdom* (2002) 35 EHRR 487.

[17] [2008] UKHL 74, [2009] AC 681.

triggering the duty is high'[18] there was no reason not to apply it to those detained with mental illnesses.[19]

A particularly sad case is *Rabone v Penine Care NHS Trust*[20] in which a voluntary patient with a number of suicide attempts had been permitted home for a weekend despite the clearly articulated concerns of her parents. Once there she went to a local park on pretence of seeing a friend and hanged herself. Overturning both the High Court and the Court of Appeal, the Supreme Court unanimously found that article 2 applied, the distinction between detained and voluntary patients being rather blurred in cases such as these. Tragic too was *Michael v Chief Constable of South Wales Police and another*[21] in which a call to the police by a woman moments before she was attacked and killed by an ex-boyfriend was not acted upon. Here the police avoidance of liability on negligence grounds was successful, but there was no escaping article 2, all seven Supreme Court judges agreeing that the matter could not simply be rejected out of hand but had to go to trial on the facts. The same was applied to article 3 in another upsetting case of police failure, this time in relation to operational failures in relation to the detection of a serious violent crime.[22] Now all these cases inevitably are imputing liability or the possibility of liability after the event. We have no way of assessing the cases that have not happened, the deaths avoided by an official sensitivity to risk that, in the absence of the Convention and its domestic arm the Human Rights Act, would never have been forthcoming. The Human Rights Act should sometimes be celebrated for the cases that have not happened as much as for those that have.

A related thread of decisions that have been made possible by the Human Rights Act are those concerned with inquests, another area

---

[18] Ibid para 41 per Lord Rodger.
[19] *Slimani v France* (2004) 43 EHRR 1068.
[20] [2012] UKSC 2, [2012] AC 72.
[21] [2015] UKSC 2, [2015] AC 1732.
[22] *Metropolitan Police Commissioner v DSD and NBV* [2015] EWCA Civ 646.

where the vulnerability of all of us is manifested in our shared mortality. Once again the positive obligation under article 2 has driven these changes, this time engaged not so much with the assessment of risk before the fatal event as with a proper investigation of it after it has materialized. The leading case came early in the life of the legislation, *R (Middleton) v West Somerset Coroner*.[23] A prisoner had killed himself and at the inquest the family pushed for a fuller explanation of what had happened than had been forthcoming from the authorities. Mrs Middleton thought that the risk of death should have been known to those responsible for her son and that they should therefore have been able to guard effectively against it. At the time the inquest rules necessitated only the blandest of statements as to 'how, when and where the deceased came by his death'.[24] Under pressure from Convention case-law and mindful of the procedural obligation it imposed on member states to investigate effectively deaths that might engage the right in article 2, the House of Lords expanded the old rule. Whereas 'how' had previously been ruled to extend only to 'by what means' it would henceforth be regarded as embracing also 'in what circumstances' the deceased had met his or her death.[25] This freed up the inquest jury to engage directly with whatever concerns it might have over the incident which had given rise to the fatality they had been asked to consider. The dead man here for example had been in prison since he had been jailed at the age of 14 for killing his 18-month-old niece. Aged 30 when he took his own life, his time in prison had thrown up a series of indicators of a tendency towards self-destruction. Now the jury's anxieties about these facts in this case could be properly recorded, and not left as a private note to the coroner which is all that the old interpretation of the rule had allowed. This precedent was

---

[23] [2004] UKHL 10, [2004] 2 AC 182.

[24] Coroners Act 1988, s 11(5)(ii), repeated in the Coroners Rules 1984 (SI 1984/552).

[25] (n 23), at para 35 per Lord Bingham, giving a speech with which his colleagues agreed.

expanded four years later when the House of Lords extended the investigatory obligation in article 2 to embrace near suicides and incidents productive of long-term injury, not inquests on these occasions of course but enhanced investigations which may in the right circumstances lead to a more public inquiry.[26] There was no need to wait for death before asking the right questions about a possible failure of care that had produced harm.

Now while inquests might eventually happen to us all, these two leading cases are of course both prisoner cases, examples of the Human Rights Act intervening to protect the vulnerable, the sort of situation that was at the centre of Chapter 9. But they belong here because this new reading of the investigative duty under article 2 has had an impact across the law. We are all open to events that expose our vulnerability, however secure we might believe ourselves to be. Perhaps we do not think this risk will manifest itself in conduct leading to our being imprisoned, albeit the figures for the prison population are now so high that this may be a false assumption. But only the most confident among us can be sure that we will live free of mental health debilities throughout our lives—and what if we are forsaken by our carers at exactly that point when we feel least able to cope? There are also the foot-soldiers in the UK's army to consider once more: the men mentioned at the start of this chapter (whose cases like that in *Rabone* can give rise to negligence actions) but those like Private Jason Smith as well. Smith joined the territorial army when he was 21 and eleven years later found himself mobilized for service in Iraq. After a brief spell in Kuwait for acclimatization, he was billeted in an old athletics stadium in Iraq in August, training in temperatures exceeding 50 degrees centigrade even in the shade. Saying he could not stand the heat, he was reported sick only to be promptly assigned to various duties off the base. Four days later he was dead, of hyperthermia (or heat stroke). It was only because of article 2 that the Secretary of State conceded the need for an inquest that did not simply record this fact

[26] R (L) v Secretary of State for Justice [2008] UKHL 68, [2009] AC 588.

but probed as well the potential responsibility of the authorities for his death.[27]

Any of us volunteering for the territorials as Smith did could have found ourselves in his position not much more than a decade later. As with the *Osman* duty, an unknown here is the extent to which human rights interventions have driven changes which have saved lives. It is surely not assuming too much to think that the holding to account of the armed forces, the police, and the prison and health services for those in their care has had some kind of a positive effect on their treatment of others, in relation to whom the lack of any litigious noise is surely a sign of success. We can see this in the way that articles 3 and 8 have been used to secure better treatments for the aged in care homes, using the prohibition on inhumane and degrading treatment in the first and the right to respect for privacy in the second to forge a new set of obligations towards the aged.[28] A glance at the Amnesty website for example gives many examples of the successful deployment of the Act.[29]

One of the most important arenas in which this respect for human rights can be demanded is the private one. The Act does extend its reach to profit-making bodies as long as they are engaged in 'public functions'. Ironically these advances have occurred despite the best efforts of the senior judiciary to prevent them. In *YL v Birmingham City Council and others*[30] the House of Lords held that a private care home did not incur the obligation under section 6(1) of the Human Rights Act to respect Convention rights when it was providing accommodation and care to a resident under arrangements with a local authority (pursuant to the National Assistance Act 1948). This was because an activity of this sort did not mean that the company was a 'public

---

[27] *R (Smith) v Oxford Assistant Deputy Coroner* [2010] UKSC 29, [2011] 1 AC 1.

[28] Cf *R (Karia) v Leicester City Council* [2014] EWHC 31 where no breach was found in relation to the closure of a care home in which the 101-year-old claimant resided.

[29] See the Amnesty International website on this for more details: <https://www.amnesty.org.uk/issues/Human-Rights-Act> [accessed 18 March 2016].

[30] [2007] UKHL 27, [2008] AC 95.

authority' for the purpose of section 6. The decision was a disappointing one for those who sought to add vigour to the legislation's impact across all walks of society, not least because the measure had appeared to have anticipated exactly this sort of situation when it set out (in section 6(3)(b)) to bring a private provider delivering 'public functions' within its remit. The lords' view that this was not a public function did not last long: section 145 of the Health and Social Care Act 2008 reversed the ruling so far as its specific set of facts were concerned, and subsequent cases have sought to recover the original intention behind section 6(3)(b) so as to give the Act an ethical bite in the private sector when its commercial operators are doing public work under contract.[31]

A curious side-effect of the attempt at a wide definition of 'public authority' in the Human Rights Act has been to create, by this most unexpected of backdoors, a law of privacy in the United Kingdom. Long resisted by the press (whose anxieties even extended to placing a special clause into the Human Rights Bill itself so as to protect the media from injunctions without notice[32]), the defenders of the usually all-powerful fourth estate could not prevent the judges early on using article 8's requirement of respect for privacy as a means of infiltrating protection for the victims of media excess into an environment previously hostile to it. This was because of the extension of the definition of 'public authority' in section 6(3)(a) to any 'court or tribunal'. This allowed judges inclined to take the privacy path anyway to say that they now had no option: the dispute between them might be between private parties (the newspaper and the person objecting to the invasion of his or her privacy) and so outside the Act but they as 'a public authority' were not and so needed to issue a human-rights-compatible remedy. This is a jurisprudence that has been driven by celebrities and

[31] There is a good overview by R Clayton, 'Accountability, judicial scrutiny and contracting out' UK Const L Blog (30 November 2015): <https://ukconstitutionallaw.org/2015/11/30/richard-clayton-qc-accountability-judicial-scrutiny-and-contracting-out/> [accessed 18 March 2016].
[32] Now Human Rights Act s 12.

other well-known persons: it is in them that the media are interested and by the same token it is they who have the resources to retaliate. The law was largely made by the battle between Michael Douglas and Catherine Zeta Jones on the one hand and *Hello!* magazine on the other over the right to publish photographs of their marriage,[33] but since then a succession of personalities from various worlds such as those of sport,[34] music,[35] and publishing[36] have sought to tame the press through the use of this new-found remedial option. Now it might reasonably be thought that this is a recherché world of litigation, about which only the affluent in the public eye need be concerned. But the media's voracious search for newsworthiness will swoop on anyone in the public eye, even if it is tragedy that has put them there. The phone-hacking scandals that dominated the news in Britain are testimony to that, with the family of young murder victim Millie Dowler being only one of a number of victims of press abuse of technology for commercial gain.[37] In the common law system of precedent, wins by celebrities count as wins for all.

The same point can be made, albeit more obliquely and in a more qualified way, about public protest. We do not all choose to engage in voluble or physical acts of dissent, or to assert our right (as we understand it) to demonstrate, and nor do we often have the necessity for protest thrust upon us. When we do, we may find that the Human Rights Act does not serve us as well as perhaps it ought: in Chapter 8 we saw examples of the way in which it has been rather more compliant to state power than might have been expected. But it does on

---

[33] *Douglas, Zeta Jones, Northern & Shell Plc v Hello! Limited (No 1)* [2000] EWCA Civ 353, [2001] QB 967; *Douglas etc v Hello! Ltd etc* [2005] EWCA Civ 595, [2006] QB 125; *OBG Ltd v Allan; Douglas and others v Hello! Ltd and others; Mainstream Properties Ltd v Young and others* [2007] UKHL 21, [2008] 1 AC 1.

[34] *CTB v News Group Newspapers and Imogen Thomas* [2011] EWHC 1334 (QB).

[35] *Weller v Associated Newspapers* [2015] EWCA Civ 1176.

[36] *Murray v Big Pictures Limited* [2008] EWCA Civ 446.

[37] See the Report of the Leveson Inquiry into the Culture, Practices and Ethics of the Press 29 November 2012.

occasion do good precedent work even here. When Jane La Porte found the bus in which she and other peace campaigners were travelling to a protest (outside a royal air force base) turned around by the police, it was the demand for the Convention's commitment to political speech and the rule of law that allowed the law lords to modify the broadly based common law power under which the police had purported to act (despite a plethora of statutory controls that they had also mobilized to help them control the crowd).[38] Had the data on police files of 91-year-old protestor John Catt all been held in one place so that there was a singular file on him (rather than merely the disparate references that actually existed) then the challenge he brought to the police system of information collection and retention might have been more successful.[39] But such 'nominal records' had in fact been destroyed some years before.[40]

We end this chapter with *Jain v Trent Strategic Health Authority*.[41] Here was a case based on a factual situation that arose before the Human Rights Act but finally reached the highest court when the measure had already been in force for over eight years. The nursing home business run by Mr and Mrs Jain had been destroyed by a sudden closure notice of their one such property, issued by the regulatory authority pursuant to an application made to a magistrate without any notice being given to them. As a result of the way the matter was processed, the Jains had no chance to contest the notice before being required to move (literally overnight) the thirty-three elderly and infirm patients who were under their care. An appeal process followed but it was not one which allowed for expedition or the stay of the contested order

---

[38] R (Laporte) v Chief Constable of Gloucestershire Constabulary [2006] UKHL 55, [2007] 2 AC 105. The claimant has not always been a winner: Laporte v Metropolitan Police Commissioner [2014] EWHC 3574 (QB).

[39] R (Catt) v Metropolitan Police Commissioner [2015] UKSC 9, [2015] AC 1065 decided at the same time as R (T) v Metropolitan Police Commissioner, at para 51 per Baroness Hale.

[40] R (Catt) (n 39), at para 52. Cf Lord Toulson dissenting ibid paras 68 and 69. Lord Mance agreed with both Baroness Hale and the lead judgment, that of Lord Sumption.

[41] [2009] UKHL 4, [2009] AC 853.

in advance of the proceedings. So when the Jains were eventually vindicated before the relevant tribunal (which was scathing about the authority's action) it was already too late for them (and their thirty-three residents). They were ruined. Their effort to secure compensation at common law foundered on the absence of any duty of care owed them by the authority that had made the early crucial, destructive decisions, an obstacle that not even the creatively sympathetic minds of five law lords could overcome. In three of the five speeches made in that forum, however, each of Lord Scott, Baroness Hale, and Lord Neuberger lamented the fact that the right to property in the Convention was not available via the Human Rights Act to deliver the compensation that justice demanded for the Jains[42]—and, we might add, the justice to which the thirty-three expelled residents should also have been entitled. This was because the situation complained of arose before the Act had come into force. Perhaps it goes without saying that the popular press did not greet the decision with hostile braying about the inadequacies of the common law and the need for human rights to protect ordinary people from state abuse.

---

[42] Ibid paras 12–18 per Lord Scott; at paras 43–7 per Baroness Hale; at para 54 per Lord Neuberger. Each also identified a breach of art 6 as well.

11

TELLING US WHO WE ARE

It is not entirely untrue to say that the British were the brains behind the European Convention on Human Rights. We saw in Chapter 4 how Winston Churchill and his former coalition colleagues in the post-war Labour government had been driving forces behind the new Europe that was then being created under American protection, and human rights clearly had an important part to play in this reimagining.[1] The Council of Europe was established in 1949 and its own website gives pride of place among its 'founding fathers' to Winston Churchill. This is how Churchill described the then unfolding European project in a speech in Strasbourg on 12 August 1949, as recorded on the Council's website: 'The dangers threatening us are great but great too is our strength, and there is no reason why we should not succeed in achieving our aims and establishing the structure of this united Europe whose moral concepts will be able to win the respect and recognition of mankind, and whose physical strength will be such that no one will dare to hold up its peaceful journey towards the future.'[2] There is a central tension evident in this quotation which has been ever-present in Britain's relationship with Europe in general and its two supra-national limbs in particular (the Council but also the later EU): is it 'us' or 'them'? In Churchill's remark, it is both: *we* are building a new Europe in the hope that *it* will then thrive. We are a parent for sure,

---

[1] For a good account which makes this point see J Norman and P Oborne, *Churchill's Legacy: The Conservative Case for the Human Rights Act* (London: Liberty, 2009).

[2] See <http://www.coe.int/en/web/about-us/founding-fathers> [accessed 22 February 2016].

but are we also a sibling, a part of the family as well or merely its creator?

The ambiguity is tied up in the legacy of colonialism. Of course many European countries have memories of having wielded global power in the past, invariably recalled in each of such places as prosperous and fulfilling times—not surprisingly since the wealth was then flowing in from exploited foreign lands with prestige and international power following, and justificatory theories of right and wrong being developed by scholars in the wake of this exploitative commerce. For some European powers, though—Poland, Sweden, Spain, come to mind—it is too long ago and too much has happened since for this memory to resonate today. For others, a more recent imperialism has been overwhelmed by defeat in war (Germany; Italy), internal revolution (Portugal), or by the humiliations of foreign occupation (Belgium; Austria; Soviet-controlled Hungary). Only a few states could even hope to continue their imperial projects into the post-war period, France and the Netherlands, for example, but neither did so particularly successfully, and both were in any event already largely shattered by the effects of their recent loss of internal freedom to Nazi Germany. The United Kingdom occupies a unique niche in this pantheon of past power: the country has been the most recent of the great powers to have been able to call the world its own; its colonial reach at the end of the Second World War was vast; it was undefeated in war—indeed (thanks not only to its own stubborn bravery but also to the strength of its allies to the east and west) it could plausibly call itself a victor; its colonial reach at the end of the Second World War remained vast; and its ruling elite had suffered no revolutionary catastrophe since the middle of the seventeenth century. No wonder it was pleased with itself. Why tie the fate of such a place to the minnows and the vanquished across the Channel?

There is a strong dose of this late 1940s exceptionalism still evident in British political culture. It may yet cause the country to leave the Council of Europe. The passion for independence demanded by it is driven by a strong but selective memory of past glory, experienced today as something that is not only within living memory but also within the reach of the future as well. 'Exceptionalism' is attractive to all countries—'Do what I say because I say it, not because I do it: I do what I want'—but very few can carry it off: Britain in the nineteenth century for sure; the USA in the second half of the twentieth and perhaps to some extent still today. But this is not true of Britain now, and nor was it in the 1940s, or even for a long time before that, perhaps since the Edwardian era. It takes strong economic power—hinged upon domination of other territories either directly or indirectly—to be able to make the rules that one wants and enforce a morality on others that one does not practise oneself while pretending to do so. Britain does not have that, has not had it for a long time. The memory lives on as an active force in the culture, however, constantly preying on the politics of the present while just as ceaselessly being foiled by the exigencies imposed by this reality of weakness. Britain has been riding both these horses since the 1940s, a fantasy island constantly being called to account by geographic and socio-economic reality.

On the one hand there was the signing up to the European Convention on Human Rights that parenthood demanded in 1950; on the other there was the very real prospect in the 1950s of litigation between Greece and the UK—made possible by the Convention—that would show up British ethics as (to put it mildly) not sustainable in the colonial context. The worry then was about Cyprus,[3] and in the 1970s the running sore became the litigation taken by Ireland in the European Court of Human Rights where a finding of inhuman and degrading treatment was eventually made against the UK for the conduct of its authorities towards detainees held under Northern Ireland's then emergency laws.[4] In recent years imaginative litigation has sought to push the boundaries of Convention responsibility

---

[3] *Greece v United Kingdom (I); Greece v United Kingdom (II)* (1958–9) 2 *Yearbook of the European Convention on Human Rights* 174.

[4] *Ireland v United Kingdom* (1978) 2 EHRR 25.

further back and further afield, into colonial Africa in the 1950s, with the counter-insurgency actions of yesteryear now drawing unexpected critical attention.[5]

There is another Europe too, of course, the source of so much recent debate in the UK but not one that there has been cause to say much of in this book up to this point. But that Europe also has much to offer on both identity and human rights. Indeed the 'Common Market' of 1957 is another example of the push–pull character of Britain's abiding failure to turn its exceptionalism into something more than nostalgic pleasure. Ignoring the initiative at the outset, the country promptly spent a dozen years or so trying to join before managing finally to do so in 1973, from which point almost immediately the pressure began to build to leave again. By then the European Court of Justice had begun to develop a jurisprudence of human rights,[6] something which the UK inherited upon entry in 1973, and this aspect of the EU's work has grown since that accession. There was the move in the 1980s into the arena of social rights under the leadership of Jacques Delors as Commission President and then further constitutional energy produced the Charter of Fundamental Rights in 2000, a document which eventually became legally binding on the EU with the entry into force of the Treaty of Lisbon in December 2009.[7] Since that time therefore the EU has had its own rights charter, and of course the enforcement of Community law is more direct, less tortuous than the implementation of Strasbourg decisions. So far as the EU's rights framework is concerned, to recall an image we have already used in relation to the country's attitude to the Strasbourg Court, the UK has throughout acted like an agitated parent on the edges of a children's football match, disagreeing with the

---

[5] *Mutua and others v The Foreign and Commonwealth Office* [2012] EWHC 2678 (QB).

[6] *Internationale Handelsgesellschaft mbH v Einfuhr- und Vorratsstelle für Getreide und Futtermittel* case 11/70 [1970] ECR 1125.

[7] See <http://ec.europa.eu/justice/fundamental-rights/charter/index_en.htm> [accessed 22 February 2016].

flow of play, calling for special treatment for their beloved from time to time, screaming abuse on occasion but never quite pulling their child away. Every European member state has its fetishes of course— the endless protocols and declarations at the end of each concluded treaty bear witness to this. Britain's determination has been to restrict the operation of EU social rights protection so far as it can, and this quickly became intertwined with scepticism about human rights to produce disdain for the whole Charter project.[8]

We should pause to ask why the European Union has embraced human rights in this way. The answer tells us a lot about the under-regarded role of human rights as a potential source of identity in any multinational arrangement. In the early days of both organizations, the Council of Europe was supposed to be the lead on such matters as human rights, with the 'common market' sticking to the boring, technical, war-avoiding issues of trade and natural resource management. The first wave of rights adjudication in the 1960s was about ensuring that all countries in this, then quite small, club stuck to the same rules, not stealing a march over each other by cutting on the costs of good behaviour. It was also about binding all its members to the new regime, showing a common commitment to rights that was drawn from and respectful of the constitutional traditions of the member states, rather than being erected in arrogant opposition to them. The later rights personality of the EU came as the organization drove itself further into the field of state-building. All proper countries had constitutional bills of rights and this aspiring single-state was to be no exception. Expansion in its remit towards much more involvement in the lives of Europeans was to be matched by the protective umbrella offered by the six 'rights and freedoms' of the Charter 'solemnly proclaimed' in 2000: dignity; freedoms; equality; solidarity; citizens' rights; and justice. The Charter's preamble talks of the

---

[8] See the Declaration Concerning the Charter of Fundamental Rights of the European Union, and Protocol 30 on the Application of the Charter of Fundamental Rights of the European Union to Poland and to the United Kingdom, Lisbon Treaty (n 7).

'peoples of Europe' being 'resolved to share a peaceful future based on common values' which involves strengthening 'the protection of fundamental rights' 'while respecting the diversity of the cultures and traditions of the peoples of Europe as well as the national identities of the Member States'.[9] Human rights are the glue that binds the polity together, giving a common colour to what is otherwise diverse, setting out an entry test for aspiring members and then providing an ethical guide for all once they are within its jurisdictional space. Europe has no king, or overarching governing unit or singular foundation myth in which everyone can share. It is a melting pot but one out of which—with the vital ingredient of human rights added—a decent cosmopolitan meal can be made, one which all feel they can eat.

In the United Kingdom, almost unnoticed, human rights have crept into the same position as a binding agent whose adhesive qualities (it is no exaggeration to say) help to preserve in place the whole national project. Like the European Union the UK is a multinational experiment. So far as the country as a whole is concerned, and in a way that is reminiscent of the EU's use of the term, human rights have become an important way of establishing a set of irreducibles in a culture that values tolerance and diversity. Unlike other jurisdictions with greater certainty over what it entails to be a citizen of a specific place, Britain has made a great virtue of not being sure of what is involved in being British. Even the citizenship was of the 'United Kingdom and Colonies' until 1983, and from that point on the national status has been divided up between various kinds of citizens (not to mention the Irish who despite being neither British nor Commonwealth have enjoyed being everything (free movement; the right to vote; automatic residency rights; access to social benefits)). All this confusion has been especially valuable in the management of the waves of immigration that have occurred since the 1950s. The emphasis in the UK has been less 'when in Rome do as the Romans do' and more 'live and let live'.

[9] See <http://www.europarl.europa.eu/charter/pdf/text_en.pdf> [accessed 22 February 2016].

A sophisticated but controversial expression of what this involves in the religious context was articulated by the then Archbishop of Canterbury Dr Rowan Williams in a speech in the Royal Courts of Justice on 7 February 2008 in which he outlined an approach to religion that sought to combine tolerance with respect for fundamental human rights.[10] But the impression given by media treatment of his remarks was of a religious leader intent on insulating all faith-based behaviour from the oversight of the law, and this caused great controversy at the time.[11] But a vital part of what Williams was saying then was about the need for a societal floor past which religiously supported bad behaviour would not be allowed to fall. This applies to cultural practices as much as it does to faith. There are limits to the variety which the state otherwise welcomes among its people, one rooted in the need to adhere to the law for sure, but the other more general, informing the content of that law and—beyond the law—the assessment that we must all make of the differences that we encounter. This second control on diversity is our sense of what our polity imposes on all of us in the name of the protection of fundamental human rights. These rights belong to no faction but are rather owned by us all. They set the basic rules in an otherwise very open-minded politico-legal culture. Now human rights understood in this way go beyond the Human Rights Act, but that measure stands as an important indicator of our society's direction of travel, towards celebration of the different (within limits) rather than an imposed homogeneity rooted in the versions of Britishness dictated to the rest of us by those in power. (We return to this problem in Chapter 13.)

Now to the various national dimensions. An enticing aspect of the country we are discussing is its uncertainty about its name. Britain or Great Britain? Neither if we wish to remember Northern Ireland. And

---

[10] Civil and Religious Law in England: A Religious Perspective <http://rowanwilliams. archbishopofcanterbury.org/articles.php/1137/archbishops-lecture-civil-and-religious-law-in-england-a-religious-perspective> [accessed 22 February 2016].

[11] 'Archbishop backs Sharia law for Moslems' *Guardian* 7 February 2008 <http://www. theguardian.com/uk/2008/feb/07/religion.world> [accessed 7 March 2016].

what of those other places for which the state has a responsibility of sorts, the Channel Islands, the Isle of Man—not quite as 'British' as the Isle of Wight, but not exactly Iceland either. The proper title is the United Kingdom of Great Britain and Northern Ireland, expanded from its previous 'United Kingdom of Great Britain' after the English–Scottish Union in 1707, but reduced by the independence of much of Ireland (in 1922) from its grandest point as the United Kingdom of Great Britain and Ireland (from 1801). The upsurge of national sentiment in Scotland and Wales that has been such a feature of politics in the past forty years has been managed by arrangements for the devolution of power that have placed an obligation to respect human rights at the core of their negotiated settlements. Both the Scotland Act 1998 and the Government of Wales Act of the same year (together with later legislative amendments) require the devolved authorities not to make any subordinate legislation or do any other act which is incompatible with any of the rights in the European Convention on Human Rights.[12] Nor can either of the law-making bodies created for each place tamper with any of the same rights.[13] Public power exercised in both places outside the devolved arrangements must in the usual way respect the Human Rights Act itself. The control here, therefore, is both the Human Rights Act and, more directly so far as the devolved authorities are concerned, the European Convention itself. So far as the latter is concerned, the devolution legislation allows (unlike the treatment accorded to Westminster's primary legislation) the quashing of (devolved) legislation which contravenes its terms. The centrality of human rights protection to the constitutional settlements in both parts of Britain has made repeal of the Human Rights Act more difficult to manage than English-centric politicians might have expected. In its recent report the

---

[12] Scotland Act 1998, s 57(2); for Wales see now Government of Wales Act 2006, s 81(1).

[13] Scotland Act s 29(2)(d); for Wales see now Government of Wales Act 2006, s 108(6)(c).

European Union Committee of the House of Lords reported, wholly unsurprisingly, 'strong support for the role of the European Convention' in both Scotland and Wales.[14]

And then of course there is Northern Ireland. As we have noted the Province had been the subject of long-running litigation in the 1970s between the United Kingdom and Ireland over the ill-treatment of detainees by British forces,[15] and disputes around human rights (often in the Strasbourg Court) had become a feature of the seemingly endless conflict that gripped this part of the United Kingdom from 1968 right through to the Good Friday Agreement of 1998.[16] The resolution of the often bloody campaign of violence in which the subversive Irish Republican Army (or IRA) engaged was predicated on a new-found expression of support for human rights on the part of the United Kingdom state which it had long opposed. Needless to say this advocacy of human rights had not been the reason for the violence in the first place; the goal of the resurgent Republican movement had been a 'reunification' of Ireland as an independent Republic encompassing the whole island. But as the likelihood of a success of this tangible sort receded, so defeat came to be masked in the language of victory on the human rights front. The Northern Ireland Act of 1998 delivered on this aspect of the Good Friday deal, and subsequent developments of it have all stood by it. Respect for human rights, exemplified in a commitment to the European Convention on Human Rights, is therefore a central pillar of the resolution of this conflict in a way that goes beyond the requirement to act compatibly with the Convention that is also (as with Scotland and Wales) a feature of these

---

[14] European Union Committee, The UK, the EU and a British Bill of Rights (12th Report of 2015–16, HL 139, 9 May 2016), at para 181.

[15] See n 4.

[16] A McColgan, 'Lessons from the Past? Northern Ireland Terrorism Now and Then, and the Human Rights Act' in T Campbell, K Ewing, and A Tomkins (eds), The Legal Protection of Human Rights: Sceptical Essays (Oxford: Oxford University Press, 2011) ch 9; C A Gearty, 'The Cost of Human Rights: English Judges and the Northern Irish Troubles' (1994) 37 Current Legal Problems 19–40.

devolved arrangements.[17] There is an international dimension too with the Republic of Ireland committing itself to incorporation of the Convention, achieved in 2003,[18] and with no current suggestion of any reneging on the promise.

The Conservative strategy document on rights, written before the party secured a governing majority at the 2015 general election, makes little or no mention of the wider UK aspects of its plan to repeal the Human Rights Act.[19] The proposals made thus far by the Tories make very clear who they think 'we' are. Over recent decades the party's reach across the United Kingdom has shrunk markedly, its unionist dimension disappearing with it. The Tory Party's now thoroughly English perspective has led it to drive through changes to parliamentary procedure which empower English MPs to vote on English matters without the aggravation of any of the Celtic fringe joining them in the lobbies.[20] A respect for human rights is not the only thing that makes sense of the country's disparate communities and nations, but it is an important one. Its value may only be fully appreciated when it is gone.

[17] Northern Ireland Act 1998 s 6(2)(c); s 24(1)(a).
[18] European Convention on Human Rights Act 2003.
[19] *Protecting Human Rights in the UK: The Conservatives' Proposals for Changing Britain's Human Rights Laws* (October 2014).
[20] T Fairclough, 'Constitutional change, standing orders and EVEL: a step in the wrong direction?' UK Const L Blog 22 February 2016: <https://ukconstitutionallaw.org/2016/02/22/thomas-fairclough-constitutional-change-standing-orders-and-evel-a-step-in-the-wrong-direction/> [accessed 25 February 2016].

PART IV
THE FUTURE

12

REPEAL

How Can We Tell?

Reporting in May 2016, the European Union Committee of the House of Lords was clearly puzzled by the way the whole debate about a British bill of rights had developed over the previous few months. The idea now 'appeared a far less ambitious proposal'[1] than it had just a short while before. What was being suggested 'did not appear to depart significantly from the Human Rights Act'.[2] After hearing the Secretary of State for Justice at his rhetorical best, the Committee found itself not persuaded but rather 'unsure why a British Bill of Rights was really necessary'.[3]

The problem when political fantasy collides with legal facts is that fantasy can never win. In a system that values the rule of law, the courtroom is a place of reason with rational argument taking pride of place over rhetoric. The legal interactions that precede such adversarial jousts are the same. From the initial solicitor's consultation through counsel's opinion to the letter before action, all is driven by a judgment about how the law will apply to the facts that are found by the judge or judges that will eventually—if things are not settled before—have possession of the case. There is no room here for the sorts of sleights of hand that draw applause at a party conference or get a busy

---

[1] European Union Committee, The UK, the EU and a British Bill of Rights (12th Report of 2015–16, HL 139, 9 May 2016), at para 45.
[2] Ibid para 46.
[3] Ibid.

On Fantasy Island: Britain, Europe, and Human Rights. First Edition. Conor Gearty.
© Conor Gearty 2016. Published 2016 by Oxford University Press.

Justice Secretary through eight minutes on the *Today* programme. The general public had a glimpse of the integrity of the legal process during the Leveson Inquiry of 2011–12: lawyers with a well-studied brief and all day to cross-examine witnesses before an audience schooled in the verifiability of assertions are a frightening spectacle for the smoothest of politicians (even those with nothing to hide).[4] Now of course, as we have seen at various points throughout this book, judges sometimes grow the law in a way that makes life easier for them and their colleagues—their calculations can be judicious as well as judicial. In the past their willingness to conform to power went even further at times, into raw compliance: we were very critical of that tendency at the start of this book. But on the key question of taking legislative and case texts seriously, these days they are likely to be unbudgeable. This is what has made life difficult for those who have argued for radical change in the field of human rights: their persuasive powers have hinged on fantasy about the current situation and wishful thinking about what can be done about a problem that does not in reality exist. The result is likely to be either no change at all or a damp squib of a 'reform'—the sort of fudge which those determined to continue to ignore facts can criticize but which everyone else who has to deal with the real world can see is all that is available.

Take the wishful thinking first. The initial big push of the fantasists/sceptics was, it will be recalled, to get rid of the Strasbourg Court, in other words to pull out altogether from the adjudicatory framework that gives teeth to the European Convention on Human Rights. The savaging of the prisoner voting case, *Hirst v United Kingdom*,[5] was as we have also seen partly designed to generate a widespread public hunger for just such a change and as we also no doubt recall there could hardly have been a more unmeritorious 'human rights victim' than John Hirst

---

[4] The Leveson Inquiry: Culture Practice and Ethics of the Press: <http://webarchive. nationalarchives.gov.uk/20140122145147/http:/www.levesoninquiry.org.uk/> [accessed 26 February 2016].

[5] *Hirst v United Kingdom (no 2)* (2005) 42 EHRR 849.

through whom to make such a case. But the Conservative Party has been quite unable to deliver on this promise. In government on their own since 2015—and so without the convenient reasonableness of their Liberal Democrat coalition colleagues—Tory Ministers have been disconcerted to discover that withdrawal from the Council of Europe (which denying the Convention's Court would necessarily entail) has become politically impossible of achievement, a fact now evident even to the more Eurosceptic of this inherently Eurosceptic political party. The intrusions of the Strasbourg Court are few and far between, and even when they arrive rarely impinge seriously on policy for any length of time.[6] The destructive impact of withdrawal on British influence in Europe and the world is now seen by all to be—to use a Europeanism—wholly disproportionate to the supposed gains achieved by such a move.

With departure from the Convention off the table, attention inevitably shifted to the Human Rights Act. Here we find uppermost the fantasies that drove much of the first part of this book—you cannot change a law for the better if it has never been what you have claimed it to be in the first place. Thus the rights set out in schedule 1 are limited to those to be found in the Convention and as we have discussed are hardly radical in their impact or subversive of the economic framework within which policy is made. The role that section 2 allocates to the much maligned Strasbourg Court is more marginal that early judicial interpretations warranted and is now correctly seen as less dictatorial than was once assumed.[7] The same is true of sections 3 and 4, where the courts are given strong interpretative powers, it is true, but parliamentary sovereignty is specifically preserved, something that section 3(2) of the Act is quite clear about.[8] Parliamentary sovereignty cannot be restored if it has not been taken away. And anyway if there are residual problems for that

[6] See Ch 7.
[7] See Ch 7.
[8] See Ch 6.

sovereignty, they result from continued Council of Europe oversight, in other words the very thing (as we have just seen) it has now been accepted cannot be changed. The Human Rights Act makes very little difference to this—indeed if it does have an impact it is probably one that reduces adverse rulings by the Strasbourg Court by giving the local courts the chance to stake out the right answers which the principle of subsidiarity can then be deployed to protect.[9] It is the same for the rest of the Act—very little of it does what its opponents have claimed.

With change limited in all these ways, it is hardly surprising that the reform to be proposed is not likely to be earth-shattering. There might be a bit of fiddling with section 2 to make it say the same thing but in a different way, and a fresh control on the judicial power of interpretation in section 3 (returning to the 'reasonableness' test rejected in 1997–8 perhaps[10]). The damages section in section 8 might be rewritten to make it even clearer that this is not an award to be made lightly (though as we have seen business has gained from this provision and may fight to retain it in its current form[11]). It just possibly might be made easier to ignore declarations of incompatibility, or new 'guidance' may be given to judges on when to make them.[12] Possible mean-spirited dilutions might include some or all of the following: removing the chance of soldiers and victims of army abuse abroad to bring actions against abuse of their rights by the armed forces; giving courts an obligation to consider the national interest when being asked to keep a foreigner in the UK because his or her rights are at risk elsewhere; removing the right of those whose privacy is invaded to sue the press for the damage done to them; restricting opportunities to be heard for

---

[9] See Protocol No 15 adding 'subsidiarity' to the preamble: <http://www.echr.coe.int/Documents/Protocol_15_ENG.pdf> [accessed 7 March 2016].

[10] See Ch 6.

[11] See Ch 8.

[12] Taking the hint from the unfortunate majority reasoning in R (Nicklinson) v Ministry of Justice; R (AM) and R (AP) v Director of Public Prosecutions [2014] UKSC 38, [2015] AC 657 perhaps, see Ch 5.

many vulnerable people subject to state power; undoing one or two cases specifically (such as *Rutherford* if its harrowing facts allow the Court of Appeal's judgment to withstand assault in the Supreme Court[13]); perhaps one or two other things. And even with regard to all these, Strasbourg will remain available to be engaged to restore the status quo not via a Human Rights Act which is no longer available but through the UK's ongoing international law obligation to implement that Court's decisions. We will be back to the 1980s and early 1990s when Ministers shouted about Strasbourg with much greater venom than they can muster today, a time of domestic judicial impotence that the Human Rights Act was designed to end. Crucially repeal of the Human Rights Act along the lines set out above will increase foreign engagement with British 'sovereignty' not diminish it.

That is supposing the changes will be tolerated by the domestic courts first. The point may seem a counter-intuitive one. Parliament is sovereign after all and it is primary legislation that is being proposed. But the plan is to prune back on the Human Rights Act, not on the common law that operates independently of it. And suppose the common law were to deliver exactly the same outcomes as those which the attack on the Human Rights Act had been designed to prevent? Tied up with this is the larger question of the extent to which changes already achieved by the Human Rights Act are now embedded in our law, and not reliant on the continued survival of the Act for their existence. A way of testing the point is to imagine that the Conservatives managed to recover their original gumption and achieve repeal of the Human Rights Act, lock, stock, and barrel, finally taking the hated European Convention on Human Rights out of the domestic equation, daring its Court in Strasbourg and the Committee of Ministers that implements its judgments to do their worst. Or imagine the party was to go even further and pull out of the Convention altogether. Neither of these positions is rooted in fundamental

---

[13] See Ch 9.

mistakes of fact, whatever view we take of their merits. The complications standing in the way of such a set of changes come in many shapes and sizes. We have a politico-legal environment that has been partly shaped by the Human Rights Act it is true but which now (whatever may have been the case in 1998) might well be capable of retaining a strong rights perspective without it.

To start with whether the repeal be radical or partial there would be the problem of what to do with laws that have already been subject to statutory interpretation on the basis of the operation of section 3 of the Human Rights Act: the partners of deceased tenants in same-sex relationships;[14] the inquests that examine more than the mere cause of death where there is some element of potential official culpability;[15] the immigrant couple who no longer need to pay a fortune to get married;[16] the family who have a chance to explain themselves before being evicted from their home;[17] the asylum seeker for whom the prohibition on inhuman and degrading treatment in article 3 of the Convention has ensured that he or she eats;[18] and so on—there are a myriad of examples, many of them covered in earlier chapters of this book. Are these interpretations now to be unravelled under the *force majeure* of repeal, either of the whole package or of the bits of the Act (section 3 for example) which drove these interpretative outcomes? Will things depend on whether the law under scrutiny was passed before or after the Human Rights Act (thus indicating a notional awareness (or not) of that legislation on Parliament's part)? What about those statutes where the Human Rights Act requirements are specifically referred to, as in the destitute asylum case, *Limbuela*?[19] Will such obligations survive repeal of their parent Act or fall away with it?

[14] See Ch 6.
[15] See Ch 10.
[16] See Ch 6.
[17] See Ch 9.
[18] See Ch 9.
[19] See Ch 9.

Does it depend on whether the repealing measure remembers to obliterate them as well?

There is a further, disturbing side to this from the perspective of those wishing to make a clean break with the Human Rights Act. The rights it embedded in UK law did not exist in a domestic legal vacuum before being laid out for all the startled judges to see for the first time in 1998. In Chapter 2 we were very critical of the record of the British judges in days gone past, not least in regards to their attitude to civil liberties (and therefore to human rights). But there had been exceptions to the norm from time to time. As early as the mid-1970s for example, a couple of senior judges had sought to weave the Convention into the fabric of the common law's own powers of statutory interpretation. In 1975, in R (Bhajan Singh) v Secretary of State for Home Affairs,[20] Lord Denning had asserted (giving judgment as Master of the Rolls, one of the most senior judges in the land) that the courts 'should take the Convention into account...whenever interpreting a statute which affects the rights and liberties of the individual'.[21] In a similar vein the highly regarded Lord Scarman had declared in a judgment the same year that it was 'the duty of the courts, so long as they do not defy or disregard clear and unequivocal provision, to construe statutes in a manner which promotes, not endangers' the basic rights to be found in the ECHR.[22] Now maybe it can be argued that here were two unusually creative figures on the bench for the times, able to spot the 'incoming tide' of European law[23] or to give an annual series of lectures on the theme of English Law: The New Dimension.[24] But if they had once been outriders, they were soon joined by enough colleagues to take the position closer to the mainstream. As early as 1980 Lord

[20] [1976] QB 198.
[21] Ibid at p 207.
[22] R (Phansopkar) v Secretary of State for Home Affairs; R (Begum) v Secretary of State for Home Affairs [1975] 3 All ER 497, at p 511.
[23] H P Bulmer v J Bollinger SA [1974] Ch 401, at p 418 per Lord Denning MR.
[24] London: Stevens and Sons, 1974 (Lord Scarman).

Fraser was joining Lord Scarman (now on the Appellate Committee of the House of Lords) in referring to the Convention in the course of a ruling on the meaning of a court and the operation of the law of contempt.[25] Ideas about human rights accelerated their creep into the 'judicial cerebellum' during the period of judicial modernization that we discussed in Chapter 3, the decade or so leading up to the enactment of the Human Rights Act. During this time, extra-judicial interventions in favour of incorporation were accompanied by efforts to develop a new judge-made head of judicial review which took rights into account. By 1995 a progressive High Court judge, Sir Stephen Sedley, felt able to note in the course of giving judgment in one case that '[o]nce it is accepted that the standards articulated in the [European] convention are standards which both march with those of the common law and inform the jurisprudence of the European Union, it becomes unreal and potentially unjust to develop English public law without reference to it.'[26]

All of this was, it is worth emphasizing, achieved *before* the Human Rights Act had even been drafted. Articulated in the limbo period after the measure's enactment but before its implementation, the remarks which we earlier noted, by Lord Hoffmann in a case from 2000 about the extent to which the common law was committed to the protection of human rights, have become one of the most frequently cited authorities in the decades that have followed, Human Rights Act or no Human Rights Act.[27] It was as though this measure enacted in the first term of the Blair government was merely confirmatory of a pivot towards rights that the genius of the common law had already been in the course of successfully executing. Not even the most ambitious of Tory revolutionaries plans to abolish the common law; in fact they are excited by returning to it its lost power. These dicta suggest, though,

---

[25] *Attorney General v BBC* [1981] AC 303. See also *Bugdaycay v Secretary of State for the Home Department* [1987] AC 514.

[26] *R (McQuillan) v Secretary of State for the Home Department* [1995] 4 All ER 400, at p 422.

[27] *R (Simms) v Secretary of State for the Home Department* [2000] 2 AC 115, at pp 131–2.

that this great beast might itself be a human rights oracle and not the creature of the past beloved of Professor Finnis and his disciples.[28]

Let us now push this point a bit further. We should recall that the 'common law' has a myriad of meanings—in the sense we are using the term here it connotes the operation of judge-made rules on not only the common law proper (disputes about the meaning of a law which originates in the cases themselves and not from any legislative intervention) but also the judicial approach to the interpretation of statutes and to the control of administrative discretion (invariably rooted in statute but also on occasion a creature of the old royal prerogative power, now for the most part deployed by government Ministers on the Crown's behalf). There are no legislative codes setting out how these second and third activities should be conducted—the courts have been making it up as they go along, just as with the first category of the 'pure' common law. If the trend noted above were to be revived post repeal of the Human Rights Act, it would be perfectly possible (probable even) that the judges would continue to deploy the Convention as a guide to the discharge of all three of their 'common law' responsibilities. A presumption in favour of respecting UK international obligations (which include various UN instruments so would be relevant even if the Convention were ditched) would be deployed to guide the interpretation of statutes where their human rights compatibility was in issue—maybe not as strong as the old section 3(1) but not far off it. The members of the Supreme Court have already been doing this kind of work with the UN Convention on the Rights of the Child so it would be a fairly easy step to expand this sideways into other arenas.[29] It would be even more likely that the courts would invoke the spirit of Lords Denning, Scarman, and Hoffmann to grow the indigenous common law of judicial review so as to embrace human-rights-related criteria such as proportionality within its set of oversight

---

[28] See Ch 2.

[29] See eg *R (SG) v Secretary of State for Work and Pensions* [2015] UKSC 16, [2015] 1 WLR 1449.

criteria. Once through this door human rights (by then understood broadly no doubt, and so extending beyond the Convention, whether still functioning in the UK or not) could quickly be relied upon to retake the ground that had been previously been staked out by the now repealed or truncated Human Rights Act. Even the mainstream common law—the cases that simply grow the old authorities and rely on no statute or engage no governmental actor—would not be immune to this rights drift. This may come as a surprise to the press whose lobbying efforts are no doubt being aimed at removing the Convention's right to respect for privacy from the domestic equation.[30] However, the way the common law has grown its jurisprudence here has been by developing pre-existing remedies in a way that coincides with the statutory protection afforded article 8's guarantee of respect for privacy, it is true, but is almost certainly capable of functioning without it. It is the same with the other Convention-based common law changes since 1998.[31]

It might even be thought that the judges have themselves been anticipating repeal of the Act by the way in which they have recently been approaching it. A marked shift was evident in three Supreme Court cases decided in quick succession in the summer of 2014. In *Kennedy v The Charity Commission*,[32] the Supreme Court took the opportunity of a case on freedom of information concerning access to information on certain of the Commission's inquiries to flag up for advocates the desirability of adopting a new approach to rights. Strasbourg decisions were not to be as relied upon as slavishly as heretofore and more attention was to be paid to, as Lord Mance put it, 'the domestic legal position'.[33] The modern principles of judicial review extended beyond EU and Convention law and were capable of operating at a deep level of scrutiny where 'a common law right or constitutional

---

[30] See Ch 10.

[31] See Chs 3 and 10.

[32] [2014] UKSC 20, [2015] AC 455.

[33] Ibid para 46 per Lord Mance (with whom Lords Neuberger and Clarke agreed).

principle [was] in issue':[34] It could do this without the crutch of the Convention. In Lord Toulson's view, since enactment of the Human Rights Act 'there has sometimes been a baleful and unnecessary tendency to overlook the common law. It needs to be emphasised that it was not the purpose of the Human Rights Act that the common law should become an ossuary.'[35] Five of the seven judges held to this position, Lords Neuberger, Clarke, and Sumption agreeing with Lords Mance and Toulson. In vain did Lords Carnwath and Wilson in dissent complain that this common law turn had been 'unsupported by any of the parties before us'[36] and as a result the judges had 'not had the advantage of full argument'.[37]

In a judgment shortly after *Kennedy*, *A v BBC*,[38] Lady Hale and Lords Wilson, Reed, Hughes, and Hodge joined in, stressing that 'the starting point' for analysis even in the field of rights needed to be the common law, even if the Convention analysis continued to govern where the end points of both were different.[39] In the very next case in which the Court gave judgment after *A v BBC*, *Barnes v The Eastenders Group*,[40] counsel were actually steered away by the justices from a Convention argument (on property rights) into the more traditional world of unjust enrichment.[41] Against this background it is not surprising that in a case in the same court a year later, one involving such an obvious freedom of speech issue as an attempt to prevent publication of a book, the Supreme Court analysed the matter almost entirely on the basis of a hitherto obscure nineteenth-century tort case, reaching the Convention and its right to freedom of expression seemingly only

---

[34] Ibid para 55.

[35] Ibid para 133. Lord Neuberger and Lord Clarke agreed also with the judgment of Lord Toulson.

[36] Ibid para 202.

[37] Ibid para 234.

[38] [2014] UKSC 25, [2015] AC 588.

[39] Ibid para 57 per Lord Reed, giving a judgment with which all his colleagues agreed.

[40] [2014] UKSC 26, [2015] AC 1.

[41] See ibid para 97: judgment of Lord Toulson, with whom all his colleagues agreed.

with reluctance, and contriving not to mention the Human Rights Act or a single Strasbourg decision across the two judgments and 122 paragraphs.[42] It is as though the Act has been dispensed with even before it has been repealed.

We can expect more such revivalist common law emulations of human rights in the future, whatever happens to the Human Rights Act; that law may well have been the ladder that allowed the common law to ascend to its current ethical heights but it is not necessary to it remaining in the lofty position it now occupies. Now it is only one step from this position to say that actually the common law is so wonderful that it ought to have superiority over Parliament itself, a position once held by the judges in eras gone by, of course, but which one might have thought had been laid to rest by democratic revolution. In fact that is not the case. At least some of the judges have allowed the enthusiasm of certain academic scholars for such a possibility to lead them to what Lord Neuberger in a Melbourne speech called 'the interesting point' of whether the courts can in fact overturn Parliament itself.[43] A mini-spate of cases in the Supreme Court has allowed the idea to grow without the unanimous disavowal that would surely have been its fate only a little while ago. On any current account the obstacles against such a judicial overriding of Parliament would need to be very high: some draconian flouting of the rule of law or what Lord Neuberger called (and even then only possibly) 'exceptional circumstances'. Perhaps these are what Lord Carswell in *R (Jackson) v Attorney General* referred to (albeit in the context of a law passed under the Parliament Act) as legislative Acts amounting to 'a fundamental disturbance of the building blocks of the constitution'.[44]

[42] *O (A Child) v Rhodes* [2015] UKSC 32, [2016] AC 219. The case that got all the attention was *Wilkinson v Downton* [1897] 2 QB 57 from which an infrequently applied rule had been deduced in later cases.

[43] 'The Role of Judges in Human Rights Jurisprudence: A Comparison of the Australian and UK experiences' Melbourne, 8 August 2014, at para 10: <www.supremecourt.uk/docs/speech-140808.pdf> [accessed 18 March 2016].

[44] *R (Jackson) v Attorney General* [2005] UKHL 56, [2006] 1 AC 26 para 178.

At present, as we have seen, the Human Rights Act positively guarantees parliamentary sovereignty, in section 3(2). But if this steer were to be removed, accompanied perhaps by a shift in the direction of a German constitutional model complete with a British bill of rights (for both of which the Prime Minister is said to be an enthusiast),[45] might not the courts be emboldened to be more assertive? It would be a neat irony if repeal of the Human Rights Act produced the very mischief which repeal was designed to prevent.

[45] 'Tories look to tame powers of European Courts' *Financial Times* 15 February 2016: <http://www.ft.com/cms/s/0/30724834-d0ba-11e5-92a1-c5e23ef99c77.html> [accessed 7 March 2016]. It is not obvious that the Prime Minister is as fully informed on the German model as perhaps he might be: R Masterman and J E K Murkens, 'Skirting Supremacy and Subordination: The Constitutional Authority of the United Kingdom Supreme Court' [2013] *Public Law* 800–20.

13

BRITISH VALUES

Shrinking into (Little) England

Who are we? As we saw in Chapter 11, the Human Rights Act helps answer that question so far as this country is concerned, by providing one strand to a larger story, that of a Britain integrated within diverse communities of a local, regional, and international character. The United Kingdom has always been outward-facing, the place itself constructed out of national alliances within these islands and thereafter growing its prosperity through a self-interested commitment to free trade. Britain long relished its position in the world as controller of colonies, creator of an Empire, and afterwards (when these had become unsustainable) as leading light in a British commonwealth of its own creation. The commitments to democracy and the rule of law that are now benchmarks of the organization of the political across much of the world can be plausibly said to be reflective of early experiments with both in an ancient England with which (and uniquely) a direct connection (via the courts, Parliament, and the monarchy) can still be made with the United Kingdom of today.

It is quite a record, but from England's point of view it is a story of domination, not partnership. Wales was absorbed by conquest, the kingdoms of Scotland and Ireland finessed into union arrangements against a background of past conflict and the willingness of the larger partner in each relationship to continue the fight. The imperial reach was always about an allegiance to the Crown that was achieved (and retained) by arms, not won by argument. Even the contemporary success of the values of democracy and the rule of law is largely due

On Fantasy Island: Britain, Europe, and Human Rights. First Edition. Conor Gearty.

to the happy accident of their being inherited by a set of American colonies that freed themselves at the end of the eighteenth century and went on in time to be able to dictate the meaning of right and wrong on the world stage in the way that Britain had once been able also to do. That time of English/British hegemony is long over, the external now a force to be reckoned with, a partner to be won over rather than a stranger to defeat into an embrace. The story has been one of decline rather than precipitous collapse, the structures of power surviving while power ebbs from their every joint. It is hardly surprising that memories of these past days linger on in the communal mind.

As this book has often had the chance to illustrate, hostility to the Human Rights Act has been part of an attempt to buck this trend towards marginalization on the world stage. The confident outward-looking British face retreats into an inward-looking English one, seeking as it does so to compensate for decline with tighter control over its (much-reduced) backyard. As with the referendum on the European Union just concluded, the antagonists of the human rights status quo have drawn their energy from an incendiary combination of the negative with the nostalgic: negative about the world outside, in this case the Strasbourg judges who control us and the nasty foreigners at home whom we can't expel on account of this law; nostalgic about a past time of social ease in Britain and dominance abroad, a period when human rights needed no tutor from far away but (as civil liberties) were a natural part of an Englishman's birthright. The national (and gender) identification at the end here is deliberate. The movement 'against abroad' and 'for the past' is very much an English project and its political and intellectual leaders are almost entirely male. (It was not an accident that John Finnis's hymn of praise to the past (with which we started Chapter 2) should have been, as we noted at the time, so exclusively engaged with the achievements of men, as well as so English in orientation.)

It is this sense of loss that has produced in recent years a movement towards the legislative assertion of 'British values'. Initially easily ignored, lampooned even, as another search for an irrecoverable (and in its adopted shape largely invented) past, this project has gathered pace in recent years, opening another front in the war on Europe and human rights and threatening further to destabilize England's inclusive political culture. The move also tells us something about how, in the new order desired by these militant nostalgists, human rights are at risk of being reconceived as a cultural weapon rather than (as at present) a collection of enforceable legal rights. The shift has origins in the Labour administration headed by Tony Blair. After the London bombings of 7 July 2005, proposed legislation prohibiting the glorification of terrorist incidents inevitably raised issues about which past events of this sort were to be regarded as part of the birth story of the nation (the execution of King Charles 1 in 1649; the 'glorious revolution' of 1688) and so outside the ban and which wrongful political violence at home (the Irish Easter rising of 1916?) or abroad (the American colonies' revolt against the British?) was properly to be caught. A modified version of this peculiar form of 'political correctness' eventually reached the statute book in 2006.[1] Some years before this, in 2003, the same government had already initiated CONTEST, a multi-pronged counter-terrorism strategy which had as one of its lead components what its authors described as PREVENT, a policy aimed at tackling the origins of violent extremism so as to prevent its occurrence in the first place. The policy was revised and expanded in 2008–9 by what was still a Labour administration.[2] The term 'extremism' was deliberately used to mark the remit of the programme as extending beyond the legislatively defined terrorists themselves, but in those early days the qualifier 'violent' ensured no spill-over into action against the wider world of antagonistic political ideologies. Quite the opposite in fact; the Blair and then Brown governments saw engagement with non-violent 'extremists' as an important route

---

[1] Terrorism Act 2006, ss 1–4.

[2] House of Commons Home Affairs Committee, *Project CONTEST: The Government's Counter-Terrorism Strategy* 9th Report of 2008–9 HC 212 (7 July 2009) has a wide range of details on the Labour models of CONTEST: <http://www.publications.parliament.uk/pa/cm200809/cmselect/cmhaff/212/212.pdf> [accessed 26 March 2016].

into achieving the effective prevention at which the strategy was aimed. This did, however, necessarily entail interaction with—and some official financial support for—'unsavoury' (albeit non-violent) elements on the outer wings of radical Islam.

The approach irked those sections of the press that are always on the lookout for unnecessary obeisance to an 'enemy within'. More importantly it irritated Gordon Brown's successor in No 10 Downing Street, the Conservatives' leader David Cameron. Early on in his tenure as Prime Minister in a newly formed Conservative–Liberal Democratic administration, he began to reshape the strategy. Speaking in Munich on 5 February 2011, Mr Cameron called on Europe 'to wake up to what is happening in our own countries'.[3] In truth 'Islamist extremism is a political ideology' which is adopted not just by 'those who support terrorism to promote their ultimate goal' but also by others 'who may reject violence but who accept various parts of the extremist worldview, including real hostility towards western democracy and liberal values'. To those who say that extremists can be used to challenge the violent, the Prime Minister's reply was succinct: 'I say nonsense.' Turning to the 'British experience', Mr Cameron continued:

> In the UK, some young men find it hard to identify with the traditional Islam practiced at home by their parents, whose customs can seem staid when transplanted to modern Western countries. But these young men also find it hard to identify with Britain too, because we have allowed the weakening of our collective identity. Under the doctrine of state multi-culturalism, we have encouraged different cultures to live separate lives, apart from each other and apart from the mainstream. We've failed to provide a vision of society to which they feel they want to belong. We've even tolerated these segregated communities behaving in ways that run completely counter to our values.

It was this 'doctrine of multiculturalism' that had led to Muslim groups being 'showered with public money' by the Brown administration and

---

[3] The full speech, which was to the Munich Security Conference, is at <https://www.gov.uk/government/speeches/pms-speech-at-munich-security-conference> [accessed 16 March 2016].

had led us as well to be 'too cautious frankly—frankly, even fearful—to stand up to' the 'unacceptable views or practices [that] come from someone who isn't white'.

The speech made an immediate impact in that it fed into a new iteration of the CONTEST strategy that followed that summer, the third overall and the coalition's first.[4] This elaborated on the connection between extremism and violence to which the speech in Munich had alluded, making clear that it was no longer to be enough for 'extremist groups and speakers' to avoid their responsibilities by 'deliberately and carefully stay[ing] within the law'.[5] All such cleverness did was produce a 'radicalisation…process by which people come to support, and in some cases to participate in terrorism'.[6] To break this escalator driving the radical to violence it was the radicalization itself ('the process by which a person comes to support terrorism and forms of extremism leading to terrorism'[7]) that needed to be stopped. Given that you could no longer recognize extremism by finding in it a necessary connection with violence, a new definition was needed, to catch it at this prior stage, early on in its upwards journey to mayhem. The government settled on 'the vocal or active opposition to fundamental British values, including democracy, the rule of law, individual liberty and mutual respect and tolerance of different faiths and beliefs'. Extremism was also specifically extended to include all 'calls for the death of members of our armed forces, whether in this country or overseas'.[8]

We shall come back in a moment to this definition of extremism but first we should note a gradual ratcheting up of the intensity of the anti-extremism discourse in the years that have followed since

---

[4] CONTEST Cm 8123 (July 2011): <https://www.gov.uk/government/uploads/system/uploads/attachment_data/file/97994/contest-summary.pdf> [accessed 16 March 2016].

[5] Ibid para 2.53.

[6] Ibid para 2.59.

[7] *Prevent Strategy* (Cm 8092, June 2011), annex A glossary of terms: <https://www.gov.uk/government/publications/prevent-strategy-2011> [accessed 23 March 2016].

[8] Ibid.

Mr Cameron's Munich speech. Liberal Democratic involvement in government initially slowed things down but even they could not stop enactment, in early 2015, of a statutory duty on a variety of public bodies 'in the exercise of [their] functions' to 'have due regard to the need to prevent people from being drawn into terrorism'.[9] The authorities specified as subject to the duty ranged across local government, criminal justice, education, child care, health, and the police.[10] Acting under another provision in the same law, the Secretary of State for the Home Department Theresa May proceeded to issue guidance to the affected bodies 'about the exercise of their duty' under this Act.[11] Here the connection between terrorism (the subject of the legislative duty of course) and 'extremism' (as previously defined) was made clear: 'Terrorist groups often draw on extremist ideology, developed by extremist organisations. Some people who join terrorist groups have previously been members of extremist organisations and have been radicalised by them.'[12] Lest there be any doubt, the guidance draws attention to the fact that the 'Prevent strategy was explicitly changed in 2011 to deal with all forms of terrorism and with non-violent extremism, which can create an atmosphere conducive to terrorism and can popularise views which terrorists then exploit'.[13] With this new law, the escalator first imagined in 2011 was placed firmly before the authorities and their obligation to prevent its early users turning into mass-killers drawn firmly to their attention, this time with the backing of Parliament and a statutory duty attached. And this escalator could start anywhere. 'Frontline staff who engage with the public should understand what radicalisation means and why people

[9] Counter-terrorism and Security Act 2015, s 26(1).

[10] Ibid sched 6.

[11] See further the Counter-Terrorism and Security Act 2015 (Risk of Being Drawn into Terrorism) (Amendment and Guidance) Regulations 2015, s 29 (1). All the sets of guidance issued are conveniently gathered together at <https://www.gov.uk/government/publications/prevent-duty-guidance> [accessed 26 March 2016].

[12] See Guidance (n 11) para 7.

[13] Ibid para 8.

may be vulnerable to being drawn into terrorism as a consequence of it.'[14] Schools needed to 'be mindful of their existing duties to forbid political indoctrination and secure a balanced presentation of political issues'.[15] Training, the pooling of resources, inter-agency collaboration are among the interventions that are stipulated as necessary with the vigilant eyes of the school inspectors, health regulators, and—above all—the Secretary of State cast over everything, ready to seize the initiative if the specified authorities are judged to be failing.[16] Since the election of May 2015, a further 'counter-extremism strategy' has been issued[17] and new legislation threatened, the purpose of which will be to 'ban extremist organisations that promote hatred and draw people into extremism; restrict the harmful activities of the most dangerous extremist individuals; and restrict access to premises which are repeatedly used to support extremism'.[18]

The government makes no explicit connection between its distaste for human rights and its enthusiasm for counter-extremism, yet the link is there to be made. All societies are naturally predisposed to defend themselves from internal as well as external threats, and democracies have been no exception. We saw some examples in Chapters 2 and 3 of the drive in twentieth-century Britain to prevent ideological opponents of parliamentary democracy from being able to deploy the openness of such a polity so as to achieve by argument an extinction that they could never have brought about by military means: there is something that rings true in a Home Secretary's gibe from the 1920s that the Communists then being harried by the law were not engaged in 'the right type of freedom of speech' to warrant protection.[19] In

[14] Ibid para 18.
[15] Ibid para 64, referring to Education Act 1996, ss 406–7.
[16] Eg paras 54–5 drawing attention to powers to intervene with regard to local authorities under Education Act 1996, s 497A and the Local Government Act 1999, s 15.
[17] *Counter-Extremism Strategy* Cm 9148 (October 2015): <https://www.gov.uk/government/publications/counter-extremism-strategy> [accessed 26 March 2016].
[18] Ibid para 112.
[19] See Ch 2.

wartime the problem of 'fifth columnists' has always been acute,[20] and in more peaceful times the challenge of counter-terrorism policy has been to defeat the violence of political subversives without in the process doing their destructive work for them.[21] Human rights law has not insulated itself from the need for such pragmatic protection. As we have seen, many of the rights set out in the European Convention on Human Rights can be legitimately departed from where this is 'necessary in a democratic society' and there is also the overarching article 17 which did for the Germany Communist Party in the 1950s: 'Nothing in this Convention may be interpreted as implying for any State, group or person any right to engage in any activity or perform any act aimed at the destruction of any of the rights and freedoms set forth herein or at their limitation to a greater extent than is provided for in the Convention.'[22] In 2003, in *Refah Partisi (The Welfare Party) v Turkey* the European Court of Human Rights extended the defensive shield of the Convention to local actions taken to prohibit the political activism of a popular political party that was however judged by the authorities to be a threat to democracy:

> [T]he Court considers that a political party may promote a change in the law or the legal and constitutional structures of the State on two conditions: first, the means used to that end must be legal and democratic; secondly, the change proposed must itself be compatible with fundamental democratic principles. It necessarily follows that a political party whose leaders incite violence or put forward a policy which fails to respect democracy or which is aimed at the destruction of democracy and the flouting of the rights and freedoms recognised in a democracy cannot lay claim to the Convention's protection against penalties imposed on those grounds.[23]

---

[20] *Liversidge v Anderson* [1942] AC 206, see Ch 2.

[21] R English, *Terrorism: How to Respond* (Oxford: Oxford University Press, 2009).

[22] *German Communist Party v Federal Republic of Germany* app 250/57 (1957) 1 *Yearbook of the European Convention on Human Rights* 222 (in French).

[23] (2003) 37 EHRR 1, para 98.

Just as with actions against both internal opponents in wartime and violent subversives in peacetime, the challenge lies in controlling the state's response, in stopping it moving from proportionate self-defence into the imposition of conformity in the name of the public interest. Naturally those doing the main work here—politicians; public authorities; the police; the prosecuting authorities—believe in the institutions they are defending, so it is asking a lot of them to discriminate between those opponents whom they need to stop for the good of the country and those whose defeat would be most welcome to them as political actors and citizens.[24] The courts are inevitably to the fore when it comes to getting this balance right, and of course they too can get caught up in the moment, as both the US Supreme Court and the UK House of Lords did when upholding wartime powers of internment,[25] with each repeating the error later as well, in the USA buckling before the chill to free speech caused by McCarthyism[26] and, in the UK in the 1980s supporting executive action against Sinn Féin's energetic use of the media to support the IRA's political violence in Northern Ireland.[27] The European Court of Human Rights has recently followed up its *Refah Partisi* decision with a ruling upholding the French ban on Islamic dress in public where this covered the face as the Niqab did (the so-called 'burqa ban'), on the basis that the restriction was necessary to facilitate the right of all to live together.[28] Though expressed in neutral terms, here is an undoubted shift in human rights protection away from tangible individual protections for the vulnerable and in the direction of support for the robust assertion in the public sphere of the values of the many, if necessary at the expense of the freedom of the few. It is

[24] C A Gearty, *Civil Liberties* (Oxford: Oxford University Press, 2007) ch 3.

[25] *Korematsu v United States* 323 US 214 (1944); *Liversidge v Anderson* [1942] AC 206.

[26] *Dennis v United States* 341 US 494 (1951).

[27] *R (Brind) v Secretary of State for the Home Department* [1991] 1 AC 696.

[28] *SAS v France* European Court of Human Rights (Grand Chamber), 1 July 2014. There is a good note by Stephanie Berry on the *EJIL:Talk!* website, 'SAS v France: does anything remain of the right to manifest religion': <http://www.ejiltalk.org/sas-v-france-does-anything-remain-of-the-right-to-manifest-religion/> [accessed 21 March 2016].

only a small step from this to the government's counter-extremism agenda.

This drift both in Strasbourg and in Britain should surely give us pause. Here are human rights wielded not as a legal protection for the vulnerable but as a cultural weapon against the different. Though the government does not explicitly refer to human rights as one of the British values to be protected from 'extremism' (no doubt considered a move too far in light of its determination to repeal the Human Rights Act), what does appear in the definition is redolent with what human rights is seen as encompassing: 'democracy, the rule of law, individual liberty and mutual respect and tolerance of different faiths and beliefs.' It is only on a truly fantastic fantasy island that such universal principles could be reclassified as indigenous to a local population to the exclusion of the whole of the world outside. In truth this is not what is meant. As David Cameron's speech in Munich showed there is a European dimension to 'British' values, albeit it has not been politically expedient in Britain for some years now to credit anything explicitly to Europe. There is also a resonance with the global values championed with great energy by Tony Blair when as Prime Minister he characterized action against extremism as not 'a clash between civilisations' but rather 'a clash about civilisation'. In this confrontation, for Mr Blair '"We" is not the West. "We" are as much Muslim as Christian or Jew or Hindu. "We" are those who believe in religious tolerance, openness to others, to democracy, liberty and human rights administered by secular courts.'[29] Earlier in the same speech the then Prime Minister had talked of the divide in politics that is as true today as it was then and which applies to domestic discussion as much as to the international agenda with which he was there concerned:

> The true division in foreign policy today is between: those who want the shop 'open', or those who want it 'closed'; those who believe that the long-term interests of a country lie in it being out there, engaged,

[29] Tony Blair's speech to the Foreign Policy Centre 21 March 2006: <http://www.theguardian.com/politics/2006/mar/21/iraq.iraq1> [accessed 24 March 2016].

interactive and those who think the short-term pain of such a policy and its decisions, too great. This division has strong echoes in debates not just over foreign policy and trade but also over immigration.[30]

And we might add 'human rights'. Throughout this book, we have seen how the law—both Strasbourg and domestic—has been able to deploy human rights to reach individuals in need of protection. There is however now gaining ground this other sort of 'human rights', seemingly promoted by the *SAS v France* and *Refah Partisi* line of cases in Strasbourg, which finds in human rights an accessory of western Judaeo-Christian civilization.[31] British foreign policy is similarly repositioning itself, continuing to talk about human rights when it wants to criticize certain countries[32] while removing ministerial obligations to have regard to international law and treaty obligations in the course of their work[33] and downgrading human rights concerns internationally when business is judged to come first.[34] Human rights without the kind of impartial enforcement that the law epitomizes become a set of merely pious declarations or a new weapon in international relations, or both.

[30] Ibid.

[31] See Ch 4 where human rights as warranting 'necessary evils'—the same development as is being discussed here—are considered.

[32] 'Minister condemns human rights abuses in Syria' FCO press release 4 September 2015: <https://www.gov.uk/government/news/minister-condemns-human-rights-abuses-in-syria> [accessed 31 March 2016].

[33] D Akande and E Bjorge, 'The United Kingdom Ministerial Code and international law: a response to Richard Ekins and Guglielmo Verdirame' UK Const L Blog (10 December 2015): <https://ukconstitutionallaw.org/> [accessed 31 March 2016].

[34] See the comments of the FCO's Permanent Secretary Sir Simon McDonald that human rights were not 'one of the top priorities' for government: 'MPs hit out at Foreign Office over downgrading of human rights' *Financial Times* 23 October 2015 [accessed 31 March 2016]; 'Britain downgrades human rights across globe, Amnesty warns': <https://www.rt.com/uk/333471-human-rights-amnesty-warning/> [accessed 31 March 2016].

PART V
CONCLUSION

14

DEFEND THE HUMAN RIGHTS ACT!

A t one level the Human Rights Act is merely one of a number of innovative laws enacted in the first years of a progressive Labour administration at the end of the last millennium, of a piece with the devolution legislation, freedom of information, and a (modest) reform of the House of Lords. One could argue that the law matters—but mainly to lawyers. The new set of guidelines for judges in their oversight of the administrative state is important to those who need to know these things and to clients who are affected by them, but not otherwise generally significant. Much of this book has been about the value of the Human Rights Act in this restricted zone. We have considered at some length its contribution to the restructuring of judicial review along more principled lines than existed before it came into force. We have observed the way in which the Act has pushed at the boundaries of the permissible so far as judicial engagement with policy is concerned. We have reflected on how it has invested the shapeless pragmatism of the common law with a new ethical purpose. Perhaps most of all we have looked on (and from the writer's perspective admiringly) at the stimulus the Human Rights Act has given to holding the government to account for its actions with regard to a range of vulnerable (and frequently unpopular) members of UK society. These are no small victories, for sure, but they are primarily legal in nature. For all its importance, there is more to the Human Rights Act than litigation, even of the ground-breaking sort (of which, as we have also seen, there has been a great deal).

On Fantasy Island: Britain, Europe, and Human Rights. First Edition. Conor Gearty.

At a second level of greater abstraction, the Human Rights Act has reached past the law and into our general approach to governance. This was something that the drafters of the legislation intended. The imposition of a duty on all public authorities to respect the Convention rights is evidence of this, as is the obligation set out in section 19 under which all proposers of government bills must explicitly state their view of the draft law's compatibility with those same rights. These legislative steers towards human rights, accompanied by the establishment (outside the Human Rights Act) of the Parliamentary Joint Committee on Human Rights[1] and the Equality and Human Rights Commission[2] were consciously designed to spread the human rights word beyond the law courts and into the very heart of the bureaucracy. Proponents of human rights often spoke of a 'culture of rights'[3] and the success of the project of 'embedding human rights in Britain'[4] has been to get public authorities generally to think about rights even in situations where legal challenges are far from anyone's mind. This has not been at the insistence of the courts: indeed the law lords went out of their way early on to relieve such bodies from the duty of checking all they do against a human rights list of rights, the judges preferring to assess the decisions they make in the round rather than through asking whether they had explicitly taken specific human rights into account.[5] This inclination to respect human rights has

[1] See HC Standing Orders of the House of Commons 152B. The Joint Committee's work can be seen at <http://www.parliament.uk/business/committees/committees-a-z/joint-select/human-rights-committee/> [accessed 30 March 2016].

[2] Equality Act 2006: see <http://www.equalityhumanrights.com/> [accessed 30 March 2016].

[3] See generally A Donald, J Watson, N McClean, P Leach, and J Eschment, *Human Rights in Britain since the Human Rights Act 1998: A Critical Review* (Equality and Human Rights Commission, 2009): <http://www.equalityhumanrights.com/sites/default/files/documents/human_rights_in_britain_since_the_human_rights_act_1998_-_a_critical_review.pdf> [accessed 30 March 2016].

[4] Ibid (the title of ch 2).

[5] R (*Begum*) v *Headteacher and Governors of Denbigh High School* [2006] UKHL 16, [2007] 1 AC 100.

grown through a process of accretion, on this occasion not into the judicial but rather the 'administrative cerebellum'.[6] As was observed in Chapter 1, the sell is not, after all, a particularly hard one. The language of fairness, justice, and inclusivity runs with the grain of our progressive instincts and even in difficult cases it is a hard-nosed (and we might assume exceptional) administrator indeed who would erect 'utility' or 'convenience' or 'the interests of the many' as insuperable barriers to the realization of such values in concrete situations.

The broadest impact of the Human Rights Act may, however, be the most important of all. This is a theme from Chapter 1 to which we can now return. The European pedigree of the Human Rights Act is as obvious as its preferment of the language of universal rights over the old vocabulary of civil liberties. Here is a law not content with the old ways, the politico-legal culture in which it was 'Britain alone' or at very least 'Britain first among equals'. The United Kingdom prepared to enact the Human Rights Act is a country that knows that it needs help and is also one that has the wit to see that help strengthens rather than weakens it in the world in which it finds itself today: not 1850 or 1950 or even 1980, but today. The nation state has survived as the key tool in the organization of the political but the battering it has taken from the global forces swirling around it means that such polities can only preserve their position through alliances, 'coalitions of the willing', partnerships dedicated to mutual assistance. And just as with people, in the affairs of nations help needs to be reciprocated if the giving of it by others is to be anything other than tactical astuteness or mere compassion. The United Kingdom should be wary of the former and does not want the latter. That leaves reciprocation, giving as well as taking, helping as well as being helped. The Council of Europe is a classic example of multinational solidarity, the Convention on Human Rights and Fundamental Freedoms its proud centrepiece, and the European Court of Human Rights in Strasbourg its emblematic ethical centre. There is far more going on here than merely this or that judgment

---

[6] The phrase 'judicial cerebellum' is that of Lord Neuberger: see Ch 4.

with which we may or may not agree. This is a project to promote a set of fundamental values which have human rights at their very core. The UK must play its part in supporting this edifice.

There is a large irony when we ask what those values are that Strasbourg promotes and the opponents of its jurisdiction so abhor. They are exactly, almost word for word, the values trumpeted as British by the Prime Minister and his fellow enthusiasts for a stronger national identity in the United Kingdom: 'democracy, the rule of law, individual liberty and mutual respect and tolerance of different faiths and beliefs'.[7] One is irresistibly reminded of the old joke about God showing people around Heaven, encountering a walled area and when asked about it God replying that that is where the Catholics are; they think they are the only people here. The United Kingdom would be fine about the European Court of Human Rights if everyone pretended it was a subset of British power, that its values were British, and that its jurisdiction was a British favour to the world. The Human Rights Act would be worth protecting even if all it did was wreak havoc with a fantasy like this.

The Act does more, though, than any of the aspects of it we have noted in the course of these final remarks. It epitomizes an attitude towards these British/European/global values, namely that they are to be taken seriously, that they are not just background music to blot out the sounds of unfairness, injustice, and inequality that in reality persist behind the camouflage offered by this fine talk.[8] Human rights offer a route to a society where all are equal before the law, where each of us has a chance to engage in political activity on a level playing field if we so wish, and in which the basics of a decent life are regarded as the minimum to which each of us is entitled, whatever our birth circumstances, our ethnicity, our gender, or our sexual orientation. Of course the Human Rights Act does not in itself achieve all this: its rights are

---

[7] See Ch 13.

[8] For an elaboration of this idea of camouflage, under cover of 'neo-democracy', see C A Gearty, *Liberty and Security* (Cambridge: Polity Press, 2013).

limited, its role in culture hardly all-encompassing, its enforcement often tentative. But it is part of this wider story, a cog in the wheel that helps keep our world spinning in a civilized way, amid all the turmoil caused by the constant movement of modern life. The past should not trump the present or our future will be at risk. The subject is too serious a one for fantasy.

TABLE OF CASES

BIBLIOGRAPHY

Akande, D and Bjorge, E, 'The United Kingdom Ministerial Code and international law: a response to Richard Ekins and Guglielmo Verdirame' UK Const L Blog (10 December 2015).

Allan, T R S, *The Sovereignty of Law: Freedom, Constitution and Common Law* (Oxford: Oxford University Press, 2013).

Bingham, T, 'The ECHR: Time to Incorporate' (1993) 109 *Law Quarterly Review* 390.

Buchan, N and Sumner, T (eds), *Glasnost in Britain? Against Censorship and in Defence of the Word* (Basingstoke: The Macmillan Press, 1989).

Campbell, T, Ewing, K D, and Tomkins, A (eds), *The Legal Protection of Human Rights: Sceptical Essays* (Oxford: Oxford University Press, 2011).

Christoffersen, J and Madsen, M R (eds), *The European Court of Human Rights: Between Law and Politics* (Oxford: Oxford University Press, 2011).

Clayton, R, 'Accountability, judicial scrutiny and contracting out' UK Const L Blog (30 November 2015).

Clayton, R and Tomlinson, H, *Privacy and Freedom of Expression* 2nd edn (Oxford: Oxford University Press, 2010).

Commission on a Bill of Rights, *A UK Bill of Rights: The Choice Before Us* (December 2012).

Conservative Party, *Protecting Human Rights in the UK: The Conservatives' Proposals for Changing Britain's Human Rights Laws* (October 2014).

Cosgrove, R A, *The Rule of Law: Albert Venn Dicey, Victorian Jurist* (London and Basingstoke: The Macmillan Press, 1980).

Council of Europe, *Impact of the European Convention on Human Rights in States Parties: Selected Examples* AS/Jur/Inf (2016) 04 (8 January 2016).

Cox, A, *The Court and the Constitution* (Boston: Houghton Mifflin, 1987).

Craig, P, 'Constitutional and Non-Constitutional Review' (2001) 54 *Current Legal Problems* 147–78.

Craig, P, 'The Common Law, Shared Power and Judicial Review' (2004) 24 (2) *Oxford Journal of Legal Studies* 237–57.

Davies, P S and Pila, J (eds), *The Jurisprudence of Lord Hoffmann: A Festschrift in Honour of Lord Leonard Hoffmann* (Oxford: Hart Publishing, 2015).

De Hert, P and Cristobal Bocos, P, 'Case of Roman Zakharov v Russia: The Strasbourg Follow up to the Luxembourg Court's Schrems Judgment' *Strasbourg Observers* (23 December 2015).

De Wolfe Howe, M (ed), *Holmes–Laski Letters: The Correspondence of Mr Justice Holmes and Harold J Laski 1916–1935* (London: Geoffrey Cumberlege with Oxford University Press, 1953).

Dicey, A V, *Introduction to the Study of the Law of the Constitution* 8th edn (London: Macmillan, 1915).

Donald, A, 'The remarkable shrinking backlog at the European Court of Human Rights' *UK Human Rights Blog* (1 October 2014).

Donald, A, Watson, J, McClean, N, Leach, P, and Eschment, J, *Human Rights in Britain since the Human Rights Act 1998: A Critical Review* (Equality and Human Rights Commission, 2009).

Dworkin, R, *A Bill of Rights for Britain: Why British Liberty Needs Protection* (London: Chatto and Windus, 1990).

English, R, *Terrorism: How to Respond* (Oxford: Oxford University Press, 2009).

European Union Committee, *The UK, the EU and a British Bill of Rights* (12th Report of 2015–16, HL 139, 9 May 2016).

Ewing, K D and Gearty, C A, *Freedom Under Thatcher: Civil Liberties in Modern Britain* (Oxford: Oxford University Press, 1990).

Ewing, K D and Gearty, C A, *The Struggle for Civil Liberties: Political Freedom and the Rule of Law in Britain, 1914–1945* (Oxford: Oxford University Press, 2000).

Fairclough, T, 'Constitutional change, standing orders and EVEL: a step in the wrong direction?' UK Const L Blog (22 February 2016).

Fisher, J, *The British Bill of Rights: Protecting Freedom Under the Law* (London: Politeia, 2015).

Fredman, A, 'Are Human Rights Culturally Determined: A Riposte to Lord Hoffmann' in P S Davies and J Pila (eds), *The Jurisprudence of Lord Hoffmann: A Festschrift in Honour of Lord Leonard Hoffmann* (Oxford: Hart Publishing, 2015) 97–114.

Fukuyama, F, *The End of History and the Last Man* (London: Penguin, 1992).

Gearty, C A, 'The Cost of Human Rights: English Judges and the Northern Irish Troubles' (1994) 37 *Current Legal Problems* 19–40.

Gearty, C A, 'Unravelling *Osman*' (2001) 64 (2) *Modern Law Review* 159–90.

Gearty, C A, *Principles of Human Rights Adjudication* (Oxford: Oxford University Press, 2004).

Gearty, C A, *Civil Liberties* (Oxford: Oxford University Press, 2007).

Gearty, C A, *Liberty and Security* (Cambridge: Polity Press, 2013).

Gearty, C A, 'The State of Human Rights' (2014) 5 (4) *Global Politics* 391–400.

Giddens, A, *The Third Way: The Renewal of Social Democracy* (Cambridge: Polity Press, 1998).

Gies, L, 'A Villains' Charter? The Press and the Human Rights Act' (2011) 7 (2) *Crime Media Culture* 167–83.

Gordon, J and Klug, F (eds), 'Special Issue on the Tenth Anniversary of the Human Rights Act' [2010] (6) *European Human Rights Law Review* 568–630.

Greer, S, *The European Convention on Human Rights: Achievements, Problems and Prospects* (Cambridge: Cambridge University Press, 2006).

Griffith, J A G, 'The Political Constitution' (1979) 42 (1) *Modern Law Review* 1–21.

Griffith, J A G, 'The Rights Stuff' (1993) 29 *The Socialist Register* 106–24.

Harris, D J, O'Boyle, M, and Warbrick, C, *Law of the European Convention on Human Rights* 3rd edn by D J Harris, M O'Boyle, E P Bates, and C M Buckley (Oxford: Oxford University Press, 2014).

Hepple, B, *Race, Jobs and the Law in Britain* (London: Allen Lane, 1968).

Herbert Smith Freehills, 'Misapplication of Statutory Scheme Leads to Damages Award Under European Convention on Human Rights' *Administrative and Public Law E-Bulletin* (15 March 2013).

Hewart, G, *The New Despotism* (London: Ernest Benn, 1929).

Hillyard, P and Percy-Smith, J, *The Coercive State: The Decline of Democracy in Britain* (London: Fontana Press, 1988).

Holme, R and Elliott, M (eds), *Time for a New Constitution 1688–1988* (Basingstoke: The Macmillan Press, 1988).

Home Office, *Prevent Strategy* (Cm 8092, June 2011).

Home Office, *Counter-Extremism Strategy* (Cm 9148, October 2015).

House of Commons Home Affairs Committee, *Project CONTEST: The Government's Counter-Terrorism Strategy* (9th Report of 2008–9, HC 212, 7 July 2009).

House of Commons Library Briefing Paper, *Prisoners' Voting Rights: Developments since May 2015* (CPB 7461, 12 January 2016).

Ignatieff, M, *The Lesser Evil: Political Ethics in an Age of Terror* (Edinburgh: Edinburgh University Press, 2004).

Independent Schools Information Service, *Independent Schools: The Legal Case*. A Joint Opinion by Anthony Lester QC and David Pannick with a Foreword by Lord Scarman (ISIS, 1991).

Ishay, M R, *The Human Rights Reader* 2nd edn (New York: Routledge, 2007).

Johnson, B, *The Churchill Factor: How One Man Made History* (London: Hodder and Stoughton, 2014).

Joint Committee on Human Rights, *Human Rights Judgments* (Seventh Report of Session 2014–15. HL 130, HC 1088, 11 March 2015).

Jowell, J, 'The Rule of Law Today' in J Jowell and D Oliver (eds), *The Changing Constitution* 3rd edn (Oxford: Oxford University Press, 1994) ch 3.

Jowell, J, 'Beyond the Rule of Law: Towards Constitutional Judicial Review' [2000] (Winter) *Public Law* 671–83.

Jowell, J and Oliver, D (eds), *The Changing Constitution* 3rd edn (Oxford: Oxford University Press, 1994).

Kavanagh, A, 'Unlocking the Human Rights Act: The "Radical" Approach to Section 3 (1) Revisited' [2005] 10 *European Human Rights Law Review* 259–75.

Kavanagh, A, *Constitutional Review Under the Human Rights Act* (Cambridge: Cambridge University Press, 2009).

Kelsen, H, *Pure Theory of Law* 2nd edn translated from the German by M Knight (San Francisco: University of California Press, 1967).

Klug, F M, *Values for a Godless Age: The Story of the United Kingdom's New Bill of Rights* (London: Penguin, 2000).

Klug, F M, *A Magna Carta for All Humanity* (London: Routledge, 2014).

Koskenniemi, M, *The Gentle Civilizer of Nations: The Rise and Fall of International Law 1870–1960* (Cambridge: Cambridge University Press, 2004).

Labour Party, *Bringing Rights Home* (1996).

Laws, J, *The Common Law Constitution* (The Hamlyn Lectures 2013) (Cambridge: Cambridge University Press, 2014).

Leach, P and Donald, A, 'Russia Defies Strasbourg: Is Contagion Spreading?' *Blog of the European Journal of International Law* (19 December 2015).

Legal Action Group, *Litigating to Save Legal Aid* (February 2016).

Lester, A, 'UK Acceptance of the Strasbourg Jurisdiction: What Really Went on in Whitehall in 1965' [1998] (Summer) *Public Law* 237–53.

Lester, A, 'The European Court of Human Rights After 50 Years' in J Christoffersen and M R Madsen (eds), *The European Court of Human Rights: Between Law and Politics* (Oxford: Oxford University Press, 2011) 98.

Lester, A and Bindman, G, *Race and Law in Britain* (Cambridge, Mass: Harvard University Press, 1972).

Leveson, B, *The Leveson Report: Report of an Inquiry into the Culture, Practices and Ethics of the Press* (HC 780, 29 November 2012).

McColgan, A, 'Lessons from the Past? Northern Ireland Terrorism Now and Then, and the Human Rights Act' in T Campbell, K Ewing, and A Tomkins (eds), *The Legal Protection of Human Rights: Sceptical Essays* (Oxford: Oxford University Press, 2011) ch 9.

Mandel, M, 'A Brief History of the New Constitutionalism or "How We Changed Everything so that Everything Would Remain the Same"' (1998) 32 (2) *Israel Law Review* 250–300.

Masterman, R and Murkens, J E K, 'Skirting Supremacy and Subordination: The Constitutional Authority of the United Kingdom Supreme Court' [2013] (4) *Public Law* 800–20.

Ministry of Justice, *Human Rights: Human Lives. A Handbook for Public Authorities* (Ministry of Justice, 2006).

Ministry of Justice, *Responding to Human Rights Judgments: Report to the Joint Committee on Human Rights on the Government Response to Human Rights Judgments 2013–14* Cm 8962 (Ministry of Justice, December 2014).

Moyn, S, *The Last Utopia: Human Rights in History* (Cambridge, Mass: Harvard University Press, 2010).

Norman, J and Oborne, P, *Churchill's Legacy: The Conservative Case for the Human Rights Act* (Liberty: London, 2009).

O'Regan, K, 'Text Matters: Some Reflections on the Forging of a New Constitutional Jurisprudence in South Africa' (2012) 75 (1) *Modern Law Review* 1–32.

Pimlott, B, Wright, A, and Flower, T (eds), *Politics for a Change* (London: W H Allen, 1990).

Rozenberg, J, *The Search for Justice: An Anatomy of the Law* (London: Hodder and Stoughton, 1994).

Scarman, L, *English Law: The New Dimension* (London: Stevens, 1975).

Simpson, A W B, *Human Rights and the End of Empire: Britain and the Genesis of the European Convention* (Oxford: Oxford University Press, 2001).

Wagner, A, 'Is this the best human rights correction ever? Or the worst' *UK Human Rights Blog* (29 September 2014).

Waldron, J, *Theories of Rights* (Oxford: Oxford University Press, 1984).

Ziegler, K S, Wicks, E, and Hodson, L (eds), *The UK and European Human Rights: A Strained Relationship?* (Oxford: Hart Publishing, 2015).

INDEX

INDEX

Wagner, Adam 115
Wales 12, 182, 201
welfare legislation 118, 137, 152–3
Wendell Holmes, Oliver 5
Whigs 49
Wilkes, John 29
Williams, Rowan 181

Wilson, Harold 38
Wilson, Nicholas, Lord Wilson of
    Culworth 197
women prisoners 143
Woolf, Harry, Baron Woolf of Barnes 42,
    43, 45, 83, 84, 150
Wright, Peter 38